Confidence on Camera

7 Steps to Present Your Power on any size screen

DEDICATION

Thanks to all my Playmates for your life support…
and most of all to the love of my life from university
and all of my life Steve, for empowering my
Confidence to Press Play on these pages – for ever
and always, love Me xx

Lottie Hearn
The Video Coach @ www.PressPlayPresentations.com
Your Coach @ www.Confidenceon.Camera
+353 (0)87 929 6575

Confidence on Camera

7 Steps to **Present Your Power**

on any size screen

Lottie Hearn

Confidence on Camera

7 Steps to Present Your Power on any size screen

First published in 2015 by
Panoma Press Ltd
48 St Vincent Drive, St Albans, Herts, AL1 5SJ UK

info@panomapress.com
www.panomapress.com

Cover design/Illustrations by Michael Inns
Artwork by Karen Gladwell

ISBN 978-1-909623-91-0

Contents

Acknowledgements

(or Lottie's big book Love In...)

Rediscovering how to play has been, and is, a joyful yet tough process. Writing this has been similar! And it would still be an imaginary screenplay without my producers and supporters. So this is my standing ovation for you all...

Many of you live by my simply amazing mother Prue's lifelong mantra for a travelling performer daughter: 'no news is good news'. So while I may not have spoken my thanks and appreciation to all of you, my #SUPERGREAT friends and Playmates who have got me to here – please know you are always a much valued part of my life. If I miss your name, I still love you ☺

Book helpers humungous thank you all so very much: Mindy Gibbins-Klein at the Book Midwife and the Panoma Press superstar team – Emma, Alison and design duo extraordinaire Mike and Karen; plus my mentors and co-preneurs thanks for your invaluable advice and support: Ciara Conlon, Shelley Taylor-Smith, Terry Brock, Valerie Pierce, Barbara Moynihan, Eamonn O'Brien, Carole Smith and Siodhna McGowan.

To my sisters Antonia and Kate, my bro Charlie and my Mummy who've watched me will my way on stage, on screen and off around the world, since the age of 10 when we had to be apart – thank you for everything we never got the chance to say... and Dad who would be very proud were he here and is no doubt toasting me with a devilish dram as you read. And to all Ross, Dogs, Hearns, Sizelands and Todds around the world for being the great fun family I never expected, and Mike and Sue - for doing it with such such quiet *(not always!)*, patient love I'm never sure I really deserved.

Thanks also to all you other fabby folk who became my global family I love so much – to my sisters since small Victoria, Billie and Danielle who shaped my mind, and big sisters and bros sharing so much ever since Alison and William, Barbs, Catherine *(see-ya-bye!)*; to all who have mentored, given advice and support, shared help, homes and happy times – so who've shaped my work, writing and life for the better along the way: Aoife, Bobby, Craig, Carolin, Damian, Gill and Owen, Ingrid, Janet, Jessica, Juliette, Kate, Karin, Ken, Leanna, Lindsay, Lizzie, Lofty, Lotte, Mark H., Marta, Mary, Megan, Nimmy, Rae, Phil and Kenz, Rob S., Sanjay, Sarah, Sharon, Siany, Simon, Stephanie, Vicky; my other CH ladies; my fellow drama queens Jo, Trish and Kelly; my HK VO variety actors; my scuba and sailing crews; my TV Pro and MFW trainers; my Coca-Cola coaches; my *Gaeltoir* Irish storytellers (especially Aoife *an scéaltóir!*); my NSAA and PSAUKI speaker supporters; all my global family from the UK, Middle East, USA, and the extended *whanau* in NZ, HK and Oz. And to all my beautiful boys who've driven me crazy and made me laugh, cry and scream, so driven my belief in the power of emotional connection and always discovering a better me – you know exactly who you are!

You've all given me the guts to make my dreams possible…

Love you, love Me xx

Foreword

by Shelley Taylor-Smith

7-time Women's World Marathon Swimming Champion,
Motivation Mindset global speaker and best-selling author.

There has probably never been a better time to be confident on camera.

Being confident hardly changes, but the communication mediums to share your work have transformed dramatically. Being confident on camera is no longer accepted but expected. It's the new norm whether on Skype, interacting via video or being interviewed for your next business move.

There are many intrinsic traits to being confident. One of the more forgotten and even undervalued qualities is being your true self. I've come to learn that being 'comfortable in your own skin' is above all the most important business resource you have at your disposal. Why? Because attitude, belief and confidence is sexier and a better seller than any body part!

And this is where Lottie's Confidence on Camera programme comes in. When I first met Lottie at a 2001 National Speakers Association of Australia meeting we had an instant 'connection'. The more we talked, the more I thought *Who is this gal? She talks with her heart and boundless energy just like I do! I like her passion exuding from every cell of her being – I get this gal!*

We connected and I knew I'd found my on-camera coach for my daunting new TV presenting role as 'Monday Motivation' Coach on Australia's then No.1 daily show *Mornings with Kerrie-Anne.*

As a seven-time World Champion, I had created global sports history as the only woman to hold a No.1 world ranking for both men and women for *any* sport worldwide. As an industry mentor, swimming Hall of Famer and double Australian of the Year nominee I've carried our flag, represented athletes, successfully fought boards for marathon swimming at the Olympics and equal female pay. I've motivated thousands as a keynote speaker around the world… but sharing that motivation on camera was still unnerving before Lottie taught me to Play on camera!

She enabled me to present my power and passion *for real* via video. She shook me up, challenged me and coached me to truly connect with and serve my audience. Now I constantly film and present DIY for online business-boosting products and I get more work on TV, radio and online.

From her pro performance and speaking background, Lottie knows how to help you discover your best self so *you can* stand up, stand out and shine! And now with this book she coaches you through her 7 Steps to Present your own power, to project the champion you on any size screen. When you commit to following this book, you commit to building your confidence on camera.

The best advice I can give you is to always remember you are human relating with fellow humans. Never stop being yourself, ensure you are making the positive connection and difference in the world that you were born to achieve. Present your true you and as Lottie always says – *"Stay Playful!"*

Shelley Taylor-Smith
Founder & Director

www.ChampionMindset.com.au
www.OpenWaterSwimmingMastery.com

SET-UP:
Why Confidence on Camera?

Talking to a machine is not a natural thing to do, yet so many folks are doing it!

Many of the machines we 'talk' to interact with us and allow us to connect and converse with others across the globe and we love them. So what is different about this one machine – the camera? Why does it take so much confidence to appear on screen? Why does the camera mystify, move or muddle us so much?

From fact to fiction, drama to documentary, the camera has allowed us to escape to a whole new world and understand the one we live in better. More recently it has allowed us to share our own world with the world online.

Some people confidently post videos online every day or happily present live-stream mobile video, virtual meetings, conference or webinar training on screen. They understand that Confidence on Camera is a necessary mindset to make an impact, enable a real interactive connection with clients and to present their powerful message to boost business online. For others, the thought of having to talk to any camera with their face on screen fills them with a dread so primordial that all confidence flees. Their whole body and logical, successful business brain shuts down – just when they need to communicate most... on the... machine...

The machine we're talking about here is your **video camera**, **webcam** or **smartphone camera**.

The camera you use to connect you to the world: to film yourself for videos; or chat via Skype; or use when you can't be in the same place as your clients or colleagues for work; or promote your business via webinars and video training courses online.

That camera can expose *all* of our flaws, our worries, our nerves, our innermost fears. And other people are watching us as we rapidly fall apart on screen.

So it's not surprising that the vast majority of people are really not comfortable with getting in front of *that* machine.

So what brings you here? What's made you pick up this book?

What Do You Want with The Machine?

- ⅄ **What do you want** to do with that camera that's going to help present your power on screen, promote your business online and increase your impact and influence on the world?

- ⅄ **Why are you on screen** – for meetings, to market 'brand you' or build a bigger business online?

- ⅄ **What fears**, if any, do you have about presenting on camera, about being the face and voice of your videos?

- ⅄ **How have you felt** presenting on camera before?

- ⅄ **What reaction**, feedback and return on investment (ROI) did you get? Was it what you wanted?

- ⅄ **Why** are you **avoiding video** and appearing on screen?

- ⅄ **What is holding you back** from or **are you afraid** of talking to the machine?

Over the years and since founding my video coaching business in Ireland as PressPlayPresentations.com and Lottie Hearn Video Coach on YouTube in 2011, I've asked these questions of many business people, professional speakers and performers. The answers have come back varied, but the top three reasons that stop people from getting on camera and creating their own videos have usually come back the same. Business people say *"No Video"* because of expected high cost, lack of knowledge and fear of presenting.

But which one do you think is number one?

Well, from years of experience, overcoming fears and making the mistakes on camera for you, I'm now saying with this book, it's time to…

Manage Your Machine Mindset!

Any fear and power you project on to this specific, inanimate object can strip you of your creative talent, expression, excitement and joy – and presenting is meant to be fun – look how much they enjoy it on TV! As the experts we are, we know exactly how to promote our products to a real person face-to-face, but *"the machine is mean", "the camera makes me look bad…"*

That mindset can make you get very serious about promoting your 'serious business' on camera. But the videos that do the best online are the ones that are fun or appeal to us as human beings. Remember your work is your expertise or passion and you are allowed to love talking about it – like they do on TV!

We're allowed to enjoy our work and making videos can be extremely enjoyable too – our videos can not only make us money, but are ultimately there to help empower and educate others. Yet so often people think of them as being *"all about me…"*

Well on camera – they're not!

You're there to provide something for me, the viewer – *I'm* the one who can choose to watch you, so you'd better help me out here! And it helps if you can make it fun…

Funny how playfulness and fun is bred out of us…

As little kids #EverythingisAwesome *(as the Lego guys would say!)* we love to play, present, perform – connect and make friends in a flash and have the guts to do almost anything.

Until we're told we can't…

Then we develop all sorts of hang-ups, built-in judgements about ourselves and others and we ignore the fact that life and work should and can be positive, expressive and fun!

We step back and observe – we watch videos, presenters, interviews on TV and online and judge… "I could do better than that" – but do you?

It's not until you step up on life's stage that you'll ever find out.

Maybe you stepped up once – made a video or online presentation that didn't work, you judged it negatively, so stopped trying. Or you've never even tried because that's the result you expect?

It's this fatalistic attitude that prevents many a brilliant speaker or business person from successfully transferring winning presentations to online video. So how do we get to be the star of our own little screen, planning, creating, presenting and promoting our powerful videos with Confidence on Camera?

It's time to make that machine and any size screen work for you.

INTRO:
"Lights, Camera, Action!"

How are we Going to Do this Confidence on Camera Learning Thing?

First we have to move aside previous misconceptions about what makes 'good' business videos online and start thinking about what makes a video that makes people want to watch. And not only watch, actually DO something after, for and with you as a result of watching your video.

As every sales person knows: **we buy from people we like and trust.**

As an online video viewer, we're so used to TV presenters bad and great, so we have to *like* the person on the screen before we'll ever do anything for them. We want them to be part of our ideal world, we want them to make us smile, we want to believe in them and be affected by their story. We love presenters who are confident in their style, credible in their content and charismatic in their delivery. We want you to convince us to take a journey with you.

So it's time to overcome that fearful adult who sees video, virtual meetings or web presenting as difficult or too techie to do and release that inner kid who looks at cameras and video technology and goes *"oooh, I want to play!"*

I hereby give you back the Power to Play!

It's time to start accessing that childlike, non-judgemental, confidence-building, playful self-awareness and exercising it, so you can discover:

- ⅄ what works for you on camera
- ⅄ how to overcome your fears, in the moment, if they hit along the way
- ⅄ how to build your plan to access your Confidence on Camera any time you need

〰〰〰〰〰〰〰〰

You have to learn to play on camera to boost your confidence about what you see of you on screen

〰〰〰〰〰〰〰〰

Why are we Doing it?

We're doing it because with some positive focused self-awareness and work from you, your story can and will make other people's lives better, richer, brighter, easier. This book is here to help you present your message via video and on camera even better than you already do.

We're not talking immediate video perfection here – it takes time to improve existing habits and build new skills. You need to start thinking what on-camera presenting you will even do, from a simple video message answering "what do you do?" to video conference (VC) presenting to the board. Only you know now how urgent and important it is for you to make the effort to develop your presenting style and technique.

You also need to recognise that you can't please everyone all of the time and if you start with that desire in mind, you're going to fail – because you're already judging yourself, taking yourself too seriously and forgetting the fun. So get over that one fast or don't bother to read on!

But with some serious preparation, planning and practice you can know who your target audience or viewer is, what they might be interested in seeing or what they might need from you. You'll discover all your business and time investment 'whys?' as we go.

What are we Going to Learn?

> *All the world's a stage, And all the men and women merely players;*
> *They have their exits and their entrances, And one man in his time*
> *plays many parts, His acts being seven ages.*
>
> **Shakespeare, As You Like It, Act II, Scene VII**

As an actor I'm a Willie Shakespeare fan, but while we may all have many parts to play and roles to take on in our business, it's the part where you play on camera that interests me!

So what you'll find are not the seven ages, but you will find **7 Steps**, each with **7 STAGES**, to empower your presenting performance on camera. These are successful theatre and TV based, but business-focused presenting techniques to help you present with impact and get your message across on screen. They actually work whether you're on camera or not, so even if you're not yet ready to make your online videos or virtual meeting screen, the book can help you with all sorts of live presenting, as well as business conference calls, or podcast and webinar VO tips too.

In the 7 Steps to Confidence on Camera you're going to:

- ✓ Deep dive into the Mind of The Machine and your Presenter Mindset – to help you overcome those limiting beliefs or fears that may hold you back right now.
- ✓ Discover how to present the power of you and your business message on any size screen.
- ✓ You'll learn about your own personal presenting style – what works for you and what your distracting habits may currently be, and what could be preventing your message from making the impact you want.
- ✓ Find out the secrets that actors use to put the 'act' into 'impact' when presenting – it's the old 'fake it till you make it!' Oh and loads of actory skills you can use when you take your TV stage. *(Well – once a drama queen always a drama queen and always looking for the ways to make you play!)*

✓ See and hear the Visual elements of presenting, the Vocal elements of your powerful voice and the Verbal – the words you choose to use. We're also going to cover how to create, write, learn and deliver powerful scripts, stories and analogies and how to share your final output with confidence, knowing that to really connect and make an impact, your most important production value in any video is simply your 'story' delivery from you.

✓ DO – LOTS! Because most of us spend 80-90% of our time picking the words we want to say and very little time practising saying it out loud, but all the best actors rehearse, rehearse, rehearse to hone their craft – "Lights, Camera, Action!" is the point of view we're taking here.

✓ Succeed and get better by having a go, to clarify your powerful messages in your conscious brain. Many business people are brilliant at writing what reads well on the website or a page, but does it sound real when you read it out loud? We're working towards what you'd actually SAY, not what you'd write.

And Why Should You Believe What I Say?

Improv. is where you make things up as an actor as you go along – it's short for improvisation. I always thought while studying drama and working on stage that I was really rubbish at it and only comics could do it well. But then I got a job for an English TV channel when living in Hong Kong, where I *had* to make things up as I went along…

Weeeeeell, I was only paid as the presenter but I had to create the shows and do everything else too – from scriptwriting, to voice-overs, to interviews and so much more! So I gave my producer a programme synopsis and they told me how much time I had on camera for any segment. There was no training back in 1994 and the budget was non-existent for kids' TV, so everything we did was sourced and created by me working with local schools, businesses, arts foundations, kids and parents.

There is no faster way to learn than when you're thrown in with children, animals, special guests and experts you've booked on, and with most local children (and a lot of adults) watching it all go off live on TV!

My motto rapidly became "*Stuff up with confidence and get over it!*" because none of the shows *were* actually live – but the producers and kids liked it whenever

I went wrong and made it fun! I learned to mess up, but be awesome and I discovered that human viewers love someone who's not afraid to muck it up and carry on, someone who's vulnerable enough to show or say they are nervous and then come across as brilliant. That's the freedom having Confidence on Camera can give you and the connectedness and fun you can have with your audience and viewers along the way. If they like you they'll join in, so you might as well create the game and #PressPlay!

I've done it on TV, I've taught others to do it, I've taught business people, professional speakers and world champions to do it on stages and screens across the world and am still doing it in Ireland today! You don't have to believe me – have a go with some of the tips I'm putting down in a book for the very first time *(well they were clogging up my simple actor brain!)* and discover the difference they can make for you today.

On camera you *need* to look and feel like you mean what you say – otherwise how are we ever going to trust you, like you or do what you want us to, after watching you? I'm not saying I'm perfect in every viewer's perception either, but I've presented enough different types of shows, written and created enough programmes and voice-overs for TV, radio, films, books, adverts and webinars, training courses and videos online; *and* coached thousands of individuals as TV presenters, VOs, customer service presenters and corporate and professional speakers over the last 20 years *(ouch, an actor never tells her age – "How old would you like me to be?"!)* to have garnered *some* knowledge of what works and what doesn't when presenting, especially on camera.

It's all about having the confidence to make a change, and yes to let go the serious and *play* at work – knowing that as viewers we *like* a person who is real, we want to watch smiley, friendly folk online, who are happy to help us along the way.

Even when you challenge or push us, we can still like you. Which for me now is just as well   ☺

How's it Going to Work?

So how's this Confidence on Camera book going to work? I hear you say!

A few people have been asking me, "How can you turn such a practical action into an applicable book?" Well, by doing just that. I've been coaching TV presenters and corporate training since the 1990s and my current company workbooks have been developed over 10 years and are still relevant, useable and practical today. In fact, along with training and learning with a number of core people and companies I'll introduce you to along the way, they have formed the basis for what I've written down for you here.

Think of it this way – the technology of how we film videos and the production tools available change all the time. Yet, just like TV or radio, it takes a presenter to be the face or the voice of that video, and presentation techniques haven't changed much in all that time.

There's still a camera, there's still a screen – you present on one, we watch you on the other.

And here's the first fact for you: the actual natural instinct when you do talk to the machine is to *not* like yourself when you first look back at you. In fact many clients actively hate it, but it is the *ONLY* way to develop your skills and get better at presenting. The first time I saw myself on TV I nearly died, but I quickly noticed what didn't work and stepped up my game *(and the receipt of the What's Hot Award from HK Magazine… too funny!)*.

So have no fear – we'll be covering ways for you to be nice to yourself and how both you and others will give you feedback, once you're ready to ask. But for now keep that as our secret as we need to go through your positive presenter self-assessment processes and how to ask for confidence-boosting feedback first. It always starts with what you like and what's good about what you do – always a positive place to begin.

It is a given in a business video that you are professional, informative, educational even – you are the expert in your field, otherwise you wouldn't be presenting the video. So think this: even if you are the receptionist who's been volunteered to be the face of the company – lucky you, you must look great and confident on camera! You already know more about the company, the business and what your business is than we do, so start from that base of confidence and reality – that is the core of what we're after, after all.

So dust off that video camera, work out how your webcam works, install and check out your smartphones camera apps, get your printer ready to copy off your bonus online .pdfs and forms and let the family know you'll be hogging the mirror in the bathroom for the next month or so!

❚❚ *PRESS PAUSE…What happens if I lose focus or get disheartened along the way?*

I know from painful experience as an actor that our ego can be a delicate and fickle thing.

Actors often need reassurance and emotional support to deliver the best performance for your entertainment. We are often pushed to experience and re-enact emotional situations that you, the audience, would chose to hide from – yet we do it on stage, screen and TV every day.

And most of the time, we *adore* doing it too – crazy eh?!

We work hard to be authentic, we have to learn to cope with rejection on an almost daily basis and we still go out and perform again another day. OK we do it for the plaudits and the praise, but that's not always forthcoming and a bad review can be heart-breaking and financially disastrous to all concerned, so interest is hugely invested in every performance.

We present it as if it's the first and last time of telling that story and you walk away with a theatrical experience and, hopefully, something gained. And if we can't be real or we don't know how, we fake it till we make it or are very good at *appearing* like we know exactly what we're doing!

Now you're not doing a play, but you are learning to Play, both with the camera gear when you **DIY** *(that's Do it Yourself)* and on the camera when you **PIY** *(that's Present it Yourself – I know, corny eh? Don't worry there's sooo much more where that came from!)* and you can benefit from this concept too. You can start mucking about with your smartphone, learning how the camera works, so when it comes to your first awareness exercise, you know what you need to do with the machine.

Playlist for a Confident on Camera Me!

Along the way you're going to find lots of Video Presenter A&E Awareness Exercises.

The A&Es are your emergency stopping points to test yourself, practise and get creative with thought-provoking and confidence-boosting exercises. And at the end of each step you'll find your Playlist for a Confident on Camera Me! This is your space to write down your learning notes and ideas from each step. The A&Es

and Playlists are built in at specific times to push you to stop, get self-aware, get your camera and have a go. YES – you can read from start to finish, but you'll get so much more from the book when you do the A&E thinking, exercises and create your own Playlists as you read…

So you'll also see an 'Online' icon which means you can get loads more advice, worksheets and .pdf bonus docs online at my website created to go with the book: **www.ConfidenceOn.Camera**

You can download docs one by one to build your own workbook, or access everything in one, when you join the Confidenceon.Camera Club. It's also a good idea to get a Video Creative notebook for all the video ideas reading this book will provoke. Otherwise there are spaces in here to jot down thoughts and A&E notes while you read.

OK NOW PRESS PLAY… ▶

CONFIDENCE ON CAMERA:
Your Commitment Pact

But before we go into the whole process of presenting, discovering how fabulous and confident on camera you will be and I start bossing you around with what you have to do in order to get there *(the director in me!)*, I want you to make a commitment to please Press Play and take Action, so say this next bit out loud:

I Commit to Empowering My Confidence on Camera

**I will go to Confidence A&E to improve my skills and
I will shout *Action* and get on camera and allow myself
to #PressPlay!**

Signed _____

I'm sharing the benefits of years of stuffing up with you here, so you can step away from fears and step up on camera with confidence. So please be open and willing to come with me on a journey of self-discovery and commit to yourself that you're willing to put in some work.

When you make that commitment, you're opening up your eyes, mind and world to a whole new level of possibility and presenter confidence you may not have really bothered about before. Possibilities are only out there for those who have the guts to create them after all.

And I thank you now for sharing them with me.

*I think a lot of the time these days people are so concerned about
having the right camera and the right film and the right lenses and
all the special effects that go along with it, even the computer, that
they're missing the key element.*

Herb Ritts

〜〜〜〜〜〜

What's that element for you?

〜〜〜〜〜〜

The Mind *of the* Machine

"Exhibitionism is different from connection.
Not everybody wants to be looked at,
but everyone wants to be seen."

Amanda Palmer - *The Art of Asking* 2014 Twitter glitterati, social media fanster,
vlogger, TED talker and provocateur *(from Sunday Times Magazine 09/11/14)*

Behind the Power of the Machine

Videos are great. They give us an opportunity to be seen without actually being looked at! We can connect with a huge global audience and if we don't want to see or hear their reactions, we don't have to – we can turn off 'Comments'. But is that really a good idea in business? Surely we need to connect and interact with our viewers and potential clients to boost our business online? So why are so many people so reluctant to use video as a number one marketing tool?

Because – as Amanda insinuates – we don't all want to expose ourselves.

(Aside to audience: And I don't mean like that, thank you!)

'Doing' a video with you presenting on camera exposes all sorts of presenting flaws we've been able to hide in the office. Or even if we're used to presenting live, no one ever sees us quite so close up all on display. Presenting is a very common fear. Presenting on camera is even worse!

From my own research over the last few years, it's the number one excuse people give for not actually making videos, before fear about costs and not knowing where to start.

And why is that?

Why do the camera and screen machines pose such an illogical threat that holds us back, when we know how good they can be for business success?

The big secret is – *it's not the machines!*

… It's YOU!

It's the very real fear of the human who has to stand in front of the machines and put themselves on exhibition. Being there causes them to create the fear and it's all about being judged, joked about, rejected. Why would we ever put ourselves through that kind of fear when we do very good business face-to-face with those nice customers we see at home?

Because there's a whole new world of wannabe customers who want and need your product and service – you could make a massive difference in their world by connecting face-to-face with them through those machines. You and they just don't know it yet, because you haven't put yourself on display.

It's not You, it's Me…

So where does this fear of the machines come from?

Human beings are voyeurs, we love watching the world, we love watching the screen. And when we watch we often make instinctive judgement calls about what we do and don't like, who we love and hate, what and who connects to us, delivering what we want in that moment, in that mood, at this time.

Whether we watch someone live, on television or online, it's really no different as a viewer – we just want to be informed, entertained and feel like we've gained something from watching you. How will you make my life better/easier/richer/more connected/more fun/more, more, much, much more? Much more betterer…? *(as we jokingly say at home!)*

Our human desire for wanting to be heard built the radio.

Our desire to be seen and communal love of watching is why television will never go away.

They connect us to the world even if we are on our own.

We can watch, learn, develop, and with the internet and online video we can respond as if we're almost there – with video messages and face-to-face live chat. Skype and Facetime let you be seen on the other side of the world, YouTube enables a platform for you to share the best of what you do, to connect with customers in a way you never could before.

Our individual need for quick and easy information and learning is why the internet is such a #SuperGreat *(my fave new word ☺)* video tool! How many people now go straight to YouTube when they want to find out 'How to…'?

A video is so fast to find out how, what, who, where, when and why?

This passion and desire to know more, *now*, is why we pay to hear fantastic speakers online, why we download podcasts, webinars and videos voraciously to absorb our favourite business guru gems.

Many millions of us prefer to watch than read – it's why virtual meetings, video conferencing and video calls have grown so fast, they're the business norm. Why spend a fortune on travel when I can talk to you face-to-face today? Video views have become the fastest growing business growth area online, with new tech enabling easy video production and millions of videos being uploaded every day – we *love* to listen and watch! YouTube is currently the second biggest search engine online, Facebook and Twitter fight them daily for direct video uploads, and we as viewers can simply connect, watch and absorb from the security of our own home, office, tablet or phone. We can see you present your service and then judge your performance and content on almost any size screen we choose.

For you producing business videos, there's the double-edged sword!

The desire to be accepted, not rejected, is why some people choose to step up and present, on whatever stage that might be; and why others choose to step back and prefer to connect another way – usually by viewing and judging others who do!

Video is so easy to access and view, we have become very picky in what we want to see. As presenters we are now much more vulnerable to viewers' opinions and judgements.

And that's something we humans love to do – to assess and opine on what we see online…

Watching TV or online is now an interactive game! *Ooooh*, the secret joy of rushing home to your favourite show, sitting with your family, or being online with friends, searching through hours of YouTube and loving discovering, and even more loving criticising, some poor person, actor or presenter on TV when they go wrong! The bloopers and the fun back stories are often the best part, even in a business video *(thanks for reminding us Wistia, Zappos and James Wedmore!)*.

No matter what nationality we are, if we like you and connect with you personally, we are more likely to buy something from you, or do what you ask us to do in the video.

Or we might interact with you or do something for you that you didn't even ask for – because we like the look and sound of you and your business message – we believe and trust in you.

We might tell you, or more likely *show* you, by sharing you and your service with all our friends. Sharing is what social media marketing is *all* about – it's what broadens your reach, so you want your videos to be shared – for the right reasons i.e. because they are good!

We aim to avoid being judged as joke video we don't like, the 'trying too hard' business video faux pas that simply annoys! That's when viewers get most vocal, vociferous and, sadly yes, even vicious when they really don't need to be… *#thankyoutrolls!*

Negativity Can Breed Success

And because of that real negativity that can appear online, not everyone *wants* to step up in front of a live audience or a video camera to present their powerful message for the screen, to post videos, or hold video meetings for business – yet so many of us have to do just that.

And you know what – whether you want to get on camera or not – it's often the negative comments that actually push you to do better next time round.

You need to share your story online to grow your business, to better serve that vast new customer base and you deserve to discover *the power you can have* when you present with Confidence on Camera any time you do!

Maybe that's why you're reading this book? You know you want to use the machines or get better at connecting through those machines. Maybe you want to work from home or hold all your meetings online; become the go-to video expert in your industry or promote 'brand you' better than you already do and you understand video can really work for you?

You Need to be Seen on Screen!

Video Marketing is a growing business to grow your business, and it's not going to go away. Whether you like it or not, video recordings can promote, sell, train and connect; they *can* be made and posted efficiently and effectively and DO build *massive* online business success.

Look at the Gen Z and screenage bloggers and vloggers growing celebrity beyond celebrity, because they've actually got something to say and know how to connect to their generation online – or even not! Some of them simply chat to connect! They may have never had office jobs, roles to fulfil, rules to adhere to. They may never have presented live or held video conference meetings or interviews – maybe they just do it in the privacy and safe comfort of their own homes. But they do it and post online and make money and a business out of it!

But you more than likely have to or do present for work – from talking to your boss to presenting to the board. You may have virtual meetings and one-to-one video or webinar calls but you don't post those online. Or if you do, your videos are maybe not seen or might not work with the impact you want… which could be why you're here now…

Top notch vloggers may not be nervous on camera, or if they are they don't care because it's all about being 'the real me' in online videos these days. But business credibility may be more important to you than being real. You may have to 'be' someone a little bit different or 'more than' just you. You may have an image to uphold, a style of presenting to adhere to that really isn't you. You can do it amongst your team, because they know – but letting it out on screen is a whole different scary presenting scene.

Well I'm here to tell you – yes… you… CAN.

And actually, unless you do, with the close-up nature of the camera and screen machines, **we will spot you not being you.** We will see it in your eyes, on your face, in how you move, your voice, your words – everything we see and hear. We spot it when it's not real and we won't like or trust or believe you or in what you say and do, on any size screen!

So why is it so easy to spot on screen? Why is it so easy to see your fear? What's the difference between presenting live in person and presenting for those darn machines?

Presenting Live vs On Screen

Some people are happy presenting live to any size audience.

You may feel OK presenting on screen, but you don't like what you see.

You may be happy to be recorded speaking live for a webinar or to be interviewed when you have a conversation and a real person connection.

Yet so many people run from talking directly to the camera lens – we don't like ourselves and how we appear on screen – we judge ourselves. It's mostly because of the *perfect presenter image* we're projected every day, those actors and TV presenters we so love to see on screen. But they are professionals – they've trained and practised for hours to be that way!

You're not going to be as good as them when you start, you may not ever be – but you are good enough to do the job you do, be the expert you are and have made a job or a business from that – and your message deserves to be shared and heard, no matter how you feel you look on screen. You'll always hate yourself more than almost any other viewers will!

It's normal to dislike yourself on screen by the way. The camera is a close-up exposure of our face, our expressions, those things that give us away – a 'distracting communication tool' even some professional speakers prefer to avoid because it so easily exposes all our presenting flaws that we can normally cover or hide when we present live! So you're not alone if you feel this way.

Face it – you are talking to a machine.

It's different, a bit uncomfortable and unusual and you may never have really thought about why before. Recording a video on your own can seem a bit dull, the performance can be draining and it does take extra work to look good on the other side. Presenting in front of a strange camera person and producer can be even worse – they're all looking at you and expecting a great performance!

But presenting on camera IS a bit of a performance. It's not actually real!

You're having to create a conversation and face-to-face connection that isn't really there.

So just like when you present live, it will take work and effort and it does take a different presenting skill. So even if you're not great presenting live, you may make brilliant videos on your own.

Simply Present Your Power but on a small screen…

Presenting the Power of You sounds like you need to be so big and expressive, like you would do on a live stage – but actually it's all about bringing everything down to minute details, to produce honest, credible delivery, but with an energy and personal charisma or charm that attracts the viewer and engages them with you. You need to make them like you.

You need to be confident, prepared and successfully self-aware to work well with these machines – just like an actor on stage or in a movie scene.

You watch them and they appear real on screen.

But just like learning the confidence to stand on stages small and big, in front of colleagues and peers, bosses and execs, clients and public showcases, you had to learn how to do it to be the best you can be. Now you may be back at the start, bringing all your presenting power down to fit the small screen, to a more intimate message – but your passion needs to shine through the machines to make you an online star! The #SuperGreat news is – it's sooooo much fun when you reach the point of going for it and pressing ▶**PLAY!**

Even at serious work, yes you ARE still allowed to enjoy it and to have a bit of fun – when you remember to play yourself, remember your passion, trust in your expertise and believe in the on-screen power of you!

To make *using* those darn machines easier, you simply understand and implement three simple things:

1. What works for you as an on-screen presenter?
2. What you can do better?
3. What do you need to do to connect to your specific, targeted viewers so you *get them to do something* for you?

You must also acknowledge, understand and accept that presenting to a camera *is* different from presenting live where the audience can see, hear and feel your energy. You may be brilliant live – you can still suck on screen!

On screen *you have to create that interactive exchange for us*, to make any impact – draw us into your world, share your personal and business stories to connect, say why, when and how you'll serve us, to drive the desire to come back and watch you again.

You need to make your viewer believe and like you enough to want to interact with you.

You must connect *through* the camera lens with Confidence on Camera to come across well on screen.

7 Secret Stages beyond the Mind of the Machine

When I was working with Sharon at TV Pro Global TV, the first private full service TV presenter training organisation in Australia, we always used to start training new presenters by looking at the psychology behind why we find it so hard to talk to that inanimate machine.

And there's a huge clue right there in the word inanimate – lifeless, inert, dead…

Kind of helps you to see why talking to it could be a bit tricky to start with!

At TV Pro we called it The Psychology of the Camera – sounds very complex for a simple concept really, and The Mind of the Machine is far more Lottie Hearn-drama-queen catchy!

So let's unmask 7 TV Presenting Secret Stages from behind the camera lens. This will help you understand how the camera relates to you and you can relate to it and through it on to screen, better than you already do…

SECRET STAGE 1: *Presenting is a Two-Way Conversation, but TV is a Screen*

The human brain is capable of reacting to a multitude of stimuli – from obvious words, visual cues, sounds, movements, expressions to more subtle moods, feelings, emotions. We gather and react to our perceived understanding of any given situation in mostly subconscious, split-second moments. Our brain reacts and neurones feed us with chemicals to help us cope with our perceived reaction – from happiness and fear, to joy and loathing.

Talking face-to-face with another person or a live audience, a momentum of energy is created between us. We can see their reaction, and assess if they understand us, feel us, hear us, are watching us, and even like us!

Sensing, hearing and seeing your audience interact allows you to assess direct reactions or moods, how they are taking your information, and if it's not what you want, you can act, react and adapt appropriately. This happens in a split second, often on such a subconscious level we don't even notice we are doing it. People constantly modify their conversation as a direct result of their perceived reaction from the other person – whether it's real or not.

Presenting Live we rapidly assess:

- ⅄ Are we creating reactions of sadness or smiles; anger or awe; jealousy, japes or joy?
- ⅄ Are they looking amused, confused, bemused or abused?
- ⅄ Are they on the journey, engaged in your stories, on their feet ready to do anything you say?!

Communication and presenting are two-way processes, so live effective communication only works when you work with the audience too – in a series of direct action/reaction/review/ reaction/action cycles. Impact is made when it is interactive – not just you talk, they listen. We need you to involve us, react to and with us, guide us to where you want us to go.

Presenting live - if you 'lose' your audience because they can't *(or won't)* understand, you'll sense it pretty darn fast! If you 'stuff up', i.e. go wrong or lose it in your presentation, often a simple encouraging smile from one nice person in the audience gives you all the support you need to get you back on track.

Our sensory perception in face-to-face communication is phenomenal – we can understand people from other lands through body language, communicate without sound and we can even do it over the phone with only a voice to hear.

But when talking to a camera, there is no face, no reaction – you are talking AT the machine!

Talking to the Camera:

You are talking at a static device, your viewers are not there – there is no two-way action/reaction cycle. Yet you **must** connect to them to have any impact, so they DO something for you after watching – to keep watching even. You are totally unable to assess your viewer, except by follow-up feedback – which may or may not be what you want to achieve. Perception is, it's risky!

Talking to a machine can turn you into one, and often a highly ineffective #trollbait one at that!

When you don't know how to cope with this, it can create mental insecurities that can show in ways the viewer can sense, see or hear straight away, and usually judges as nerves.

Unless, of course, you're being insecure on purpose, as a fun part of the story #we-love-self-deprecation-on-screen! So we need to learn to **#BeFlawsome**... Much, much more on this later in the book, but right now I do want you to think about what you've seen on screen that you've judged to be 'nerves on show'.

SECRET STAGE 2: On-Screen Nerves are ALL on Show

Have you seen or presented any of these potentially perceived nervous moments:

- X Stiff or annoying body movements – so tense, tight or repetitive they unnerve you?

- X Flat face – dead or scary staring eyes; no smiles or no expression, animation or joy?

- X Weird voice – tense or uneven; wobbly or high; dull or monotonous tones?

- X Lost lines – obviously fluffed or forgotten script or words; what did you really say?

- X Lack of spontaneity – over-rehearsed, nothing different or exciting, challenging or fun?

- X Lack of energy – flat, dull, boring, lacking interest so you miss the message?

- X Watching or presenting, feeling it's sooo bad you have to press STOP!?

Because we humans are so good at spotting anything that doesn't quite seem right, or those nerves that give us away, any good presenter needs to know how they manifest their nervous habits and why they are so distracting or uncomfortable for their viewer to watch.

It's the main reason people stop watching.

You will need to recognise your mental insecurities and plan how you can succeed despite them to best connect you to your viewers before you start, so jot down what you think yours might be in your first mini-Presenter A&E...

Quick Presenter A&E
Presenting Live vs on Camera – I think my
Machine Mind fears could be…

To overcome your nerves and not let these nerves show on screen (*or to self-deprecatingly cover them up when they do show up!*) does require a bit of basic acting work. You need to substitute your natural, live action/reaction subconscious skill with a bit of #PressPlay imagination. You need to let yourself play with your performance and get creative before you can release any connecting presenter power!

But is also comes from KNOWING the point of what you're doing and why.

SECRET STAGE 3: KNOW WHAT YOU'RE ON CAMERA FOR

For every video, every recording, webinar, vlog or time on camera you need to KNOW:

1. **Who are you talking to?** – target your one ideal viewer

2. **How do you want to be perceived?** – by that individual viewer

3. **What product or service are you promoting in this video?**
   – one specific item

4. **Why your 'product' can help them?**
   – why they should watch you?

5. **How will it/you help them?**
   – how will you serve them/help them succeed?

6. **What you want them to do after watching?**
   – your Call to Action (CTA)

7. **Whose opinion ultimately matters?** – Point of View (PoV)

Think of the idea you have in your head and take a moment to jot down some notes.

How well did you do off the top of your head, without much thinking?

You need to know that every viewer wants to know:

"What do I get/learn/gain from spending my time here now, watching you?"

Your videos will have the biggest business impact only when you give them that.

Knowing this from the start will help you decide on your core message and what style, mood and presenting personality your viewer will expect to see – therefore, what you need to do to find that in you.

And by thinking and jotting down notes, you're already starting to Press Play in your mind!

SECRET STAGE 4:   Stop Talking at the Camera Talk through the Screen

You have to stop talking *at* the machine and pretend you are talking *through* – *to someone real*. This will give you the energy to connect past the machine and boost your energy and confidence before you even start.

Help your on screen confidence by thinking of the camera lens as an eye to view you through – like the cover of the book! Make that eye contact and serve what your viewers want to see on the screen.

Press Play on your Imagination:

- ⌃ So how is your viewer ideally reacting?
- ⌃ Make up their reaction as your BEST, #amazeballs reaction – the one that has them on their feet, energised, ready to do/say/react and act as you want.
- ⌃ Then perform it with energy and Play!

By replacing the static energy with your imagined or ideally perceived *reactive energy* you can connect through any camera lens, because you are boosting your energy, which we see and sense as more real on the screen.

You come across as more real and believable, because it IS really you – you have imagined the live conversation, the actions and reactions, you have played the whole communication scenario towards the result you want. You are confident in your connection by making it real.

〰〰〰〰〰

**Connect through the camera by making it real for you
– by talking to your reel* person!**

*No responsibility taken for poor use of puns… in your perception ☺

〰〰〰〰〰

SECRET STAGE 5: Viewer Opinions are not Your Presenter Truth

You're good at business homework research, right? So you probably have a pretty clear picture of your target market for your video – your ideal client, right? The thing is, even if you think you've got the perfect video or webinar recording to hit that target market, not every ideal client is going to react to it the way you do, or the way you want them to.

Or maybe you don't know your target market quite as well as you'd like to, or think you do!

You may not like it, but they may not like you – and you know what? That… is… OK.

It's purely our own personal opinion that every single one of us is entitled to have *(though not always to share if it's derogatory, derisive or damaging, please!)*.

An opinion is purely our *perceived reaction* to something we see, hear or do. We are allowed to *perceive* things however we want because that is the message we take in and react to. And that message may be from a split-second moment, a minute or a whole hour – our brains keep the action/reaction process going over, and over, and over… We are given stimuli and our brains to comprehend, understand, advise on what action to take. We translate your message to check how it does/can/will affect our lives and therefore react however we choose – because NO ONE else has our personal reaction, depending on our mood that day, or understanding.

Even when that understanding may be wrong…

Yes, come on – you know you're right, even when you're wrong!

But you also know you can sometimes misunderstand a message or pick up mixed messages, and sometimes you misunderstand, lose interest, even react with heels-dug-in *"No way, NO!"* At others it's a resounding, big fat *"YES – WOOHOO!"*

So remember, other people's opinions do not have to be true to you, but you and your opinions do! You have to believe in what you're saying to be of any use, or to enable you to serve and help your viewer. You have to believe with passion in what you do.

We *will* make judgement calls about your presenting, both good and bad – because we can – but not all judgements are negative and many can help us improve. We need our viewers' opinions to make sure we are delivering what we say and what they want to see more of.

The *Brave New World* author Aldous Huxley said, *"There are things known and there are things unknown, and in between are the doors of perception."*

Well, presenting is all about not knowing what your viewer will think as you present, but creating your own perception from your own business knowledge and experience anyway!

On TV and video every single person has their own personal perceived reactions – opinions of what they want, like, expect, choose to watch and act upon. While most people call it judgement, I've often found that to be limiting and often perceived as derogatory, derisive or damaging. So to be less defensive we're calling it simply: **Perception!**

SECRET STAGE 6: Know Whose Point of View (PoV) Rules

Presenting has two points of view, or simply for gratuitous TV acronyms' sake **PoV = Point of View**.

1. Your PoV = what you want.
2. Your viewer's PoV = what they want.

As your viewer, whenever I watch you in a business video I can perceive you however I want.

I can judge you if I like, or you can influence me. I can choose to do something for you when I like you, especially when you help me like you. But ultimately all I *really* care about is my own PoV – with my WIIFM? reaction.

WIIFM is an old sales and marketing acronym for What's In It For Me?

〜〜〜〜〜〜

My Perception = My PoV = My WIIFM? – "what do I get from watching you?"

〜〜〜〜〜〜

Yet when *you* first start planning that very same video, you always start with your own perception, PoV and WIIFM:

- ⅄ "What's this video going to do for me?"
- ⅄ "How will this video help improve my business?"
- ⅄ "Will this video connect me to a bigger/better/new audience?" etc.

But whose PoV and WIIFM actually counts when you're presenting on camera?

In your PoV, you may have a *superimportant* message that you want to get across to me – you may even think it can help improve my life! But I'm the one with the choice here – it's my screen, I control the mouse or remote control in the end, not you. Any time I can:

 Press Stop   **Press Pause**   ▶ **Press Play**

So whose POV is most important – yours or mine?

YOUR PoV
ON CAMERA

MY PoV
ON SCREEN

Whether it's a video, webinar, online meeting, VC presentation or vlog…

For *any* viewing on any screen

ONLY I CHOOSE

to Press Stop, Pause or Play…

Your **PoViewer has the power…**

So help them choose to watch you!
Help me LIKE you!

SMILE!

SECRET STAGE 7: First Impression - Annie "You're never fully dressed without a…"

Our time is so precious these days, you have to help us choose to watch you. More than likely we'll only stay watching you if we get a positive first impression of you – something you do that grabs us and draws us into your world to hear more.

Remember, we make judgement calls within seconds of seeing you on screen. It's an instinctive reaction so you've got to grab us fast. Now, we've all heard *"there's only one chance to make a first impression"* – but on screen, you have lots of different videos, you can do lots of different meetings and webinar recordings, so actually each time you get another chance to make a first impression. Your first topic may not have grabbed my interest, but your second or third one might, so I might give you another chance.

You might have to help me like you a bit more though – and what's THE BEST thing you can do on screen to help me with that first impression? Yep – from my very first acting audition aged 10 for *Annie* in London, to you right now… "You're never fully dressed without a…"

Yes – SMILE!!!

Did you know a smile is the first instinctive 'other people' reaction we have as a baby?

Why? So the first impression we have from an early age is that we're absolutely adorable and people pick us up and look after us! It's so deeply ingrained from our ancient Neanderthal brain, when we'd die if someone in the tribe didn't care for us, that we don't even notice it any more. Even if you're not a baby person, try holding back that smile when that baby beams out at you!

As adults, if we see someone smiling our instinctive, natural, reaction is to smile back. And it works from you presenting on one side of the camera through to me watching you on screen! Same with laughter – it's infectious. If you've ever had giggling fits on stage with another actor *(we call it 'corpsing' – literally dying on stage of laughter!)*, you'll know just how infectious it is.

Smiling and laughing is good for you too – it releases endorphins in the brain, which relax us and make us feel comfortable. No wonder we all love a good laugh and a smile. OK, not everybody smiles, but you can learn to!

How #SuperGreat would it be if the first impression you give your viewer makes them feel great? SO SMILE ON CAMERA! I'm shouting that at you because I see too many clips where people don't, and it gets me down 'cos it's so easy and simple to do.

Starting your video with a smile, or sharing a smile within the first **10 seconds** – *which you will often now see written through the book as **10″** –* is an immediate ice-breaker, a connector, and leaves a positive first impression. It doesn't have to be huge, it could just be when you say your name, but DO connect to your smile. Get the connection to me, and then you can get on with the core of your message.

There are times when a different approach will work, when you need to decide what perception you'd like your audience to have of you, who you need to be. And you can actually manipulate that, but if your video is a simple intro to you, your website, your welcome video, focus on finding your smile for an immediate connection with your audience.

~~~~~~~~~~~~~

**Avoid negative judgements and get viewers
on your side from the start.**

Start with a smile ☺

~~~~~~~~~~~~~

BONUS SECRET STAGE: *Confident Camera Connection Makes it REAL!*

Most people tend to watch online videos on their own screen. But no matter who we watch with, how or what we watch, the next secret of TV presenting is this: every viewer wants to feel like the presenter is talking directly to them.

LOOK AT THE CAMERA AND THROUGH THE LENS = EYE CONTACT!

Face-to-face we like eye contact – the ONLY way you get it on screen is when someone looks right at the camera – connecting eye contact through the screen. Sharing that very personal connection makes me feel you're talking directly to me, makes you more REAL and so helps me like you.

Professional actors and presenters have confidence to make eye contact when they need to *make* it real – so it becomes so. And a play is called a *Play* for a reason in my world! When we watch TV we expect actors to be believable in their role and factual TV presenters to *be real people* – educating, informing and entertaining us about real and interesting things.

If we don't get the connection with them, we simply turn over or turn off.

We all love to see an actor or presenter with a personable personality who connects to us for real – we spot a fake mood or fake smile a mile off! We can also spot when you go wrong, but we *will* forgive you for it when you stuff up well, when you make it entertaining and do it in a down to earth, real way. It's part of being **#Flawsome** after all! *(you'll find out in a tick…☺)*

And now most TV is online too and we can actually interact while watching multiple devices. There is so much more clamour for our attention, so you've got to do something special to hold on to my attention as your viewer!

Or do you?

Maybe you can simply strip it back, be more real to simply get real?

So let's get really real – you can't get real until you know how to do it! You've got to go over the top to start with to find where your on-screen energy balance lies. You have to ham it up acting luvvie to know when it actually feels real…

How can you come across as REAL without over-acting?

Remember, to a viewer you are simply a conveyor of information, but if you can entertain them too, you're on to a winning video. When you have a very dry video story to tell, or are unsure how to tell your story, you may have to put in a bit of an acting performance – it may suit your story.

At others, the simplicity of your corporate message may be all you want to convey.

BUT the on screen presenter big hint here is:
just because your business may be a Serious Business,
we don't have to be serious about business all of the time!

In fact you're far more likely to create a positive interaction with your viewer by presenting in a more entertaining, enlightening or intriguing way. Let different aspects of your personality show. Be confident with your choices – you'll find out exactly how when you identify what areas you want to work on, so you can step into any Confidence on Camera Step when you need.

Your Confident Mind of the Machine A&E

It's time to check and exercise your self-awareness, to build your work-book of ways to Play on camera. So here's your first mini Awareness & Exercise: A&E, so get Playing!

My Viewing Playlist for a Confident on Camera Me!

Think about when you are watching a presenter as a viewer, whether TV or online:

1. Do you really care what or who you're watching, or are you just looking for yourself?
2. And whose PoV is really most important to you, theirs or yours?
3. What first impression judgement calls do you make?
4. How much time does the presenter have to make an impact on you?
5. How long do you give them to say what you want to know - your WIIFM?
6. How often do the presenters you really like smile?
7. Who do you like just because they make you smile?

Now, next time you leap to judge a presenter, think how you'd feel in the same situation and give them a moment more. Give them a smile and they may smile back at you!

What Works on Camera?

Who presents well online and on TV?

Before you pick up your camera, you need to do some research.

So we're going to get subjective here to recognise what works on camera and who does it well online and on TV in your PoV.

NB. I know I said earlier that you can't mimic other people and try to 'be' them as it isn't real, but you CAN take what works for them and adapt it for your own use. So here comes the fun part and homework for this chapter...

You must now watch TV and surf videos on YouTube and Vimeo...

"Yes, honestly darling, my video coach said it is homework!"

Now – it's not just any TV or videos mind you! You need to watch clips and programmes with presenters in that you feel might suit your style, or that give you inspiration, or that you simply like to watch.

Your Favourite Presenters on Screen

1. My favourite TV presenters are

    _____

2. Now think what is it you actually LIKE about them?
3. What words would you use to describe them?

    I like _____

    because _____

    _____

    _____

If you want you can see my list online. Lots of fantastic BBC TV presenters I grew up with like David Attenborough, to comics like Tina Fey from America, Dara O'Briain from Ireland and YouTube business stars like Marie Forleo's Marie TV and James Wedmore, or successful social media influencers and business guides like Chris Brogan, Ann Handley, Gary Vaynerchuk or Myles Dyer in the UK or Jeff Bullas or Alvin Phang the other side of the world.

I'd like you to make your own notes in your workbook *or download the .pdf:*

My PoV Favourite Presenters Online and on TV	▶

1. Presenter Name: _____

   URL/TV Show: _____

   I like because _____

   _____

   _____

2. Presenter Name: _____

   URL/TV Show: _____

   I like because _____

   _____

   _____

3. Presenter Name: _____

   URL/TV Show: _____

   I like because _____

   _____

   _____

...AND FOR FUN - WHAT ANNOYS OR DISTRACTS?

I also want you to start noticing when you *don't* like a presenter. What annoys or distracts you when they present on camera and when you watch them on any screen?

What reactions do you and others around you have to them?

Chat about it, discuss, debate – it can get very vehement at times, we're all secret armchair judges on TV and that's coming up next.

Stop! Judgement Time!

Now comes the part that most people instinctively jump to first – **what irritates you on TV?** So let's have a judgement moment now, just to make you aware of the habits, as I'm *sure* it's not something such a lovely person as you does at all…!

- ⅄ What have you seen on TV or online that really doesn't work when you watch?
- ⅄ What makes you want to press Stop – what is it they do, or don't do?
- ⅄ Is it the presenter or production issues?
- ⅄ Does the size of screen you watch on affect your opinion?
- ⅄ Are you ever happy listening to them, as long as you don't have to watch?

Now be specifically perceptive here, not willy-nilly negative "just cos…."

Develop simple clarity behind your like/dislike reasoning.

- ⅄ What distracting habits irritate you, big and small?
- ⅄ They may well be habits you've seen yourself do, they may be something new.
- ⅄ It may be what you sense, what you hear or what you see.
- ⅄ What specific habits have you seen/heard presenters use that irritate you?
- ⅄ What is it about a specific presenter that makes you want to turn them off?
- ⅄ What things do you notice you may do yourself?
- ⅄ What impact do you think that could have on your audience? *(YES - you might irritate them too!)*

Now get consciously specific and think about:

1. What you see – the Visual aspect.
2. What you hear – the Vocal aspect.
3. The choice of words – the Verbal aspect.

Be direct with what distracts you, instinctive about what irritates.

Notice details, get precise as to why, be clear on exactly what annoys you and why.

You can also note if there are any production distractions – lighting, sound, backgrounds etc.

Common Distracting Habits of Presenters

Specific Distracting Habits I notice are...

Visual – *e.g. repetitive hand movements/body shifting/ dead eyes/stiffness etc.*

Vocal – *e.g. repetitive voice pattern/too quiet/mumbling etc.*

Verbal – *e.g. crutch words/no key point/rambling/unclear message etc.*

Production Distractions for Me:

Set up: _____

Lighting: _____

Sound: _____

Awareness over Judgement

OK, so you've now noted what you do/don't like in the presenters you've looked at.

It's your personal perception PoV, so anything you say is OK, by the way – it's just between us!

But before you go off slandering, slating or slagging (*as we used to say in Oz – that's Australia not the yellow brick road place!*) these presenters with your friends, spare a thought...

When you were watching was your first natural instinct to find *what you didn't like/what didn't work for you?*

    ⅄   Were you a judger first?

    ⅄   But where does that leave your thought patterns?

    ⅄   What kind of mindset does that put you in?

    ⅄   Yes, a negative one.

I asked you to think about what you liked *before* coming to the negative, irritating things.

From now on you will simply identify what Visual, Vocal or Verbal habits distract you in a presenter – what is within their control at the time and separate from production issues.

This takes away the stress of judgement or self-judgement and replaces it with simple self-awareness. It's judgement in a confidence-building 'be kind to me A&E: Awareness & Exercise' structured way.

Too much choice has caused us to be fickle with our viewing whims. So it simply means we need to make the best, most positive, hard-to-be-rude-or-mean-about impact to stand out. We need to be the viewers' choice presenter from our first actions and words. We need to help them like us, so the most important rule *(for now and within business reason…)* of The Mind of the Machine is simply…

On camera and on screen… **Anything Goes!**

Some things **work** with **impact**

Other things **dis**trac**t**

Which would you prefer to do?

Positive Presenter Feedback 101

Be prepared – just like you did to presenters you watched, you may get some sledging *(Aussie cricket term)* from some folk when your videos are up. So I want you to start giving specific feedback in a positive way, right from now, for every presenter you see – this will build your confidence too:

1. Look for the things you LIKE first.

2. Only then review the dislikes or irritations and get specific to avoid generalisations.

3. Also stop using the words 'irritations', 'dislikes' or 'annoyances' – DO use 'distractions' or 'distracting habits'.

It's your personal perception, but when you use more positive language when being critical or judgemental, the more constructive your choice of words can be and the more positive and confident your mind becomes. Be constructively kind to others, and especially, be kind to you.

So let's take that positive mindset and bring the spotlight on to you – go get your camera 'cos it's time to step into the spotlight and Press Play with Confidence on Camera **Step 2: The Presenter Mindset**.

STEP ONE:

The Mind *of the* Machine
Learning Review *and* A&E

My Learning Stage Notes:

My things to think about from the Mind of the Machine...

_____

_____

Live vs on screen perceptions?

_____

_____

My 7 Secret Stage Notes I want to remember...

1.

2.

3.

4.

5.

6.

7.

Remember 'My Playlist' notes are YOUR notes to remind you of what you need to know from each Step. Future Playlists may get more specific for you to Play!

The Presenter Mindset

Since everything is in our heads,
we had better not lose them.

Coco Chanel

Before we do get deeper into your Presenter Mindset to maximise your success on screen, I've broken this Step, and each chapter Step from here on, into 7 Stages for you to appear on.

(I know, more cheesy theatrical puns – I'll stop soon I promise, it's just the excitement of getting all this down on paper to share with you!)

They're not secrets this time, simply common sense practical knowledge picked up along my way from and with many amazing people, which together all help build you towards your confident mindset for on-camera - success from self-awareness, to making connections, to making an I'mPact…

STAGE 1: *The Power of You Self-Awareness Video Presenter Self-Assessment*

Stage 1 is actually all about stepping into your video spotlight, as it's a *practical* video recording **A&E** = **Awareness and Exercise**, self-awareness exercise.

You've already learned it's impossible to improve your presenting without some practice, so go film a clip on any camera, or pull up a video of you that you have done before. It can be less than a minute and no need to be perfect *(in fact, be as natural or tense as you are)* because you're going to learn how to give yourself an honest, positive, confidence-focused presenter self-assessment. This Video

25

Presenter Assessment is where most of my clients start – and it is allowed to be fun too!

Online

The 7 Step Video Presenter Self-Assessment Process

There are seven key Steps to assess your presenting with Confidence on Camera and it will take about an hour of your time to complete. So book yourself quiet time to do this properly – invest in yourself to get the best results.

NB. You really only need under one minute of clear smartphone or webcam close-up video and make sure it's no longer than two minutes for self-review. You can present on any topic you wish, so no need to spend hours creating the perfect script for it – that's later in The Verbal Impact.

▶ **Press Play** - *7 Step Self-Assessment*

Start with Steps 1-5 – and complete the accompanying Video Presenter Self-Assessment form you'll find with the instructions online. Then you Press Pause – read this below before carrying on with **Step 6** and **Step 7.**

❚❚ **Press Pause after Step 5**

So you will have now watched yourself four times… that's more than many presenters do when they first start off as it is normal to hate doing it! But you are probably now starting to notice things that *do* work for you, that it's *not that bad* as your first impression, judgement perception may have been when you first watched yourself…

This is the time to pat yourself on the back and say, *"Job well done, yes, I'm actually OK/quite good/very good/a natural/wondering why I'm still reading this book"!* And yes, you know why: because that dark little judgemental devil on the shoulder has also spotted some things you don't like – or in preferred positive speak *"things that I can do better"!*

So before the next Step in the exercise, take a moment to step back from your self-judgement and agree to be purely objective, kind and positive about yourself.

▶ **Press Play for Step 6 and Step 7**

Only then, move on to Step 6 – to watch again for distractions…

Finally, end your self-assessment on a positive with **Step 7:**

- ✓ How could you present even better?
- ✓ What potential presenter perceptions you might want to project?
- ✓ What great words could viewers say about you?

It may seem like overkill, but going through this process with self-assessment at the very start gives you the confidence to avoid judgement and think purely objectively about yourself. Some things will take some work to change, some things can be improved immediately as long as you are aware of them. This is purely a self-awareness exercise, and the more specific you are with what you like about you, what habits can be shifted and what deep-seated fears need work, focus and practice to shift, the better.

Remember to go online for these instructions and my Video Coach Presenter Assessment form to complete yourself and build your workbook. Or when you want, you can ask about a personalised Video Presenter Assessment from us – "invaluable" and "first place to start for immediate improvement" to quote assessment fans!

The 7 Step Video Presenter Self-Assessment Process: steps 1-5 ▶ Online

1. Record your video to view

Watch yourself kindly! Make positive notes!
Look for what works/what you like...

2. Immediately write down what you LIKE about yourself?

Use positive descriptor words. How could viewers describe you?
E.g. real, friendly, calm, endearing, persuasive, analytical, challenging, driven, open

_____

_____

Do you like your look/style on screen?

_____

3. Watch again with sound off – look only at your Visual Impact:

How do you look on screen? WHAT WORKS for you Visually?

_____

_____

_____

_____

_____

_____

4. Watch again with the sound up - listen to your Vocal Impact:

Do you sound like you mean your words? What works Vocally?

_____

_____

_____

_____

5. Listen once more and this time focus on the Verbal Impact:

Close your eyes and listen to the words you actually say.
What Works Verbally?

_____

_____

_____

_____

6. Now watch for any 3 Vs distracting habits or incongruent moments?

Start with focusing on just **ONE** key habit for each of the 3 V's:

Visual _____

Vocal _____

Verbal _____

7. Watch the video one last time to think what more could you do? What could be better?

How can you make any distractions better?
How can you be even better on screen?

What potential personality styles could you project
with a bit of imagination?

What words best describe you on screen?
How do you want to be perceived?

So now you have a detailed specific self-assessment and you've seen how specific you can get. So how did you do? Did you like yourself? Did you go to what you didn't like first each time? Did you get down on yourself at all?

If you did, that's perfectly OK – this is an ongoing process, and the more you get on camera, the more confident you will become at reviewing yourself, letting all your 'mistakes' (as you perceive them!) go and start to appreciate just how good you are and can be.

You're allowed to be critical of yourself to learn, but you MUST also do it in a positive, self-supportive way. If you find it really hard, ask someone else you trust to tell you what they like about you when they watch it. Say there's no need to point out distractions – they can simply tell you what they like and what words they would use to describe you. But before you do ask, you might want to finish reading this chapter about your Presenter Mindset, pitfalls and power building, so you can go into sharing your presenting work with a superconfident connection!

STAGE 2: *Confident Connections – from your Mindset*
3 Cs make a Real Connection from you to your Viewer

You may have noticed doing your assessment that there were moments of brilliance and connection, moments of not; you may have sensed when it was real and when you were faking it; you will have spotted far more 'bad' things than anyone else would have done – but did you also spot your potential as a presenter with personality?

You, as a *Presenter with Personality,* are simply someone conveying information who is a:

1. **Confident** speaker who serves a clear, defined, positive, helpful message.
2. **Credible** representative as The Expert in your field – believable, trustworthy, convincing.
3. **Charismatic** person who is acceptable, but also appealing, charming, captivating.

These are the **3 Cs of connection** to your viewers.

~~~~~~~~~~~~~

A professional TV Presenter is ALL of the above – how about you?

~~~~~~~~~~~~~

Once you have self-belief in these 3 Cs then you can add your emotional investment to create the mood of the piece, an actional driver from your mindset that gets the viewer to do what you want and the impact you actually have on the viewer who will take action.

It all starts with your self-belief in your 3 Cs – how real are they in you?

A Real You = comfort in Confidence + Credibility + Charisma
+ Emotional Connection – the sensory and feelings investment from you
+ Actional Connection – to state clearly and evoke what you want
+ Impact – to get the action you want

Remember, in the end it's simply about the perception we have of you on the screen; even if you don't feel all of these things, you can help yourself *look* like you do, and that is why we are here – to practise and help you fake it till you make it and it actually does become real!

Confidence:

How we perceive confidence in you presenting is that perception that allows your viewer to be easily, effortlessly entertained, informed and confident enough to believe in your offering to take some action on it. You need to make it easy for us to watch you – we never want to be nervous on your behalf!

All TV presenters must incorporate entertainment as part of their informative presentation.

Television is confident delivery of facts or fiction + entertainment to engage. Think of you as MeTV*

*yes MeTV is a website to watch old TV shows, but think of this as your own channel!

But is business entertaining?

When you think of your time on camera as being a mini TV show and you realise your job is to engage, interact with your viewers, then yes you *must* entertain your viewers. Or pique interest before they turn you off at least!

Entertainment does not necessarily mean TV quiz or game show style hosting – but why not if that suits your business? For some, going music host, talent show or children's programme host might work when you have the courage and inventiveness! You are allowed to enjoy yourself while filming too – this comes across as supreme confidence.

So in your business, what can you do that is different and entertaining to hold their attention, while you deliver your important facts? It may not seem appropriate right now, but a bit of fun may be what your business needs to demonstrate your confidence. Create your own version of entertainment like Zappos.com or the Wistia.com team.

Most of us simply need to think of the best documentary, news or lifestyle show presenter.

So again, go watch TV and research YouTube presenters you like. Marie Forleo TV, James Wedmore, Zoella and Alfie Deyes all started off with their own cameras in their own space – just like you are doing today...

Confidence Connection:

✓ Nothing is blocking the Confident You but you!
✓ You can create the confidence to imagine being entertaining/great/amazing/interactive/emotive/challenging/leading/intriguing/demanding/fun etc.
✓ You have been these things at some point in your life
  – you DO know how it feels
Pick what works for you!

Credibility:

A credible online presenter focuses on answering the questions that viewers want answered by an expert. A TV interviewer researches and structures every chat to get the best information on air in an allotted time. They focus on the most interesting or enlightening things they think the audience wants to hear.

Really smart interviewers know their topic so well they can go off track to get the latest extract, most fascinating information or gossip, and easily get back on track within the time. They also ensure they promote any items their guest is there to talk about. It's always a two-way street. So remember that if you are ever interviewing or co-presenting a video, LISTENING is key!

When presenting on camera, looking, sounding and being fascinated in the topic is a must, or why should we be interested in you?

Credibility Connection:

✓ You ARE the expert in your field
✓ Believe in what you say
✓ Say it like you mean it
**Your credibility comes from your knowledge
and skills you have built up to today.**

Charisma:

Because TV and video represents **a human medium** as a form of entertainment, we like presenters with a charismatic personality. But what is charisma, who has it?

The Oxford English Dictionary online definition is:

✓ 'the quality of being trusted and believed in'; 'convincing or believable'; and even shows 'street cred = acceptability' – a basic human craving.

If you search for charisma with your computer Thesaurus you also get words like:

✓ charm, personality, appeal, magnetism, allure, attractiveness and captivation.

So what does it mean to you? Why do so many people think it is so elusive?

Charisma is purely that part of you that makes people stand up and pay attention. As intellectual and informative a video may be, it still requires a suitable presentation style to enhance and effectively project the subject through to the viewers with as much impact as possible. The biggest impact comes when we see your confidence and credibility combine with your own style of charisma, we feel we are watching the real you... it's that split-second positive PoV judgement call that we *like* you.

When you know which side of you best suits your theme, you can present the best, most suitable you at any moment. That performance enhancement allows you to let your charisma shine.

DO I have Charisma? ☺

"But what if my charisma doesn't shine? What if I don't have any?" I hear you shout quietly…

Charisma comes in many, many forms and is in the eye of the beholder, as they say. But if you are contemplating video as a promotional tool, then you already have a business, product or service that you believe in, that you want to promote, yes? So you probably have people who believe in you, yes? So ask them about the charisma they see in you. Ask why they believe in you, ask what it is you do when you share your passion that makes them feel that way. What piques their interest when you share your ideas and help them live? If you have one friend or family or colleague who listens to you, who takes your advice, who smiles at you when you talk, then you have your own charisma too. All you've got to do is translate that energy on to screen.

Everybody has their own charisma, even if you don't believe in yours yet!

For anyone saying not everyone has charisma, stop listening to them and go find someone who thinks you *are* acceptable and trustworthy, or charming/ fascinating/worth listening to/ valuable/ #SuperGreat! They are the person who can help give you the confidence to let your charisma shine.

But my Charisma really doesn't shine? ☹

If you're really in that low self-esteem/lack of confidence situation, you need to know when and how to ask the right people, or negative feedback can knock you down. Understanding why and knowing how to get people to give you feedback which empowers, enables and boosts your confidence is extremely important when you are starting off. So if you want you can skip on now to Step 6: Sharing with Confidence, where there is more on how to ask for positive feedback. Remember, you have already done it for yourself, so now's the time to be kind.

The main thing is, not everyone is going to like you *(and that's OK!)*, so focus on your target viewer and decide which side of your personality matches the information you want to share with Confidence, Credibility and Charisma!

> ### Charisma Connection:
> Watch other TV presenters to see what works on camera or what habits annoy you...
> ✗ Copying and imitating someone else's style may not work for you!!!
> ✓ Use your own personality to get your message across!
> **Your charisma is yours alone – now it's time to shine!**

Confidence in Being Me – why every presenter needs to be themselves

- ⅄ Every person can present – we communicate every day.
- ⅄ Everyone has a personality – we do all have someone who'll listen to what we say.
- ⅄ Everyone has charisma – within their safety zone where they feel comfortable.

But why do some things work for one person when they present, and when you say them, they sound sooooo wrong?!

Because each of us has to discover our own voice, our own way of saying things on camera and have the confidence to say it out loud. And the way we say it is not always the way we write it down. Your written word for business may be far more powerful and convincing to read than your spoken business word on camera. But we don't speak how we write, so you need to find your business voice in a whole new way. It's time to simply 'chat' business online.

Watch and listen to the way in which your 'good presenters' express themselves and the words of the script with their own interpretation.

- ⊀ What style works for them?
- ⊀ Could that style be useful for you?

Because every one of us has different aspects of our personality and preferred behaviour styles, we do need to discover and match our presentation style. Our voice and our script need to represent the video core theme, but it can show different sides of you: you can demand, challenge, enthuse, excite and flirt all in one video, on different lines – but which side of you suits the message you're sharing? Be YOU – not a carbon copy or half-hearted image of someone else you'd like to be.

The best presenters learn to use different sides of their personality and are easily able to hide any discomfort (usually physical and vocal distractions, repetitions or blockages of energy) even when they don't like what they have to say. If you've been given this job to present someone else's words, this will be very useful for you. How you make that connection is coming up on page 56.

The success of a presenter depends largely on their ability to:

- ⊀ express themselves as naturally and spontaneously as possible through the script
- ⊀ chat on screen and engage me
- ⊀ share the information in an easy storytelling way
  – take me on your adventure!

Confidence on Camera is knowing the impact that has on your viewer.

Engage me, enchant me, inspire me… Capture me, captivate me, charm me…

Make your impact on me with your best 3 Cs!

Constant expansion of your research arena and repetition of exercises and scripts will encourage a natural growth of confidence and ease, elevating you to your maximum performance level for your credible, charismatic appearances.

3 C Presenters Keep Going to the End!

As Coco Chanel said, *"you'd better not lose your head – or get too stuck inside it on screen!"*

Our nervous habits manifest themselves in all sorts of ways – from not blinking to how you hold your hands, from a tight voice from not breathing to 'crutch words' like 'Uhm' or simply forgetting what you want to say. But one of the biggest production headaches working with a new or unconfident presenter is when they get nervous or flustered on camera and decide to just stop talking when they feel it's all gone wrong. They hold their breath and we see it all collapse to a stop in graphic close-up detail!

Nothing is more disheartening, even irritating, for a production crew when you've just been so 3 C natural, coming across sooo well on screen, than when you mess the whole shot up by stopping! Unless a director says "*Cut!*" **the camera is still**

rolling, so you have to learn to do the same. We can always cover visual stuff-ups with a cutaway 'B-roll' shot and a clever edit, but you might never get that spontaneous brilliant spark of energy so good again. So…

No matter what happens on camera… KEEP GOING!

Stopping mid-sentence or thought makes a clip hard to edit.

One take always has a natural flow and is stronger than a video with lots of edits – unless you have done that on purpose as a specific editing/artistic reason.

When shooting your own PTCs, keep going to the end, even when you do go wrong. And when you *do* go wrong – go wrong well!

Stuff Up Well! * *(*Aussie phrase again – means a casual "gone wrong" or mess up, but often on a huge scale!)* Having fallen flat on my face in many a public arena, and carried on regardless, and faced many a rejection as an actor and performer, I know you CAN develop the mental flexibility and strength to cope with whatever is thrown at you AND keep going – as long as you're willing to laugh at yourself, be a human being and get over it!

And I'm talking right in the moment, right then and there. To keep on keeping on to the end without that horrific *'OH NO I've stuffed up!'* look on your face, sound in your voice and mental block in your mind that freezes your brain in fear – that horrible live TV mess-up moment!

Most of the time online you probably write your own scripts, yes?

So we only know you stuffed up when *you let us know* – by showing us your embarrassment, flusteredness, stress or nervous habits.

So my motto since I first started in kids' TV is: we have to learn to…

~~~~~~~~~~~

STUFF UP WITH CONFIDENCE AND GET OVER IT!!!

~~~~~~~~~~~

Stuff Up with Confidence Secrets from your Viewers' PoV

1. You are a human being and I will forgive you if you stuff up well and appropriately – whether with humour, frivolity, honesty or grace.

2. Beating yourself up the moment you stuff up only leads to more nerves – I see it all.

3. You must learn to let it go, breathe, apologise if necessary and keep going to the end!

4. Stuff up self-deprecation works – I'll laugh with you, not at you when you do it well, because it can be hilarious and fun!

5. I'll support you through your disaster when you get over it, because it's real.

6. You become more 'normal' like me – I might not have the guts to do what you're doing on screen, so you might even seem more charismatic, captivating and compelling too!

7. Stuff up well – I think you're #FLAWSOME!

#BeFLAWSOME

To use my favourite courageous-sounding word you've already heard, I picked up from a 2013 magazine and adopted my own *(thanks The Irish Times!)* Any time you feel it all *go wrong* – remember to be…

FLAWSOME = when flaws show, make them awesome!

Being #Flawsome *(OK drop the # now!)* and 'stuffing up' with confidence – giving a small apology, a smile or a huge laugh at your ridiculousness, whichever is appropriate – and simply carrying on when you go wrong and getting over it, is hugely appreciated by any audience.

Being Flawsome on TV

It's also something TV producers love when you're a guest interviewee on TV – that you are aware and confident enough to overcome any *"disaaaaster darling!"* situation and simply keep going. And if it's live TV, webinar, GHOA or Skype call, you're a winner all ways round as everyone involved will love you for releasing any tension the stuff-up has caused if you can laugh at yourself!

You'll be even more of a star if you are not only Flawsome in a disaster zone, but if you can deliver your chats in snappy sound-bite form. Or as Patricia FrippVT.com the pro speakers' speaker trainer says, be "quotable, Tweetable and repeatable" – say your point, get in your 'CTA' and then you can stop. More on that in Confidence on Camera Step 5.

Now, let's get theoretical on our next stage to understand:

✓ How we instinctively notice nerves, stuff-ups, flaws in each other?

✓ What little things give us away?

✓ Why it is so important to get your message across to have the impact you want?

STAGE 3: Confidence in Congruence – what we worry about and why?

The Congruent Message Theory

While developing Train the Trainer (TTT) skills and learning how to be a corporate presentation trainer with Maura Faye Workshops Australia, we were great advocates of using Professor Albert Mehrabian's theories of communication. They are regularly used and quoted by communication trainers across the globe.

But the thing is, it was only since his theories have been easily available online that I realised I was actually on the common communication trainer band-wagon Mehrabian loathes – misquoting the concept of his '7%-38%-55% Rule'.

In case you are going "HUH?" I'm going to tell you a little bit about Mehrabian, as he and his UCLA students are still in the forefront of research into non-verbal communication studies. And if you've heard this rule before and wonder what I'm on about, bear with me and you'll find out what I mean.

So Wikipedia states: **"Albert Mehrabian** (born 1939 in an Armenian family in Iran, currently Professor Emeritus of Psychology, UCLA), has become known best by his publications on the relative importance of verbal and non-verbal messages. His findings on inconsistent messages of feelings and attitudes have been quoted throughout human communication seminars worldwide."

You can discover his findings in his books *Silent Messages: Implicit Communication of Emotions and Attitudes*, *Non Verbal Communication* and *Tactics of Social Influence* for anyone with a theoretical bumper burning brain!

So far, so nice, so here's the theory…

MEHRABIAN's % of COMMUNICATING A MESSAGE =

Mehrabian's studies looked into "the relative importance of verbal and non-verbal messages" in face-to-face communications – checking the preferences for audience likes, dislikes and how an audience garnered understanding of each, or any, live presentation or communication. This led him to two key conclusions:

1. Any face-to-face communication comprises of three key areas:

    a.   Non-verbal physical behaviour – i.e. our body language, facial expression, gesture

    b.   Tone of voice

    c.   The words we say

Mehrabian designated a percentage of how *'important'* each is for viewer understanding when delivering a message that involves a **connection with emotions and feelings** – *as you will do on camera every time*:

  a. = 55% of your message

  b. = 38% of your message

  c. = 7% of your message

At Maura Faye Training we called these the **3 Vs elements of communication**

  a. VISUAL – what we see

  b. VOCAL – what we hear

  c. VERBAL – the words used

2. Congruence is key

For any message to *really* be heard and to be understood so it has an impact, the 3 Vs have to be working together to succeed. Just like ducks in a row flying in perfect V formation… led by the lead 'duck' the Visual impact. This is the concept of 'Congruence': everything has to match and work together for your message to be heard – without any distractions.

Without this the message makes little or no impact on the listener, they can zone out, misunderstand and are unlikely to take any action you want at the end.

The 3 Vs Model

Here's the model I like to use in my workbook:

38% Vocal
Tone of voice/variety

55% Visual
Body language
Facial expression

7% Verbal
The words you say

Even better my favourite piece of research in 2001 by UTS (University of Technology Sydney), indicated that the power of the Visual could equate to up to 70% of any message, 25% Vocal and only 5% Verbal.

Through my own experience and research, I've concluded that when it comes to communications on camera and through a screen, whether presenting for TV, video, webcam, online training, meeting, interview – basically on any camera and any size screen – the Visual Impact has an even stronger bearing for most people. We're voyeurs, remember! And the smaller the screen, the more important it becomes to keep visuals clear and keep it simple.

When you're presenting on radio, naturally the vocal and verbal aspects have more impact, because the strong visual element is taken away. This is even more true for voice-overs – when your voice has to convey all of the message over, and beyond, the visuals on the screen. How you use your voice carries a huge percentage of the understanding and connection to your message – *Vocal Impact coaching is covered in the next chapter* ☺

Mehrabian – Momentous Messaging Misunderstanding

I only relatively recently discovered my momentous messaging misunderstanding from Mehrabian's Wikipedia pages that: "The '55%-38%-7% Rule' has been so overly interpreted in such a way that some people claim that in any communication situation, the meaning of a message is transported mostly by non-verbal cues, not by the meaning of words *(or that the meaning of all the words can somehow be overridden by the Visual and Vocal Impact)*.

"This generalisation from initial very specific conditions of his experiments is the common mistake made with regard to Mehrabian's rule."

Mehrabian's theories were actually *only* talking about when we are communicating 'feelings and attitudes' and that these percentages are only really relevant when the Visual, Vocal and Verbal are **IN-congruent – i.e. mixed messages**. *"The non-verbal cues are very important in conveying the speaker's attitude towards what they are saying, notably their belief or conviction..."* but it's **when we mix up the meanings of the words with a visual or vocal cues that don't match the message gets confused** – whether consciously or subconsciously.

Because the camera is a visual medium it is even more relevant and imperative to understand:

~~~~~~~~~~

When the non-verbal behaviour and tone of voice don't match the meaning and mood of the actual words you say, we tend to believe the visual and vocal stimulus and don't hear your verbal words.

We watch your incongruent distractions and any impact is lost.

~~~~~~~~~~

So never mind understanding the words, the brain actually overrides the verbal words actually said and replaces them with what it sees and hears first!

This means that any Visual, Vocal or Verbal habit or perceived 'tick' you may have that is incongruent to your actual words and message WILL cause a distraction – even if you don't mean to, or notice, your own distracting habit. It's why I keep getting you to ask questions and do A&Es – we're building your awareness of what works and self-awareness for you. It is imperative to create three V habits that support your message, mood and style. Ticks don't have to be distracting though – if they are congruent they can allow the viewer to feel good about your message, hear it all and enable a positive attitude reaction to you – and you're more likely to get what you want them to do for you = SUCCESS!

Our subconscious brain notices any mismatch long before we consciously notice and we can get irritated, even irate about some habits that presenters have. Think of the last time you saw someone live who had an annoying habit for you. Was it Visual, Vocal or Verbal? Did you have to work to keep focus or did you drift away and miss what they had to say?

We can spot disparity in a split second and our gut instinct is to mistrust or disbelieve the speaker, whatever they say, so our brain literally judges and switches off the trust connection.

All of this has always led me to wonder quite *why* we focus *so* much on writing the perfect text in business, when actually we should be spending more time rehearsing *how* we say those words and what our body does when we do, to make sure they match! And remember, I'm a drama queen, so I do love and appreciate the written word – in fact the Verbal Impact chapter is the biggest in the book, because I understand the power of the written and spoken word.

But because of that I appreciate it when you can clearly write what it takes me three lines to say! Verbalising everything for dramatic effect and theatrical texts and scripts have been so much a part of my life, I love to read and say things out loud, to hear if it makes sense *(and sometimes it doesn't because I write as I chat!).*

But I suppose scripts have always been written to be said, as well as studied to be read.

So that's a new learning skill for those who blog brilliantly or write so well for web and online business…

We don't speak how we read!

You need to *write for the performance* and you need to be confident with your attitude to congruence – *you have to believe it feels right when you do or say it* – which may mean you have to perform a bit, as I've already said! Performance, rehearsal and improvisation are the norm for me, I've done my 10,000 hours of practice during years of training and performing. It's what actors and performers do and TV presenters have to have the flexibility to do at the drop of a hat. But here I'm doing the hours for you, shorthanding a life of experience and stuff-ups I've so gloriously made, so you don't have to! So please indulge a quick TV story here if I may?

Creating my own Congruence on TV Story

In Hong Kong *Tube Time* was the daily 4-6pm kids' cartoons and entertainment show with a continuity link presenter – you know the one reading your letters and birthday messages, showing your paintings and messing around with guests between the shows! As that presenter I had to create the show, write my own scripts, keeping it fresh and exciting to maintain viewers with different daily schedules. We would pre-record the whole week's continuity links, as if it was a live show, in two to four hours on a Thursday. Between that and my other two shows, it took a lot of organisation, which I also had to do: get guests on certain days, find prizes, create competitions, research local kids' events, find local stories *and* do the admin, so the last thing I had time to do was actually *write* a script as well!

As a result… and don't tell my producers… *I didn't!*

On air – when we were 'live on screen' – I'd simply let the chat flow.

I'd create a solid plan in my head of each section – of what had to happen within a certain time frame, jotting down and knowing how I'd start, how I'd end and what was the key point of that link, whether it was 10 seconds or five minutes.

It being a kids' show, creating congruence with my message had to be and always was fun! I had freedom to mess around as much as I wanted to… well almost!

But it was also important for me to bring in educational and enlightening items for the kids to know about. So I would promote local theatre events, sports activities, school, community and charity events for kids. These had to be specific, detailed and factually correct, so written down and read, or referred to, or remembered – there was no autocue for kids' TV back then.

Advertising during kids' TV 4-6pm was banned on all channels in HK back then, so getting your event on to *Tube Time* became a premium promo tool when kids were your market, because you knew I could sell your event for you well. I was often jumping from one crazy cartoon to a birthday hello to a very serious message – all within the same minute.

Sometimes I had to totally change my whole persona, my expressions, movements, way of talking and tone of voice to match the message that my guest or organisation wanted to get across – in a split second. I did it instinctively, before I even knew about Mehrabian. To me it was like playing a role as a professional actor, except this time it was me playing a different side of me. I had to match my attitude to the mood to the message.

By being congruent with choice of words and my way of saying them, I made an impact on my target market. Ratings and viewer interactions went up when I was on, so that's success to me!

Feeling Congruence with Mehrabian Attitude

If you think about it logically, we all do it naturally; think of how a child wanting to get its way will flip from one personality to the next and the next, trying to win you over and get what they want! We, as adults, have simply forgotten that we are allowed to play and have these different sides of us already there – so rather than having to learn lots of difficult TV presenting techniques, you are simply accessing the interesting, best and different sides of you!

Part of the reason I'm banging on about this is that I really do feel we need to get more emotional, be even more passionate about the work we do to have a successful business story on screen. In order to make an impact and get a reaction from our audience we MUST involve our real feelings and attitudes when presenting. Otherwise viewers will see so quickly if you are not being real or mean what you say.

I always say to my video coaching clients: **because online video is *all* about appealing to viewer feelings and attitudes, almost anything goes on camera, within the confines of your shot and congruence of message.**

Anything you do or say *can* work, but as we've learned there are certain incongruent habits that distract your viewers, whether consciously or subconsciously, and they can be superquick to turn you off!

~~~~~~~~~~~~~~~~~~

Presenting is never a case of rights and wrongs
It's simply messages that work and habits that distract
– which would you prefer to deliver on screen?

~~~~~~~~~~~~~~~~~~

So while Mehrabian's theories may be misquoted, the concept of feelings and attitudes congruence is completely relevant when presenting – all your ducks must be flying in a row or we can all go off course!

WHY Congruence Connects Through the Camera?

When you are incongruent in person presenting live and you don't have a big screen, you can get away with it more often – it's also easy to move, turn your back and step away when anything goes wrong. You can also refer to your notes – the audience will wait for you if you have them on side.

But on camera you appear on a very small screen, often in very close close-up! You are restricted to how much you can move, how you move, using your face, head and shoulders as your biggest form of expression – and you've got to remember what it is you want to say!

(Thank goodness for the move to one-minute expert videos and live video streaming, eh? We all need to make easier, more impromptu videos, or short 'n' sweet LIVE presenting clips, rather than long edited spiels!)

Also, remember **watching any video screen - it's only in 2D.**

Because of this, the first thing that hits us is *always* the Visual Impact, so it must carry the core of the message. Close-ups work when delivering a personal message, approach or plea as we can see the whites of your eyes and you are always talking one-to-one with a viewer on screen...

And again, while you're not face-to-face with us, you're acting as if you are. Your impact is *all about* how you make us feel and our attitude to you on screen. If you're addressing us on a screen, then talk to us! What you say and how you say it is what affects us most – we can even forgive some crummy production when you help us. But if your choice of words is one thing and your face, body, hands and tone of voice say something else, then what will we believe and be influenced by?

Because of this, when you do something on screen that annoys us, I reckon the Visual Impact can be up to 85% of your message!

Visual Incongruence Really Irritates on Screen!

If your Visual habits are distracting or irritating for us, then we notice. How many presenters have you seen flapping their hands around for no reason, or holding their body in one position while saying how excited they are to be talking to you? Grrrrrrrrr!!!!

Once our conscious brain spots the repetition, a distraction or incongruence, we focus most of our attention on the distracting habit and stop listening to what you are saying. We then hear things wrong in your voice and pick up on misplaced phrases or words. And you know what happens if you annoy us enough, or forget to be #Flawsome… We press ■

Your job as a congruent, confident presenter is to work out WHAT works for you on camera:

✓ what body movements, gestures, facial expressions…

✓ what tone of voice you want to use…

✓ what words match the mood you choose?

MAKE IT EASY TO WATCH YOU – STOP US PRESSING ■ STOP ON YOU!

When do you Press ■ Stop?

I've had a fun TV research question on the go now since the mid-1990s for every potential TV presenter I've assessed or trained. When absent-mindedly looking for something to watch:

How long will you watch a presenter before you turn off, turn over or turn away?

.... seconds

Think about your own TV viewing habits –

do you notice distracting habits or not?

When it comes to hogging the TV remote control and how fast we channel hop, with over 20 years and thousands of answers, my conclusions may already be as apparent in your house as they are in mine – sorry gents!...

- Men seem to give an average of only one to five seconds attention when absent-mindedly channel surfing to find something to watch on TV. But if they find a lovely lady *(or lad, so's not to be sexist!)* to 'like', they can stick to them until they get caught or bored before moving on! *(oh yes you do, sometimes so do we to be fair* ☺ *but…)*

- Ladies are a little more patient, giving three to 15 seconds if we are simply looking for someone to grab our attention on TV. Women mostly stop on the people who make us smile - they hold our attention the quickest, longest and it's a natural human instinct to react to the smile.

And now online…

How long will you watch a business video for?

If the presenter annoys you or you don't like it, how long before you turn off?

I turn off after _____ seconds of a video when there's something I don't like.

What's your preferred length of video time when surfing for interest?

How long do you prefer your videos to be? How long will you watch?

I will watch _____ minutes of video when I'm interested.

How long will you watch if it's for personal development?

I will watch _____ minutes of video when I'm learning something new.

NB. Please do contact me with your answers for my ongoing research – thanks!

Of course we'll all watch fun videos till the cows come home – when we're entertained and amused we lose track of the time. But for business videos, which are rapidly outpacing blogs and articles, our attention span is getting shorter and shorter – it's halved between 2013 and 2015!

2015 online trends seem to suggest that one-minute/one-and-a-half-minute videos are ideal for quick watching daily, but no more than three minutes, unless we plan the time.

If we're *really* interested or have planned, we're happy to watch a TEDxTalk length long-form video over 10 minutes, up to 18/20 minutes. But we still do prefer shorter if watching more than once a week.

But when we're learning something new, especially something we've paid for, we expect to invest time in for our money. So we'll follow a webinar or video happily for 45 minutes to one hour – as long as we can DO something with it along the way: make notes, copy what you're doing etc.

This is a good lesson when building videos into your training programmes – unless you are doing highly technical, detailed visual training, you may be better to film a series of shorter videos with action exercises in between – a bit like I'm doing here, constantly getting you to think, write or do.

Three to seven seconds of Incongruence is enough to turn you off!

From my drama training and TV remote control hogger research I developed my presenter viewing 'Three to Seven Second Rules' (3-7" Rules) well before I got any presenter training. That is also how little time we actually have to make a first impression, according to adult communication experts.

> **Lottie's 3-7" Rule: PART 1**
> Three to seven seconds is enough time for viewer first impression judgements – perceived levels of eye contact connection, congruent message and mood matching energy levels they see you present on screen.

My 3-7" Rule: Part 1 grew from the average time both male and female trainees took to be distracted by irritating incongruences, whether conscious or not, or stop paying attention both when channel surfing on TV or watching fellow presenters during training – coincidentally, both for live presenters and when watching on a TV or computer screen.

The other relevant regular training comment was when classmates could see each other both live *and* via the TV screen (even if I asked them to watch each other on screen) some always said, "Yes, but when I watch them doing it live I'm not so distracted by their habits because I can see all of them, not just the close-up on a small screen."

Viewer perception was "they seemed more alive in person and I'll watch them for longer" live vs on screen, where distracting habits and flaws were easier to spot close up. It was especially easy to see nerves in repetitive hand gestures or on the face, but a smile always helped ease the nerves.

People might put up with a lot more distractions from a live presenter, but we are distracted within three to seven seconds on the small screen – and if you don't change it, we're gone!

Repetitions of visual movements are most distracting because everything seems much more obvious on the small screen, even when movements start off congruent to our message.

3-7" Rule Rehearsal Playlist A&E

1. Notice what you do when you move/repeat a vocal or verbal pattern.

2. Notice when you do something twice, then a third time within 3-7".

3. Stop – breathe, smile…

4. Drop the movement, change the voice/word.

5. Do something different – no more than three times in 3-7".

6. Do something different again…

7. You can come back to your natural instinct move again – as long as you avoid the Rule Part 2!

The Screen is 30% Mean!

The way in which we move and the appropriate energy we put into our presenting directly affects the viewer's attention span and therefore our impact upon them. As a result a lot of people drop their energy levels when talking to the camera, as they think they need to make things smaller than on a big stage. In some aspects we do, but your energy level is key to congruence here.

The mean machine and TV screen 'steal' about 30% of your natural energy

Simply by recording and delivering your physical presence and message through the camera, the view is only 2D on screen, as you may have noticed I mentioned once before – did you spot this thought then?

As a result we need to boost that extra 1D that's missing through recording and watching via the machine – that's your one dimension 30%+ not One Direction folks! **Confidence on Camera needs your 1D 30% extra energy boost.**

BUT – you still need to fit that energy within the confines of the small screen – so staging and set-up of your shots is key. You can boost energy by 30% using:

- ⅄ your shoulders and expressions in a close up
- ⅄ with your face, body and flowing easy-moving arms in a mid-shot
- ⅄ and by bigger gestures or the slow TV amble walk in a long or distance shot

Screen your energy to fit within the screen.

On Camera Congruent vs Incongruent Presenting breaks down to this:

1. You **can do or say** *anything* on camera, within the confines of congruence + camera shot + image i.e. where and how you can move and behave to match your message
    - actors have a 'mark' or 'spot' where they have to stay so they remain in the camera shot
    - you also have to be appropriate, which I hope goes without saying!
    - your message and actions must be even more congruent on the small screen

2. There are **Things that Work** on camera – know what works for you?
    - within a certain time frame and suitable style
    - grab attention in the 3-7" Rule: Part 1
    - boost energy 30% extra

3. Then there are **Things that Distract** your audience – know what you're doing?
    - the things Mehrabian was saying can irritate us
    - the 3-7" Rule: Part 2 = even if a habit is congruent with your words…
    - a habit repeated 3 times within 7 seconds is already a distraction!

The Congruence Confidence A&E

Here's a quick test for you to really get what I mean – as you already know, actually *doing* something always reinforces any adult learning and we retain far more information by getting involved ourselves, hence producing the online A&E that goes along with this book and leaving you spaces to write in here. But for this one you can follow along a DO – so please do join in the simple drama class!

Say out loud the words "*I'm excited*"

Did you actually say the words out loud?

How did they really come out?

- Did you say them with energy and enthusiasm, or quietly to yourself, lacklustre and dull?

Now think of how that would look in someone else:

- What would their body and face and voice be doing for you to think they didn't mean it?
- What makes the Visual and Vocal congruent/incongruent with the Verbal "*I'm excited*"?
- What do we need to see in someone saying the words to make us believe them?

Now have a go at saying "*I'm excited*" out loud again:

- First as if you *really don't* mean it…
- Now as if you *really do*!

What did you notice this time?

- What were the differences in how you actually *felt* when you said the words?
- Or did you just read them and not bother saying them out loud?

HA! I know you may have done, because most of us are lazy, but to reach the point of presenting on camera with confidence, you **will** have to open your mouth, so let's have another go...

This time, I want you to say "*I'm excited*" with a big smile on your face and the exclamation mark in the inflection of your voice. Think of a time when you really felt it, at a moment in your life when you actually were… Be a big kid and play with the words... Go on, go O.T.T. as in…

"I'M EXCITED!!!!!"

Did you end up doing anything instinctively with your body as a result of putting in the *real* feeling?

I had a giggle, my shoulders went up and down, my office chair has just gone wheelie round the desk and my brain is now starting to wonder what it is I'm excited about – *WOOHOO!*

It's caused me to smile as I write! I have created a real physical and mental state simply by being congruent with the Visual and Vocal tones to match the Verbal words – i.e. my 'script'.

Aim for Complete Congruence

1. Your script must contain words that evoke emotion and have feeling – avoid blandness!
2. Match the emotion and feeling by setting the visual scene – production wise.
3. Think of the time you felt the emotions for real – how did you behave?
4. Use vocal patterns and tone to match – say the words as they mean.
5. Use body language, facial expression, gestures, movements that back up the words.
6. Act it in rehearsals – commit to the words to make them real.
7. Create a completely congruent message – backed up with your 3 Cs!

And remember – boost your energy that 1D 30% extra through the machines.

Go on – have a go at being over the top with the *EXCIIIITEMEENT!!!*

It may seem mad, but it will look Flawsome on the screen!

STAGE 4: *Creating your Confident Mindset*
Confidence Knocks and Building Blocks

Right – we've talked about judgement and perception enough when we were looking at other presenters. We've looked at turning judgement about yourself in to Flawsomeness and we also know you already know the answers to some tough truth questions:

1. Who's going to be hardest on your presenting style?
2. Whose PoV counts?
3. Judgement calls come from what first impressions, what habits?
4. How long do you have to make an impact and how long before a habit distracts?
5. What judgements could be made about you?
6. What can you be to help you – the 3 Cs?
7. What will help your message be heard – the 3 Vs?

So that MUST help us with our own confidence as a presenter.

Well, it's tough love time folks.

To be brutally frank, none of this knowledge truly prepares you for your very first 'bad' review. It really doesn't. It always hurts, but your confidence resilience is what gets you over extreme negative feedback. Otherwise, any negative comment like the "fat and ugly" I've had myself on YouTube will knock you so far for six that it's easier to not bother again. Trolls aren't worth connecting with by the way, they are just a waste of energy, so ignore them, leave them be. They're the ones who want interaction – never give them the satisfaction.

As every actor knows, you HAVE to learn to trust in yourself that you have done a good enough job in the moment. Everyone's a critic after all. So STOP looking at reviews and start looking to yourself for validation!

Who has ever watched themselves on TV and immediately gone *"Ooh, I'm good! I like me!"*? Very few people, right? And they are among the normal ones, I'm telling you.

So your new mantra is going to be:

"I can't please all the people all the time and I'm good enough for me!"

As your on-camera confidence grows, you'll start to know when it feels right – so trust in that review and only a few key Confidence on Camera coached positive feedback givers.

Reduce your Fear – Crave your Confidence!

A quote presentation trainers the world over always use is one you can never find the exact reference for:

"The greatest human desire is acceptance and the greatest human fear is rejection."

And as Franklin D. Roosevelt put it in his First Inaugural Address:
"The only thing we have to fear is fear itself."

Now, surely putting yourself out there online via video for the masses is asking for it?

Well, to now nab a professional speaking oft-quoted acronym:

FEAR is simply - **F**alse **E**vidence **A**ppearing **R**eal

Some fear is human instinct, logical nature, because it can *actually* kill you – snakes, poisonous spiders, fire, deep water, or more modern-day flying – all the everyday things in Australia!

Other fear is created from lack of learning or nurture or copying others – putting your face in water, non-poisonous spiders, public speaking, theatre critic reviews, being on camera. Some is simply irrational – pink fluffy slipper fear anyone?!

FEAR is *all* in our mind.

Sadly some fears can be exacerbated in some situations and by some really negative critics from our life. What was that moment, or who's that one person you feared so much once, that when you think of it or them, your whole body starts to shake, adrenalin kicks in, the heart starts going, palms sweat, knees knock – the whole nine yards.

Well THAT is the power of our mind and the physical chemical reaction your brain puts out there, *just* from remembering that time. Sometimes just a smell can do it and it takes a while for us to calm ourselves down. You may even have felt similar when presenting on stage or as soon as that camera lens turns towards you...

But FEAR is *all* in our mind.

But I reckon...

If our mind is where fear is...

surely that's where our confidence is too?

YEP – CONFIDENCE is all in our mind and accessible whenever we want to create it – it's just a darn site harder to make an acronym…

Confidence
Over
Natural
Fear
Is
Definitely
Easier
Now
Choosing to
Embrace it!

OK then – send your better suggestions on a postcard!

So choose to create your own confidence at super scary times, just like I did…

Fake It Till You Make it Story

Max was the scariest thing I'd ever seen! And he was lying there, right next to me, belly out, bright and bold, poised to pounce at me at any moment I thought… And then he said the fateful line: *"OK time to hold Max!"* My adrenalin spiked and I was almost out of my chair!

My mouth dried up, sweat dripped down my spine and all I really wanted to do was cry – I was working my fears up to the max for Max!

But then I did hold him, because I had to, and a strange thing happened.

He was gentle and smooth, cool, soft, yet firm and I started to quite like him, then the conversation started to flow…

Now – that's nothing to do with *50 Shades of Grey*… simply a story from when I was in a position where I so wanted to run away, but I absolutely could not.

I was presenting the *Environment Watch* section of one of my kids' shows *Action Hong Kong* and (mostly because he knew I was petrified and that's good TV!) my producer had said I HAD to hold Max – the harmless black and white striped with red and yellow common garden snake that helped you keep nasties away – rather than the black and white many-banded krait snake that could 'kill a child in a matter of hours'. All the safe snakes were being killed off, so we had to give them a hand.

I couldn't get away with just looking at him or I'd lose all credibility, so I had to get over it in the moment on TV. Watching myself back that weekend with mates, we laughed because we couldn't see ANY of the fear I've just described. Everyone said how cool I looked and that they would never have had the confidence to hold him, how brave I was etc. – HA!

The penny dropped – it's just like the old actor's adage, when you have to you *can* **fake it till you make it!**

When you have to overcome the fear and do it anyway and you see how much of your nerves you *can* hide on camera. And when you're Flawsome – yes, I did giggle and mess around with *"Ooh, I'm a little bit scared, kids!"* – you have to laugh at yourself and just get on with it.

Once you laugh you let the tension go, forget your self-inflicted worries and fears – then you wonder why you were ever afraid in the first place!

Choose Confidence!

✓ Choose to lose the False (or in our made-up minds Fictional) Evidence

✓ Shift your perception and you can do anything!

Perhaps my acronym should be:

CON-FI-DENCE = CON the FIctional eviDENCE!

> **Choose Confidence on Camera**
>
> Aim to:
>
> 1. Please yourself as your most constructive critic.
> 2. Do your best with the knowledge and skills you have right now.
> 3. Know you can always improve, but what you're doing right now is OK.
> 4. Know what works for you and what habits distract.
> 5. Be confident when you have delivered enough to suit your video aims.
> 6. Note you can always film another one.
> 7. Believe the more you do the better and more confident you become.

Self-Awareness Helps this Happen

BUT – ensure you never get too cocky on screen, unless that is a character you are playing. There's nothing that puts us off faster than an overinflated ego or sense of 'me first' self-centredness. Being selfish here when you're learning is OK – you're spending time focusing on yourself right now, that could be considered selfish, but you're learning! Self-centredness is more narcissistic – if your self-review is glowing with praise yet people seem to be turning your videos off, then something is going a bit wrong! Self-centred focus, talking about me, me, me or only 'telling what we do best' can come across on camera as arrogant, uncaring, dismissive.

So even when you are superbrilliant on screen, check your humanity and connect with your Flawsomeness, rather than lording it over us. Your verbal language choices have a huge impact here – but that's Step 5. Follow the 7 Steps process and keep focus on your mindset to now find out *how actors connect the concept of an emotion, mood or feeling to actually* **make the feeling real.**

STAGE 5: Emotional Connections Make It REAL
How to Connect Concepts + Feelings

According to vast volumes of adult learning concepts we learn in Train the Trainer training, people perceive and process new information in an infinite variety of ways.

But all of these range between:

1. Experience – our own personal engagement; and
2. Conceptualisation – our ideas, language, abstract approaches to learning, thinking, absorbing and imagining.

When the experienced feelings and more abstract conceptualisation are fully connected and congruent, we make a connection in our on-camera/on screen performance. Then we can get viewers to make a connection between their 'watching' or reflection of your video content and the 'doing' action you want them to do after. The easiest way is to use an emotional pull to connect them to us, to the message and to the desired action we need.

The viewer needs to feel the emotional pull – hear it, see it – indulging their kinaesthetic, auditory and visual ways of taking on and absorbing information. You need to use all the 3 Vs, 3 Cs and more because when they become emotionally invested, you have made an impact.

But you have to connect emotionally first, or they'll never believe you!

It's a step beyond congruence and into performance until you can do it instinctively for real.

You need to show that you are connected with the words you are saying, that you fully understand, appreciate and know the importance of how your words can affect your viewer. You need to demonstrate your interest, passion and unique personality on camera through:

✓ your **Energy** – the 30% extra!

✓ your **Body** – knowing how it feels to move naturally

✓ your **Face** – looking like you mean it!

Drive the M³ Mind-Muscle-Memory

When we start training as an actor, we learn to connect the concept of a script to the real emotion required to invoke feelings and reactions, from both our fellow actors and our audience, by learning to develop what I now call our:

M³ = Mind-Muscle-Memory Bank

We learn to:

1. Notice how our muscles move and feel with any mood.
2. Understand how we move, talk, express and know how our energy, body and face feel.
3. Learn to stand and move naturally, create poses that connect the visual to our mind.
4. Rehearse and exercise so when we perform, the emotional display is instantaneous.
5. Do it without getting fully emotionally involved.
6. Never be paralysed by emotions on stage
   – we can overcome stage-fright.
7. Allow the emotion to drive how we move, our tone of voice and how we say the words.

Then we avoid forgetting our lines and physically draining ourselves on stage every night!

Good actors do this so naturally we never notice that they're 'acting'.

Knowing how our whole body is affected by emotion is one of the first skills an actor develops.

Why M³ = Mind-Muscle-Memory is REAL

Our bodies hang on to all sorts of emotions and feelings, allowing us to have total sensory recall at any moment we choose – we can and often do actually re-live an experience. On screen that shows in your eyes as you remember a feeling and that can engage us as a viewer and force us to pay attention to you. Micro-expressions of fear can give us away or confidence can help support an emotion on screen, so we need to develop the positive visual displays you can use.

Your 'performance ready' **M³ = Mind-Muscle-Memory Bank** needs practice to grow, so when you need to access a mood, your body knows how it feels and your brain comes up with the right words. It can easily be learned using my Emotional Connection A&E on the next page.

~~~~~~~~~~

Feel the feeling

for real to make a real connection to your viewer.

This is the base of not only your Confidence, but your Credibility and Charisma too.

~~~~~~~~~~

Emotional Connection: Mirror Me A&E

CONCEPT: How Do Feelings Feel and Show?

Remember when I asked you to say *"I'm excited!"* and to notice the difference it makes when you say what the words actually mean? Then you boosted that energy the 30% by adding in the real FEELING of the words and *showing* us what it means to you.

Well now we're going to dive into deep detail to *really* observe yourself and see:

- ⅄ what that looks like
- ⅄ how it feels
- ⅄ how your body changes and what your muscles do

Develop Feelings by Doing with Emotional Connection A&E

It's time again for a quick 7 Stage Acting Exercise – *"I'm Excited!" part 2.*

Yep, your Playlist A&E details are online!

Now – rather than doing this on camera yet, simply find your nearest wall mirror and forget about any camera restrictions on movement for a moment and simply **remember how "I'm Excited" really feels** and **see how it actually looks**…

This mirror exercise will help you discover how to develop your

M³ = Mind-Muscle-Memory Bank.

NB. How your body moves automatically has an effect on your voice when you let it too, so chat out loud to yourself during the exercise while feeling any emotion and hear how it carries through. This is one of the obvious reasons why incongruence is so easy to spot when you know how…

Emotional Connection Mirror Me Playlist A&E

1. Think of a time when you were really excited?
   When did you think or truly say *"I'm excited!"*
   - ✓ Get it?... Got it?... Good _____

2. Who was with you?
   - ✓ How did they look? What were they doing? Were they excited for you?!
   _____

3. Stand up, feel it! How did it really feel in your body, on your face
   – how did it make you feel – really remember that feeling in the
   moment and **feel how it felt**. Look in a mirror – see how you look
   _____

Fix your feelings in to your M³ Mindset Bank

4. Allow your body to move as if it is back in the moment "excited"
   - how would you move? Your head, neck, shoulders, back, hips, legs,
   feet, arms, hands
   _____

5. How do you express it in your face? What happens to your face?
   Your mouth, eyes, eyebrows, forehead, cheeks, chin
   _____

6. File, or Mindset, your reactions in to your Mind-Muscle-Memory-
   recall-bank.
   - ✓ Say the feeling out loud - tell yourself what you were "Excited!"
     about out loud
   _____

7. **M³ Mindset the feeling** - see it, feel it in your body and we
   will hear it in your voice!
   - ✓ Let your mind be free to choose the right words for you right now
   - ✓ – trust what's right!
   _____

M³ Mindset the feeling and the words you want to say will naturally come!

Your M³ Mindset is your most powerful tool for projecting *whatever* feeling you choose, for creating congruence and for appearing confident and fully in control whenever you like.

Actors learn to create theirs so open your M³ Mindset Memory Bank today!

~~~~~~~~~~~~

My M³ Mindset is my own personal Emotional Connection and it is REAL

~~~~~~~~~~~~

How to Create your Confident Congruent M³ Personas

Honour the viewer – know their WIIFM and M³ match the best you to tell the video story. You must make that side of you, or persona, on show congruent with that script.

To connect to your script emotionally you must KNOW what image you are trying to portray...

Ask yourself:

- who do I need/want/choose to be perceived as?
- how do I need to feel to get this message across?
- how do I need to look/sound?

Remember, it is a 'given' that you are:

- ✓ Professional
- ✓ Informative
- ✓ Interesting
- ✓ The expert in your field

... about what you present – **SO TELL YOURSELF YOU ARE!**

It is our duty as a presenter to feel our message and make our audience feel enough to bother doing something – our Call to Action (CTA).

~~~~~~~~~~~~

This is your Emotional Connection IMPACT!

Start with making part one of your I'MPACT – I am…

You can be whoever you need to be to present this video…

~~~~~~~~~~~~

My Emotional Connection List

To help you out I've created a whole list of adjectives, feelings, ways of being from warm, spontaneous, to direct, serious, to committed, quirky to sexy, to fun! Pick your words for the A&E…

Emotional Connection List

I AM _____

_____

_____

_____

warm	hard-hitting	compassionate	conservative
committed	dynamic	laid back	animated
spontaneous	demonstrative	direct	inquisitive
intellectual	enthusiastic	intense	flirtatious
purposeful	encouraging	serious	down to earth
earthy	patient	funny	demanding
adventurous	precise	stylish	cautious
assertive	deliberate	energetic	chatty
restrained	formal	unconventional	grounded
outgoing	analytical	driven	amazing
sporty	competitive	touching	funky
witty	controlled	expressive	outrageous
perfectionist	honest	sociable	passionate
cheeky	determined	curious	direct
quirky	amiable	focused	realistic
caring	challenging	astute	thrilling
straightforward	sophisticated	humorous	coaxing
startling	natural	healthy	intriguing
persuasive	arty	suave	sexy — sex sells!

The extended list is online and always feel free to add more words.
The more you expand your list the wider range you will have as a presenter.

Emotional Connection: Video Presenter Playlist A&E

1. Pick out all the relevant words you or others say you are/can be.
2. Pick 10 that relate to how you want to be perceived for your work.
3. Order them 1-10 of words you'd most like others to say about you on screen.
4. Pick three to five (max!) that relate to a specific video story you want to tell.
5. Pick the one key mood as the overall driving mood of this video.
6. You now have your overall mood theme and your ideal positive perception words.
7. Now do your Mirror Me A&E for each of these moods you choose – Try, then simply be…

And remember effecting this effect is the first step to help you fake it till you make it!

If any script doesn't encourage or instil great emotion in you, then use this exercise to help you boost that 30%+ energy and connection even when you don't feel it for real – your viewer will think you do!

M³ Emotionally Connect – You to your Script to your Viewer

✓ Effect the Effect = have emotional impact, then fake it till you make it!

✓ Create the reality inside of you = M3

✓ Use the mirror or camera to practise and make it real for me to see too!

STAGE 6:   *Confident Actional Connections Connecting WIIFMs them to you and CTAs*

We've connected concepts and feelings to help you appear more appealing.

The next step is to connect what you want them to do after watching you with *how* you can actually influence that. It's not being manipulative – we already know if your viewer likes you, they are more likely to do what you want.

This is simply another acting technique we use on you from the theatre and the big screen that you don't even know yet that we do!

So let's link what we want, our WIIFM, to what we want them to do for us – our **Call to Action** (CTA).

ACTIONAL CONNECTIONS & OBJECTIVES
are the why, how, what of what we want
CTAs tell the viewer they want it + what to do next!

The Actor's Objective + Actional Connection Story

Every actor has an **Objective** of what they want other characters on stage to do or feel – it becomes the basic need of the character and it runs throughout the performance. The objective (your CTA) is created by the director giving **Actions** to follow, to DO… to effect an emotion in your fellow actor and the audience.

The Action is always a Verb – *"what I can do…"* to the other actor on stage to provoke a reaction in the moment that creates a chain of action/reaction, action/reaction of emotional feelings, creating the audience emotional buy-in. If you can't get the actor to do what you want one way, you try another – and we *can* chop and change our mood within seconds using our Emotional Connection skills, like a child wanting a lolly!

Every actor studies traditional Stanislavsky acting techniques at some point for why each character is motivated to act and react as they do, within the confines of a script. I also spent two years in Australia studying Practical Aesthetics (PA) – a more radical, modern, extremely analytical acting technique created by David Mamet and William H Macy based on the Stanislavsky method. We would spend hours breaking down every single line, action/reaction, to make sure we were 100% clear on what we wanted, so the audience would never *see* the performance. Instead they'd get emotionally involved in a series of spontaneous reactions that looked and sounded very real every time. We were no longer 'actors' – our character became a real living soul.

NB. If you're interested, you can train in PA in New York, Sydney and Scotland, or you can read *A Practical Handbook for the Actor* by six amazing pro actors and coaches who all worked with Mamet at his phenomenal Chicago Goodman Theatre Company. Deep stuff, but it taught me so much more when it comes to these techniques for on-camera work – it's more than just presenting, speaking, telling your story. You need to get passionately, emotionally involved to make an impact – it's real life instead of being on a stage!

As the presenter with your own script, you have far more freedom than an actor, but still need to choose and be clear on your essential video Objective (CTA what?) and your Actional Connections (CTA how?) before you start.

~~~~~~~~~~~~~~~

Emotional Connections are perceived concepts + your real feeling...

Actional Connections help you perform to evoke real feelings in the viewer...

Objective CTAs are the ideal RESULT you want from them!

~~~~~~~~~~~~~~~

Creating Your Objective CTAs + Actional Connections

Let's think about them for a specific video idea you have:

1. WHY I want to connect the viewer WIIFM to my Call to Action = **My CTA Objective**

2. WHAT my viewer will get from watching me is **their WIIFM = Their Objective**

3. HOW I *evoke* that reaction is the conceptualised verb *I will DO to them to make them feel* = **My Actional Connection**

Remember we want to connect conceptualisation + feelings to make enough impact to **effect an action to act.**

The Objective CTA + Actional Connections Online A&E

So talking of acting – it's time again for you to go off and do some thinking and planning again, to see how easy it is to create your Objective CTAs and Actional Connections.

Again these exercise details are all online where you'll find the seven steps to create your CTAs, your Actional Connections and a list of action verbs actors use to help effect the impact. This A&E will help you solidify what you need to know and do to really get your viewer buy-in and commitment for each video.

So what way of presenting can help you achieve your goal? What words from the list CAN you DO to your viewer?

I CAN _____

☐ inspire	☐ outrage	☐ shame	☐ command	☐ bewitch
☐ buy/sell	☐ shock	☐ restrain	☐ bemuse	☐ humour
☐ dazzle	☐ empower	☐ plead	☐ cajole	☐ prepare
☐ encourage	☐ flatter	☐ control	☐ tease	☐ entreat
☐ contradict	☐ revive	☐ influence	☐ demand	☐ reproach
☐ change	☐ challenge	☐ torment	☐ rouse	☐ WOW!
☐ beg	☐ coax	☐ electrify	☐ uplift	

Know you can affect your audience & you WILL create an effect in them.

Both Emotional + Actional Connections affect how you write your script.

Think how strong words affect you…

How much more fun is it to:

⅄ intrigue rather than just interest

⅄ astound instead of just tell

⅄ energise or enthuse more than just encourage

Get creative, play with your words here, but ensure the words you write in your script are words and feelings you can use comfortably. If you have written your script before this planning, review this process and check your message style and wording is real for you and is congruent with your Objective CTA and Actional Connection target market mission.

~~~~~~~~~~~~~~

**Strong Objectives + Actional Connections
drive the result!**

~~~~~~~~~~~~~~

STAGE 7: Make the IMPACT

My Irish Productivity Coach queen, Ciara Conlon, reminded me recently about how rocking our RAS is! I'd *known* about it for years in theory and regularly got people to recognise it in themselves, but I'd never known its official name – our **RAS is our Reticular Activating System**.

Again, it's an ancient part of the brain that allows us to see, quantify, clarify and prioritise things in our world, again in a split second. It subconsciously notices things, so we can consciously decide what we want or need, or what could be dangerous, and therefore what to give top priority to, to survive and succeed. We notice, we react, we take action when we want.

It's the part of my brain that kept noticing Fiat 500 cars once I decided to get one!

What we bring to the forefront of our mind and consciously label as 'urgent and important' can either cause us to leap to judgement, negative reaction or self-serving positive action.

It works for our words too, so we need to allocate positive RAS language to succeed. Making this a Presenter Mindset habit is a HUGE step to enable you to overcome camera fears, negative performance patterns, critical judgement and shift the mental blocks that cause us to procrastinate or stop dead on a project

Positive language not only makes an impact on your viewer – we've also learned what you say to yourself makes a HUGE impact on you. Go read online how positivity actually affects your health if you're not believing me now!

SO RAISE YOUR RAS FOR POSITIVE IMPACT WITH THE I'M-PACT!

To make an Impact, take the I'M-PACT...

We now know why we want to make an impact on our viewer:

1. Our WIIFM.
2. Their WIIFM.
3. Whose WIIFM is most important.
4. Which WIIFM we use for max impact.
5. Our Emotional Connection.
6. Our Actional Connection.
7. How we use this to create max impact.

So now it's time to make an impact and commitment in your own mind by taking the I'M-PACT!

Or my *'I Am, I Can, I Will Pact'...*

My I'M-PACT for your presenting – *'I Am... I Can... I WILL...!'* – is your kick up the wotnot to give you a positive boost when you need and to RAS notice any fears if you don't do it and successes when you do.

You get your I am… and I can… through your Emotional and Actional Connections. The I will… is what you want to get from your viewer – your Objective CTA.

By connecting all the sections in your own head and saying what you WILL achieve out loud, you are giving your conscious brain the oral and aural stimulus to kick your confident mental support into gear, to remember, to succeed.

The I'MPACT ONLINE WORKSHEET A&E

So before you wrap up this chapter, do get your I'MPACT Impact worksheet online, complete and add it to your workbook.

The I'MPACT IMPACT – I am… I can… I will… ▶

To make the Impact you want…
Create your own I'M-PACT before you go on camera, online or on any screen!

Emotional Connection: Who do I want to be?

I AM: _____

My M³ mindset to create the perception – so viewers have trust,
belief and confidence in me!

Actional Connection: What must I do to my audience to reach my objective CTA?

I CAN: _____

The action I need to do, to create that perceived reaction in my viewer

Objective CTA: What do I want my audience to do/say/feel
as a result of my presentation?

I WILL get my viewer to: _____

_____

This is the point for me of my video, for my confident mindset
– this result WILL happen!

Connect with Confidence, Credibility & Charisma.

The Presenter Mindset
Learning Review and A&E

" To truly laugh, you must be able to take your pain, and play with it!"

Charlie Chaplin

My Learning Stage Notes:

1. My Video Presenter Self-assessment - what works?...

2. My Confident Connections - 3 Cs...

3. My Congruence - focus for me!..

4. My Confident Mindset - turn fear to…

5. My Emotional Connections - M3 exercises…

6. My Actional Connections - WIIFMs me to viewer you + CTAs…

7. My I'MPact - to make an impact, take the I'M-Pact…

Be #FLAWSOME - Stuff up with confidence & get over it!

You can use these Mindset tools to create your own Confidence on Camera, and actually any time you present in public, when you are willing to:

- ✓ Trust your brain
- ✓ Believe in yourself
- ✓ KNOW you can and will!

The Visual Impact

We have all, at one time or another, been
performers, and many of us still are
- politicians, playboys, cardinals and kings.

Laurence Olivier

Confidence in your body to negate your nerves

People always ask me why I mention nerves when I talk about the Mind of the Machine but don't really talk about them when discussing the Presenter Mindset.

But we've just learned about the RAS, right?

So there's your answer!

If we keep discussing nerves when setting your Presenter Mindset, what will you keep focusing on? Yes, NERVES!

We also know the power of the M^3 – so as soon as we start talking about nerves, we tend to get all nervous! As my true-blue Aussie best buddy and mentor 7-time World Champion Marathon Swimmer and Master NLP coach, Shelley Taylor-Smith, always says, "Don't think of a Blue Tree... to NOT think of it you have to first create it in your mind." As I found out when working with Shelley, our minds are extremely powerful things! She's used her Champion Mindset™ to beat the boys swimming around the world and to help heal diseases that should have killed her.

And she's not my only buddy who's done the same is she, Vic and Ali?!

So because of that, I prefer to first link nerves to the machine that creates those fears in your head – where you now know you have the confidence to overcome those fears! And focus on your positive power and Flawsomeness – so you can laugh in the face of and belittle any nerves *(I won't even allow them a capital N!)*.

So the word 'Nerves' is now out of the window.

Instead focus on releasing that energy – re-focus, re-brand and re-work it.

Let's turn that useful nervous energy in to *Re-Energised Energy* you feel confident to use…

~~~~~~~~~~~~~~~

Release your 'nervous' habits – avoid the word and set your energy free!

~~~~~~~~~~~~~~~

Now we can actually talk easily about their actual impact on any size screen without the emotional engagement.

So Step 3: here is all about 7 Stages of The Visual Impact and how, if nervous habits do hit, you can make a RAS shift in the moment to make them look better and you feel more confident.

STAGE 1: How Do Visual Nerves Show in Shot?

On-screen nerves can most often show as:

Body Language – movement, gesture, feet, spine, shoulders, head, breathing, not breathing!

Facial Language – expressions of fear in eyes, mouth, forehead, redness, tightness on face/neck

Remember what works on camera is CONGRUENCE – connect the visual elements to the message to prevent mixed messages or distracting habits!

Visual Impact of You in Shot or 'In Frame'

Think how most business videos are shot and how they are 'framed' – what fits in the shot and how you are seen through the camera lens on screen? The four most common shot set-ups are:

WS = Wide Shot	MS = Mid Shot	CU = Close Up	XCU = Extreme Close Up

- ⋏ **Wide shot** = full body or legs up, with full gesture room
- ⋏ **Mid-shot** = usually waist up, with arms and hands in shot
- ⋏ **Close-up** = chest up, with shoulders and head and some gestures if you raise your hands
- ⋏ **Extreme Close-up** = tight on your face, no gestures, so all action must be done by your face

The closer the camera zooms in, the less space you have to move all your body and the more we focus on your face and eyes. Your movements are restricted within a certain fairly small space, so all movements must therefore be steady, even, flowing – nothing too jerky or too large. The tighter zoom-in shows all your expressions, so the more you *can* give your nerves away. But can also make more impact when you energise your face instead – your eyes are the window to your soul after all!

You now have so many congruent expressions to use with all your Emotional and Actional Connections A&E hard work, so zoom in until we see the whites of your eyes and make your real face work for you. Your mindset is going to be in such a confident place and so involved in telling your story for a *fantastic* reason that we'll miss any small nervous giveaways!

And you've always got your smile!

STAGE 2: Negating your Visual nerves
So What – Do Your nerves Show?

When we think about what gives us away when we are nervous, most of us pretty much know what that thing is – come on, fess up time! What is it?...

Now say *"So what!"*

It only matters if you let it – you can change it in the moment, as long as you know how to within the shot and how to help prevent the viewer from seeing it in the first place.

On screen your nerves are mostly spotted by our viewer RAS as a visual distraction and some people have obvious nervous habits: a repeated gesture, movement or sway. But others have more subtle giveaways we've discussed – like the sweaty palms, a tight chest, back or shoulder tensions or aches, dry mouth. The viewer's subconscious brain picks those up on screen too.

Think about it: if your hands are clammy, what might you do to try and stop them being clammy? Yes, you might rub your fingers over your palms – no one will spot that, right?

But if it's in shot – WRONG! Human peripheral vision is phenomenal and our RAS instincts kick in when we spot something on the edge of shot. As the viewer I'm relaxed in my environment – so I will quickly notice any nervous habits and distractions that you show, especially within the 3-7" Rule.

Online viewers might even start looking for "What will this person do next I can laugh at… or shall I just press ■!" so you need to get over your nerves before you even start!

Why 'Get Over' your nerves?

However, good nerves news!

There is one fantastic phenomenon about us as humans: we really are sociable, pack animals and most of us are happy to follow the herd. So when one of us is willing to go out on a limb and speak up for what they believe in, i.e. present a video that can help us, we do WANT to support them. Especially if we're interested – as we must be if we've pressed Play on your video, meeting or webinar.

Most of us do actually *like* to find the nice or good things in other people. It is in our human nature to greet negative with negative, positive with positive. We can turn negative to positive.

Or if it's really a total disaster, to laugh at it, or go away.

Some nervous habits are actually quite endearing and get the viewer on your side when you're Flawsome with them. So *get over* the worry of yourself – it's not about you! Smile through your nerves, laugh at yourself and we can end up rooting for you to succeed.

This is really where my catchphrase *"Stuff up with confidence and get over it!"* comes from. You remember Max the snake in Hong Kong – well, when I saw myself on the studio monitor, seeing myself be so scared holding him, I simply had to laugh at myself! All that worry and nervousness for nothing, all that FEAR and stress created purely in my mind, all those silly worries I chose to let go of in the moment and ended up having such fun with.

That was my AHA! or light bulb moment…

✓ It's OK to be nervous
✓ It's OK to have nervous habits
✓ When they come up... use them with confidence – BE FLAWSOME!

How much stronger a connection do you have with your viewer then?

Show you're human – they still think you are *WOW!* because you've got the guts to step up to present, not run away! That same fight or flight adrenalin spike that causes nervous tension can actually be used by you in the moment to create energising energy instead, when you focus on what you *do want* instead of what you don't – i.e. nerves.

STAGE 3: *Energise Your nervous energy*

To me, it's now strange that even the thought of a camera can cause many folk to start sweating, feel tight in the chest and start backing off across the room – Neanderthal fight or flight syndrome in fast action! But I understand it because I've seen it; that action manifests visually and can be anything from an actual physical backing away, to blocking body, arms or hands, to the smallest of head movement backing off.

So how do you help yourself USE your nervous habits and turn them into energising and activating habits on camera?

✓ Recognise when we feel it
✓ Acknowledge it is OK to feel
✓ Learn to harness it!

Turn that nervous energy into Energising Energy to create something great!

What nerves Do You See? – Playlist A&E

Energising your nerves starts with awareness, so you'd better be up for some more A&E exercises, a bit of fun – on with that judge's black cap and let's play with nerve spotting!

So...

1. Think of how nerves can manifest themselves for a moment
   – in you or what you've seen in others.

2. Focus purely on the VISUAL Impact on screen – what we actually SEE in someone.

3. Think of a standard TV mid-shot – from your hips or waist up – how much can you see?

   ⋏ remember they are mostly a Distraction within the 3-7" Rule, but as we all have our own PoV, we are allowed different opinions of exactly how distracting they actually are!

4. What do you think the common habits are?

5. Why are these habits so visually distracting?

6. How do these habits give away your nerves?

7. What could you do to make them better?

Watch for these habits in TV presenters and on YouTube videos.

Grab your workbook to make your own notes, or write in the gaps as before.

Turn Your nervous energy into Energising Energy A&E

Now you are getting fully aware of what a viewer can see.

So take another moment now to jot down in your workbook what your nervous or 'giveaway' habits are and how you can turn them into energising, more confident-looking energy, that actually makes you feel better, adrenaline fuelled for successful action and more ready to stand and 'fight'!

My Potentially Distracting VISUAL Habits + Energising Exercises	
My Nervous Habit is:	*I can hide / disguise / make it better by:*

My Visual Impact Mantras

1. Awareness I am doing the Habit in the Moment is imperative – *"I Am Aware of ..."*

2. Habits – body, gesture, expression – must be used to enhance the message instead of distracting: *"I Can change/shift/adapt my habit."*

3. Breathing controls it all! *"Breathing Will allow me the confidence to do so!"*

STAGE 4: What Does Your Viewer See?

Now you know what you see, let's take a look at what your viewer actually sees and get specific with what common nervous habits actually appear most often on screen, or as I call them…

The 7 Habits of Often Distracting Presenters

Over years of research and the amazing teams I've worked with we discovered that there are really only 7 common core distracting visual habits for presenters, and I knuckled down the pet peeves on screen over the years. I'm not talking production distractions again I'm talking my '7 Habits of Often Distracting Presenters'.

They are in no particular order and it's not just what irritates or distracts me, these are just the most common 7 habits I've seen, and researched that others have seen too. And yes, smarty-pants reader, this is wordplay on Stephen Covey's *7 Habits of Highly Effective People* – it's so effective after all!

The 7 Habits of Often Distracting Presenters A&E

Have a go at completing the table below from your own 7 Habits perspective – what do you think the 7 Habits could entail? Think mostly Visual, but some may entail Vocal or Verbal too...

When I do this exercise with people in a workshop, we get all creative after brainstorming in groups, we design posters to represent the characters, we actually act out the habits, over-exaggerate and stuff up with confidence big time, so have some fun with this.

The 7 Habits of Often Distracting Presenters *(or common nervous habits!)* ▶			
The Habit	Why are they Visually distracting?	How do nerves show?	What would be better?
1. The Scruff			
2. The Fidget			
3. The Body			
4. The Energizer Bunny			
5. The Stiff			
6. The Mouse			
7. The Handler			

Shift and adapt your body + gesture + expression habits to work for you!
Use Visual Habits to Enhance your Message!

Once you've had your own 7 Habits ideas, you'll probably want to read exactly what, why and how these habit characters distract so much – and learn habit 'fix 'em' solutions to make them look better. So both the form above and my fully completed version are online to find solutions that may help you!

So What DOES your Viewer See?

By the way, you CAN DO all of these 7 Habits on camera when done for a specific reason and within the 3-7" Rule! Just notice when you do them and when you start to feel uncomfortable or when they don't fit the words you are saying – congruence, congruence, congruence! Gently shift the habit for something else that works.

Pay attention: notice if you fall into these habits for prolonged moments when you present and make that change right in the moment with confidence. By the way, your gentle recognition and acknowledgement of your potentially distracting habits also builds credibility and charisma – it's all connected!

Remember with any habit use the 3-7" RULE:

✓ Avoid three repetitious moves or poses in that time

✓ Gently change the habit or pose within 7"

✓ Be aware of your habits that could distract and do something different!

STAGE 5:   How Should I Stand?

This Stage is all about how you stand on your stage – in a way that helps you feel confident.

The *only* way you are going to NOT give away subliminal, distracting or mixed messages is by:

1. **Using your body as a tool to be a congruent part of the message**
   and in between…

2. **Find a neutral, open way of standing, sitting
   – find your moments of still.**

Confident Open and Neutral Body Energy

When clients always ask, "How should I stand?" I usually say, "Stand for your OBE!"

It's a story I tell when speaking professionally to give a fun subliminal connection between standing at an important time in your life and appearing open and relaxed on screen.

Like collecting an OBE British Honours Award from the Queen, as my step-dad and step-brother have both done, but as my mum always said "Don't worry if you don't have one – it stands for other burgers* efforts!" (*Replace burgers there with a similar sounding very English swear word – she is a naval wife after all!) And of course I make: **OBE stand for OPEN BODY ENERGY**

How to Stand for your OBE A&E

It's a way actors learn to stand early on – it's a relaxed starting position you can move anywhere from here. It also gives nothing away! At Maura Faye Training in Australia we called it the Open Body Position (OBP) or Neutral Stance; it's actually the way our human frame is supposed to stand relaxed fully supporting our skeleton and muscles. It feels safe, solid, and secure when you stand correctly – just not so stiff as in front of the Queen! Try standing for your OBE now and get the details online:

1. Stand open, relaxed, feet under your hips, balanced, grounded
2. Arms are down by your sides, hands relaxed
3. Now add a small, friendly smile on your face
4. You give off no mixed messages in your Visual Impact, because you look neutral
5. You are absorbing and eliminating any negative energy
6. You can also breathe properly to support your voice, oxygen can flow to your brain to allow you to think
7. Tension goes when you learn to stand this way, as you instil confidence and you are ready to move to any position with energised energy.

What About When I Sit Down?

For OBE when sitting, master the standing OBE online so you know how to feel comfortable and powerful standing, then you can learn to sit without slouching.

Sit tall and **forward** – we must always 'be on the front foot' energy wise especially when sitting.

To sit:
1. Be forward on the chair, almost sit on the front edge, with hips tilted up and forward.
2. Use your back and stomach muscles to hold you up, place a cushion behind you for added support – NO slouching!
3. Spine is straight, supported and pulled up strong with shoulders down and relaxed.
4. Place feet flat on the ground directly under your knees, or one foot flat and the other slightly back for better balance; lean into your front foot for energy projection.

5. Hands rest palms down on your knees or on the table (but not supporting your weight).
6. Lengthen your neck, hold your head upright – proud and with slight smile!
7. Always set the camera up so it is eye height or above – avoid the dreaded double chin when we look down into a camera. DIY camera set-up 101!

Check page 205 with your laptop set-up too.

When you are comfortable sitting openly, without visual discomfort or effort, you can start to add asymmetric positions that suit your chosen style. Double benefit – they look more interesting for the viewer when you do 'sit-pose' well, in a natural, easy way and it's more comfortable for you.

Do note that the pose WILL portray a Visual Impact message, so you must match your sitting position to your Emotional and Actional Connection moods + Objective – e.g. to evoke concept + action *"friendly, relaxed, mate next door; to ease the viewer into calling me!"* try one arm up on the back of a chair.

GET USED TO YOUR OBE

Please DO remember – you CAN stand or sit any way you want, as long as you are congruent, comfortable, moving with ease and flow, sitting or stand tall, upright and forward towards the camera. But never slouch or get stuck solid still!

Getting stuck in one position can also give you away, send mixed-messages if not congruent, not a look good for your viewer and may put them off – so give yourself the best possible chance to make an impact by practising your OBE.

The OBE may feel a bit strange to start off with because we have all developed our own unique ways of standing or sitting to be comfortable to avoid aches and pains, hide nerves *(or so we think!)* and be in our safety zone, especially with our hands covering our 'vulnerable' parts, as I mentioned before! So keep remembering to stand openly and keep at it – practise your OBE during those boring moments in life: waiting in queues, standing in lifts, standing in front of the boss – you know when.

Persevere – it WILL feel comfortable after a couple of weeks as you ingrain the habit to your subconscious brain and undo distracting standing or sitting habits of a lifetime. It can take from 21-40+ days to ingrain a new habit, when you work on it every day, and once you've mastered it, I promise you will find it useful in your life in so many ways!

Once you are comfortable with this you can start to use the TV asymmetric positions that look better on screen, but use the same starting point, resting point and moment of still points with your body, arms, hands and spine.

As an OBE Master you can pull this out any time you want to appear completely neutral to your audience and give absolutely **nothing** away – both at work or at home. Honestly it works – especially during those high stress, nervous or emotional times when our Visual Impact body movements are most likely to give us away. That may be on video, virtual meeting, online training or Skype seminar; or face-to-face with a live audience or a nerve-wracking interview online or tense end of year review.

STAGE 6: *Warm Up Your Body as Well as Your Mind*

Your mind may be ready, you know now how to stand or sit for your OBE, but one simple thing people often forget to do is to warm up the body as well as the mind.

We've done all this work on your mindset – refocusing your nervous energy – but your body could be still half asleep, so time to get moving with a Warm-up.

Why Warm-up?

Most people forget this and often come to video shoots right from work, or sitting writing scripts, and don't realise that the tension they are holding in their body is one of the first things that we'll see when the camera starts to roll.

Professional performers always relieve any tension before stepping on stage and you need to get in a physical and mental mindset ready for "Lights, Camera, Action!"

ALWAYS warm up your body as well as your mind.

Most people don't realise it but we often hold and block our energy in our bottoms… Check if your cheeks are clenched right now!

It's actually the first place to check before opening your mouth.

If your bottom is clenched there's a knock-on effect – your leg muscles are probably already tight, so is your spine…

So most likely are your lungs, shoulders, arms, neck and probably facial expression too…

That may be an extreme, but clenched bottom and tightening your tummy (self-perceived 'looking thinner' on screen) simply create bigger tension that is often the root of other tension, and eventually leads to your brain tension and you falling apart on screen!

Quick Warm-up A&E

Even if you can't do a full body warm-up, try these tension releasers – please do them carefully as I accept no damage liability if you take them to an extreme! *(That goes for all the tips in here – always do anything I advise within safe limits for your mental and physical health – please always be kind to you!)*

Breathe in through your nose and out through your mouth for all of these exercises and if sound gently escapes when you do, that is OK, you're gently warming up your voice too…

1. Stretch your body, relax tense muscles in shoulders and arms by squeezing them tight, then letting them fully go, stretching and shaking them. This is the actors' really quick **Tense + Release** method to remove stiffness in a flash.

2. Loosen your spine and neck with a gentle stretch to either side and roll it if you can.

3. Throw your arms back wide and do gentle spine twists to release spinal energy.

4. Jump up and down a couple of times and shake out your legs and feet – the energy dance! As you jump and land, let your breath and a gentle "HUH!" sound escape from your mouth – this helps wake up your lungs, breath and voice too.

5. Release face tension *(yes we hold it there too!)* by making strange faces. Move your mouth wide, small, tight, pouted, wide grinning; wiggle your jaw side to side; chew up and down – go on, really gurn!

6. Open eyes wide and blink to refresh them – get ready to focus through that camera lens.

7. Finally **squeeze yer bum and let it go!** – a phrase intended to make you smile and an action for laughs to let it all go! You can do this with your tummy too if you hold tension there – just be a bit gentler than with your bottom…

HOW:

⅄ as you breathe in, clench your bottom really tight
   – go on squeeeeze!

⅄ as you breathe out, smile and let it go

⅄ repeat this slowly, getting faster, loads of times – until
   you're laughing by now!

NB. My 'bum squeeze' is a great quick tension release any time you present because nobody knows you are doing it except you and it often makes you smile ☺   And not because you're thinking of squeezing mine, thank you very much, but whatever makes you laugh!

Why Tense + Release Works

By tensing and releasing face, neck, back, arm, leg, thigh, tummy and bottom energy you can:

1. Re-energise your body and mind so you're set and ready to present.
2. Energise your brain to think and remember the script.
3. Relax – give yourself time to enjoy it = boost your credibility and confidence.
4. Pause – give greater congruence to your lines and let viewers absorb the info.
5. Move – connect your visual image to words more by using specific moves and gestures.
6. Add the required 30% more feeling, energy and animation into the words, release energy past shoulders, up into full facial expression AND find time to **SMILE!**
7. Allow your lungs to expand freely so you can breathe!

So now you're physically warmed up, and I've been talking about breathing, I'm going to guide you how to breathe.

This is the ONE thing that can relieve and ease any issues in the moment faster than anything else – no matter which of the 3 Vs you want to ease…

STAGE 7:   Breathe in to Your Bum!

Now you'll have to excuse me for being a bit rude, but how to breathe properly to project a voice was drummed into me many years ago. And yes most of us do have to learn to do it right! Also, once I've squeezed and released it, the mere thought of thinking about breathing in to my bum still makes me smile and forget any worries I might have in any moment.

And that is the whole point – natural, proper breathing automatically makes you feel better!

So what do I mean by this?

Without breathing what are we? Yes, exactly… but people have passed out on stage from not breathing properly! Others spend their whole life holding their tummy in – training stomach muscles to be tight, without knowing it takes those muscles to relax to breathe normally.

I've done it so I know; if you've never let your tummy go, I bet you breathe in to your lungs.

Proper Performance Breathing is THE core and cure of releasing energy to focus your performance body, soul and mind

For anyone who's done yoga or seen voice or singing coaches on TV talent shows, you may have watched them coaching performers to breathe in to the belly and expand it into the back of the ribs. You may have even joined in. We used to spend hours with our voice coach in drama class, lying on the floor with hands on our tummies contemplating the minute movements of our navels. Or upright, hands down the back of our spine to feel the minute muscle movements in the back as you breathe properly, fully, controlled. Yes, controlled while huffing, panting, projecting sounds, numbers, letters, often with a tiny plastic bit between the teeth called a bone prop, to make your mouth work with proper diction – yes extreme breathing exercises!

So these days I prefer thinking of simply **breathing in to your bum** because then you'll probably either smile, giggle or even better have a good belly laugh. As soon as you do that you'll breathe from where you're meant to and you'll feel in an instant which muscles it actually takes and where to breathe to for better breath, and therefore voice and mental control, without the painstaking navel contemplations.

Now You're Laughing – quick A&E

Have a good belly laugh now – go on, push yourself to snigger, giggle and laugh out the air in your lungs and feel what happens as you do…

1. Did you feel your tummy muscles spasm in as you laugh? That's your diaphragm moving there.
2. Now laugh bigger!
3. Can you feel your lower back muscles getting in on the game?
4. When you really go for it your hips and bottom get involved, yeah? It's not called rolling around laughing for nothing, is it?... as you lose balance on your chair!
5. Notice how those muscles get involved to counteract the diaphragm being forced up, to keep you supported – so you're less likely to fall off your chair.
6. Did you notice what happened at the end of each laugh?
7. Did you naturally have to gasp in the air to the very bottom of your lungs?

If not, you weren't laughing hard enough my friend, so have another go!

OK, that was a bit of a laugh, but why do you need to learn all this breath control in the first place?

As I keep saying, the key to releasing nervous energy *IS in your breath control*.

You really do need to discover where you actually breathe from, what breathing allows your voice to sound steady or boom and your brain to remain in control, reacting fast in fight or flight mode to get you out of a memory glitch pickle.

Some ways of breathing actually *cause* your distracting habits physical reaction.

So you need to learn the difference between the breathing that leads to distracting habits – visual giveaways, a red face, tongue-tied, blank on your lines – and the breathing that allows you to be confident and in control.

Breathe: from distraction to control

And how better to learn the difference than to actually have a go and for you to physically feel the sensations, to notice how you feel after breathing in different ways.

So grab your workbook (and bottom!) to make your own notes as we do some breathing A&E. And please – I hope it goes without saying, stay in control, never push these too far.

If you feel at all light-headed, sit down immediately and breathe easy.

CONFIDENT BREATHING A&E

Let's learn how we breathe.

✓ Stand or sit in an Open Body Position with your arms relaxed by your sides.

✓ Breathe normally for 30 seconds – note your natural preferences:

⅄ Do you prefer nose or mouth?

⅄ Do you breathe shallow or deep?

⅄ Do you breathe high in lungs or low in your tummy?

How Does Breathing Make Me Feel A&E?

Now, follow steps 1-3 below, doing an extreme version of the breathing for only about 10-30 seconds each. Take notes on how you actually end up feeling both physically and mentally: any tightness, light-headedness, aches, mental blocks, dry mouth etc.

If you feel any pains or dizziness, stop and rest immediately.

1. **Short & Shallow - 10-20 seconds**

    ⅄ Breathe in and out quickly, using only the top part of your lungs

    ⅄ Allow your upper chest to heave in and out as if you are puffed out from exercise

    ⅄ Feel what happens when you speed it up, as if you have been running

2. **Deep & Noisy - 20-30 seconds**

    ⅄ Breathe in and out deeply, using the bottom part of your lungs

    ⅄ Use your tummy to really push in and out

    ⅄ Let your breath push out any voice if it wants, a sigh, a humf, haaaaa, whatever sound

    ⅄ Feel the weight of the world in your overly loud and deep breathing

3. **Deep & Slow - 30 seconds**

    ⅄ Breathe in and out steadily and evenly

    ⅄ Use all of your lungs in an easy, steady, gentle sigh

    ⅄ Allow your tummy and upper chest to move as if you are ready to go to sleep

Add this online sheet to your workbook if you want.

How Does Breathing Make Me Feel?	▶
How do I breathe?	**Result – how it makes me feel?**
1. Short & shallow	Physical: Mental:
2. Deep & Noisy	Physical: Mental :
3. Deep & slow	Physical: Mental:

How Should I Breathe?

Most drama schools used and still use the voice bible from the doyenne of voice coaching, Cicely Berry. Her book *Voice and the Actor* is must-read material for anyone serious about improving their voice and has many of the exercises I mentioned for true navel contemplators! How do we breathe for confident control? We need to use the control of the diaphragm, the muscle just under our stomach that pushed up when you laughed – the one that spasms when you hiccup. We can squeeze it in and out to boost our breath, can tighten it for a short, sharp burst, or learn to use to control our breath coming out in a steady flow.

7 Steps to Diaphragm Breathing

1. Stand in your OBE Position – standing allows more lung expansion – and put your palms on your back, either side of the middle of your spine
   ⅄ point your fingers down to your bottom, thumbs around the sides of your hips
   ⅄ spread your fingers and thumbs wide across your back
   ⅄ be ready to feel any small movements when you breathe
2. Take a steady, slow, deep breath in through your nose and notice if your hands move
   ⅄ if not shift them slightly upwards around your waist/lower chest and try again
   ⅄ remember to breathe out gently through your mouth each time too!

3. Breathe in steadily and slowly, focusing on breathing in to where your hands are low down first, only then allow the top of your lungs to fill with air – without overfilling!
   - if you still can't feel movement in your back, move your hands to your sides
   - still can't feel it – move one hand round on to your lower tummy
   - it can take practice to breathe in to your bum!
4. Think of your lungs pushing your hands out and breathing steadily, moving your tummy not shoulders, neck or upper spine
   - once you can feel your hands moving out on your back, sides or belly, you're breathing in to the correct place
   - if you can't it's OK – try doing this lying down and watch your tummy as you breathe
   - the main aim is to keep your shoulders relaxed and down – stop breathing in to your upper lungs only – if only they move, you're breathing too high
5. Count a slow 5 as you breathe IN through your nose
   - if you can't breathe in for 5 you are gasping in air too fast and probably only breathing in to the tops of your lungs – SLOOOOOW down… take it easy!
6. Count a slow 7 as you breathe OUT evenly through your mouth – no noise yet
   - aim for a steady and even breath without forcing anything by the end
   - do you notice how your diaphragm muscles under your ribs push up to squeeze the air out as you get to the end of your breath?
7. Always breathe in through the nose to avoid getting a dry mouth and clacking gums!
   - this is important to learn if you are a natural mouth breather

Once you feel you can breathe at a controlled steady pace, note how you feel.

Stretch out any muscles that might be a little tense – this may be new after all – and see if you can control and extend the count of your OUT breath from 7, to 10, to 15.

How do I breathe?	Result – how it makes me feel?
Diaphragm Breathing	Physical: Mental:

M³ Your Breathing Too!

Pay attention and start training your breathing mind-muscle-memory so you know you are in control and can use your easy breath to give you greater confidence any time you need.

Always stay relaxed and take your time – breathing should be easy!

1. Breathe in and out without forcing the last air out of your lungs – stay controlled and notice when you are easily breathing deeper and deeper down in your lungs.

2. Aim to feel your lower stomach getting involved in the breathing – the easy feeling.

3. As you breathe naturally deeper, think of easy breathing in to your bum!

4. Can you feel your hands expanding more around the back of your lungs/spine/bum?

5. Can you feel your fingers moving and muscles expanding as you breathe lower down?

6. Can you feel the air going down into your abdomen, without forcing it?

7. Make sure your shoulders are staying down as you breathe deeper – feel your shoulders drop and relax as you do, feel your spine relax, feel your brain clear and your M³ grow…

If you are having trouble, lie down on the floor and do this like we used to in drama class, it does actually help as you can feel your lower back sink into the floor and watch your tummy rise gently up and down as you relax and breathe properly. But no blaming me if you're caught asleep on the floor!

Visualise M³ Breathing if you need

For a more visual M³ boost, think of seeing a baby asleep… their tiny tummy goes up and down so naturally. That is how we SHOULD breathe but often it has been taught out of us in that desperate need to look thinner in our own vanity!

It's almost impossible to hold your tummy in and breathe how you need to, to present with confidence and breath control, to support your voice and give enough oxygen to your brain to allow you to think quickly on your feet.

This is how we *instinctively* breathe when ready in fight or flight, in the 100% focused moment.

Breathing like this can actually psychologically make you FEEL more confident, because you are in control – of your breathing, of your mind and body and of yourself.

Practical Breathing

And you have to practise this breathing exercise each day for the next month to embed the feeling of confidence and control. Do it during the boring moments when you are practising your OBE position, or just before you go to sleep at night.

Envisage and feel the air expanding through your lower back, into the base of your spine and into your bottom. You can even do a couple of quick knee bends, to sink your breath even lower as you breathe out.

Natural Shortcuts

Yawning and laughing are great for breath control too; you naturally breathe exactly where we want you to, so if you still haven't got it, do a couple of great big yawns, full mouth open, and feel where the air naturally goes.

This also gives a massive oxygen boost to your brain, allowing you to think clearer – so always good for your mind and soul ☺

Then give yourself another laugh – you deserve it! Laugh all of the air out of your lungs until nothing is left and feel that air rush in as a result. This is why laughing at yourself in a sticky spot is physically and psychologically so good for you – you get the fresh air and oxygen you need!

Benefits as an actor

When you can feel that sensation and you feel completely in control, relaxed, calm, centred, focused and your brain is alive with oxygen and ready to go, then you are breathing like an actor or singer, so give yourself a pat and keep practising; you'll need this breath control to support your Vocal Impact.

〜〜〜〜〜〜〜〜

SO Actor Breathing Numero Uno...
Breathe in to your... uhm... BUM!

Aspire to breathe control, body and mind at oxygenated ease

Breathe easy and smile on screen!

〜〜〜〜〜〜〜〜

**Quick Bum Breathing A&E Review
– how does Bum Breathing make you feel?**

_____

_____

_____

_____

_____

_____

_____

If you have words like clear headed, alert, awake, relaxed, stronger, ready, centred, stronger voice then you're breathing how you're meant to be.

If not, go back to focusing on breathing in to the bottom of your lungs and feeling your hands moving in and out nice and evenly around your diaphragm. You'll have plenty of breath control from there, and a few good deep breaths, huffs and blow-outs will give you the oxygen boost you need to the brain to feel confident before you present.

Remember, we could be changing the habits of a lifetime to get you to really _breathe easy..._

The Visual Impact
Success Review A&E

My Playlist Learnings for a Confident on Camera Me!

The key learnings in this chapter have been all about Step 3: Your Body and your nerves and how you can help yourself create a negative or a positive Visual Impact PoV – which would you prefer?

I want to leave you with some thinking here, to review your A&E notes to get that brilliant brain of yours noticing what can and will make a difference to your visual Confidence on Camera.

Ask yourself:

1. What are my habits with my body?

2. Does my body work for or against me?

3. How can I use all of my body to best effect when I present?

4. Am I habit aware? Do my body, hands, arms, face distract my audience?

5. How can I stand and sit to feel most confident and suit my video style?

6. What can I do to prepare?

7. How can I breathe for a confidence boost?

My Notes for me – I Can…

_____

_____

_____

_____

My Playlist for a Confident on Camera Me! Online

STEP THREE:

7 Actor Stages to Empower my Visual Impact

My Learning Stage Notes:

1. **Frame** – your shot + mind to look your best!
   Pick your happy frame and SMILE!

2. **Negate nerves** - focus adrenalin into connecting to benefit the viewer.
   You're helping them!

3. **Release my energy** - Know your nervous habits, re-energise and let them go!

4. **7 Habits** – what works for you?
   Use "Eye contact" = connect. Smile, laugh, breathe…

5. **Use OBE** – feet, knees, hips, spine, shoulders, arms, hands, head, neck, face.
   BREATHE…

6. **Warm up** – tense + release muscles, stretch, shake, jump HUH,
   bum squeeze - BREEATHE!

7. **Breathe** - learn to M^3 Breathe into your bum
   – focus your mind, laugh, boost confidence.

Be #FLAWSOME - Stuff up with confidence & get over it!

And if you're wondering about the Visual Impact of DIY setting the scene – where and how to film, basic lighting and sound tips, equipment, what to wear, how to look good etc. – flip to the end of the book and you'll find all that non-presenting related Visual Impact in Step 7: Confidence in Planning, Production and Promotion on page 189.

STEP FOUR

The Vocal Impact

Begin at the beginning," the King said,
very gravely, "and go on till you come
to the end: then stop.

Alice in Wonderland, Lewis Carroll

An Actor's Voice is a Powerful Tool

As Shakespeare's Marc Anthony said in *Julius Caesar*, it's now time to…

"lend me your ears" to develop your voice!

Our acting voice is our well-honed, powerful tool.

We train to speak clearly, to articulate with good diction, to learn about how our voice adapts and changes to create different characters. We learn how our voice can physically, emotionally and mentally affect and influence others, from animals to human beings.

We learn how moving, shaping, tensing different areas of our body and muscles changes our voice; how our mouth and breath control vocal clarity and diction; and which muscles help us to protect and project our voice from the back of the stage to 'the gods' – the very highest seats at the far, far back of the theatre. As a voice-over (VO) artist talking all day, we really learn how much vocal variety we are capable of when we listen, and how to take care of our voice.

Now, voice training as an actor was another daily torture to learn how and where our voice reverberates in our body: the mouth, the head, the nose, the chest, the belly, the bottom (yes, back there!). There were chewed-on fingers, bone props, bitten tongues, sore jaws, shoulders, arms, legs, knees, feet. But we had to learn so we could maintain our voice, to use it without stress or strain, so we could use it night after night and perform again and again.

You *can* become far more powerful and commanding through minute changes in muscle tension and focused breath control. And you can learn the basics of how – without all my drama class palaver. So now it's time to focus on your voice and listen, really listen, to how you use it and discover its hidden power.

So let's just get stuck into the 7 Vocal Stages for this Step of the process…

STAGE 1: *The Power of the Voice*

A voice can have a powerful effect on us.

A professional speaker at a National Speakers Association Australia conference told me that *"your voice gives eyes to the blind"* – I loved that concept! It reminded me of my Dad telling me stories when I was little… I'd close my eyes, listen to his crazy voices play and let my imagination fly! A good voice aids that imagination.

Which voice still rings in your ears as that powerful, confident sound that influenced you? What was it about *that* voice that makes you feel the authority/ go weak at the knees/want to do anything they say?!

Now think more recently to watching something online: how often do you actually *stop* watching a video or webinar, but turn the sound up so you can *listen* while doing something else? Think of the power of podcasts, voiced webinars and virtual interview recordings.

What works for you? What doesn't?

And what about you…

- When was the last time you listened to your own voice through a recording?
- If you have, do you like it or do you find it hard to listen to?
- What do you like about your voice? Can you hold an audience with the gravitas or warmth of your voice alone, or do you want to make it work better for you?

You CAN train your voice to become richer, warmer, deeper, stronger, more flexible to adapt to different scenarios, settings and rooms for recordings. Knowing what you want your voice to achieve will affect how and when you use your voice – a hugely powerful tool at your disposal, once you recognise and implement the power of what works for you.

The power of your voice is not just about how loud you can talk, it's about how much of an effect your voice has on us – what in your voice causes or demands we listen?

Even when you know your voice and how you use it, some people will love it, others will hate it, but as long as we understand you and can hear you clearly, you give yourself the chance to be a voice that people love, by paying attention to what works.

So let's exercise with some acting voice games to develop vocal capabilities, your mental flexibility and vocal quick thinking. Let's assess what we like in a voice, then test and assess yours to learn how you can improve the power of your voice. All instructions are online along with loads more docs to build your Vocal Impact section of your workbook – it's growing fast, isn't it?!

Playlist: 5 Actor Voice Games to Develop Vocal Variety A&E

These five actor voice games will help your story-telling abilities, get your brain used to timing without rushing and remind you to warm up your Vocal articulators – if you can't speak clearly, we're never going to hear you, but more on that later… If you do nothing else for your voice than warm up with humming and the Tongue Twister exercises, you must do these to kick start your voice before presenting.

5 Actor Voice Games to Develop Vocal Variety:

Start collecting your stories – your own are best for you, so write them down!
It's imagination, creativity and Vocal Play time!

Story Games	My Notes
1. My Soap Box Story Use emotion - passion, love, rant! Practice timings – 30 secs/1 min	My fav story is… My rant is…

5 Actor Voice Games to Develop Vocal Variety:	
Story Games	**My Notes**
2. Bed-time Story Read kids book – with voices! Can use news stories Practice timings – 30"/45"/1 min	My fav book is… My fav news source to match my style is…
3. Story Games to buy online Storydice The Winner Matrix The Story Bus books	Story games for me are…
4. Just a Minute Talk to a timer for 1 mintue Practice timings – 30 secs/1 min No hesitation, repetition, stopping!	Topics I can talk on are…
5. Tongue Twister List Use the list to warm up your mouth Articulate clearly before speed Use those hard ones to say!	Tongue twisters I need to use are:

Make your voice your story-telling tool – use vocal variety, practice, Play!

These are great voice games to play with others or practise on your own. Do regularly record your voice telling the stories to check on your skill improvement.

STAGE 2: Auditory M³ = Vocal Mind-Muscle-Memory

Your Voice Connects our Memories

Your Vocal Impact connects you to your audience in a deeper subconscious level than the Visual Impact because hearing is usually one of the first things we learn to do. It is harder to assess why we can be irritated by or really like someone's voice, but hearing a voice you don't/do like can actually transport you back to a terrible/wonderful time in an instant and automatically turn you off/on to that person – even though you've hardly heard them, you really don't/do want to hear what they have to say! You often stop/start listening from a judgement call, made from and directly linked to auditory muscle memory.

Remember all of us hear slightly differently with our different shaped heads, body mass and shape, so one person's favourite voice might be someone else's nightmare! So it's OK, whether you like a certain voice or not is purely personal preference and you're allowed to speculate as to how you hear *your* favourite voice.

But, as always, let's start by thinking who has a good voice in our own head and why we think so. Grab your workbook or make notes as usual as we have a few exercises to get through in this chapter. Oh, and you'll probably be talking to yourself a lot in case you want to warn those around you – no, you're not going mad!

My Ideas of a 'Good' Voice A&E

So what do you think makes up a 'good' voice for you?

_____

_____

_____

If you have jotted down things like: clearly spoken, warm tones, powerful or interesting variety, easy listening, smooth or lyrical, musical voice, then you have at some point opened your ears and heard some of the parts that *do* make up a voice, which we'll come to in a moment.

But first, I'd like you to think of some famous Voices, or Google Best Voices and see which ones you like (*or don't – you are allowed not to!*) and yes think Voice with a capital V – who really is the best for you and specifically why?

_____

_____

Being an actor, many of my favourite voices are actually other actors and professional speakers, which makes sense as we are voice coached from a very early stage. Also, as I started before every performer had a mini-microphone on stage, I had to learn how to project my voice to the back of the theatre, hall or room, and that hurts if you don't do it properly, without forcing your voice and stressing your vocal chords, so I appreciate others who can do the same!

I enjoy rich, deep-toned voices, velvety and luxurious – you might prefer a lighter voice. Remember none of us hear or actually listen to a voice in exactly the same way.

People Listen in Different Ways

When I taught English to Japanese businessmen and their wives in Hong Kong, they would often not look at me or close their eyes. I used to think I was boring them or they were just plain rude, until one very high-profile businessman, who would literally turn his head away AND close his eyes, very politely told me it was to *"enable my ears to work better to hear you"*…

What a great phrase eh? By blocking the potentially distracting visual stimulus, it allowed him to hear my pronunciation, articulation and vocal tone more clearly, so that he could better understand my foreign language and emulate how I said things.

This AHA! moment changed my whole perception and made me even more interested in how and why some voices 'work' and some simply don't. Our voice has a musicality that the subconscious picks up tiny vocal nuances, varieties, tones we don't even realise are there, or may be missing. Your voice is literally your mouthpiece for your storytelling, an instrument to play, that can flex to a variety of different styles.

~~~~~~~~~~~~~

So – our voice is a muscle which, like any other, needs warming up, exercising and resting when it is tired!

~~~~~~~~~~~~~

Why do we Listen to a Voice?

We've thought about your favourite voices. What do you think interests you about a voice? It is probably the vocal variety that does so, and any dull, monotone, non-varying voice probably annoys you, or sends you to sleep. Well, again, that's actually key to your voice…

VOCAL VARIETY CREATES AND HOLDS INTEREST!

And having eye contact is key to that vocal variety.

Variety is actually subconsciously created by visual cues when we talk face-to-face with someone or an audience live. As we discovered in ConC Step 1, we can see when they're giving us rapt attention and when we lose it, so we vary our voice accordingly. It's an ongoing cycle.

It does relate to our content and our enthusiasm for what we are doing and saying. If we are bored, our voice can express that feeling without us realising, so we *sound* boring.

Sounding Bored

1. Try saying "I'm excited" but think bored!
2. Slump your body, head down, flat energy.
3. Hear what happens to your voice?
4. Low volume, mumbled, dull, total lack of interest…
   INCONGRUENCE again!
5. Now stand for your OBE – look up, smile, be congruent…
6. I bet you sounded a lot less boring then!
7. You will have used different volume, clarity, notes, style of voice.

See, we can turn it around in a split second when we notice we have lost audience attention. We can do something different with our voice: make a change, go higher, lower, louder, quieter, harsher, softer, adapting our voice to suit our script and the mood we want to set.

We do this most naturally when we tell stories or have a specific mood or goal we want to achieve.

Think of hearing stories as a child, how much more fun was it when you put on silly voices, like my Dad did for me? Can you remember a time when a voice lulled you to sleep? Was it at a time you wanted it to, or was it when you needed to stay awake, but the voice was so samey, it was hard to keep focus? When I'm too overtired to read, my wonderful husband often reads to me in this monotone, quiet voice he puts on. No, not saying he's boring – he does it on purpose! But be aware that when we present, sending someone to sleep is definitely not what we want, so where does the interest in your voice lie?

Why the Machines Flatten your Voice

Most people hate listening to their voice recordings. That's because 60%+ of how we actually hear our voice is it echoing and resonating beautifully around the cavities and fluids in our own body and head. Recording through a machine takes away that lovely echo and rich sound quality we actually hear.

Talking to the machine flattens your energy and can flatten your voice immediately, if you let it. You have no eye contact, so the M³ Emotional and Actional Connections are so important and relevant for your voice too – you have to imagine the reactions of that real person you are talking to, to hold your own interest!

We need to be aware of when to shift in our vocal storytelling and of our own vocal flexibility to create the power of our voice on camera, especially when doing a voice-over (VO). Things that sound different cause us to take notice, a finger snap can jolt us awake, so can a change in vocal volume, inflection, pattern, tone.

NOTICING VOCAL DISTRACTIONS

Simple exercises can quickly help once you know what your vocal strengths and 'distractions' are. Some are easy to change when you want. Others, like speech impediments, take specific voice coaching I'm not covering here. We're discovering more about a voice 'quality' – the vocal power that can easily be adapted. So before we go there, let's have a bit of fun and get all human judgemental again and think whose voice *really annoys* us!

My personal Distracting Voices – the ones you forget to listen to what they say, because you're purely distracted by the tonal *how* they say it – are: Pee Wee Herman, Justin Beiber, Nicki Minaj (when she plays her music 'character', but not when she acts funnily enough!), Lady Gaga, Miley Cyrus, J. Lo, Kim Kardashian's inflections, Lee Evans' high-pitched tone. Funnily enough, most of my vocal pet peeves are musicians or character voices who sing and perform brilliantly, but in my view don't bother with their speaking voice!

When we practise playing with our voice and noticing how we speak normally versus what we *can* do when we play, our presenting voice improves as we've primed it to do so. So let me be a little more specific with some other famous, but often Distracting Voices and why I feel that way.

Voices I find particularly distracting:

✗ George Bush Jnr American President had a repetitious vocal pattern that nearly always ended on the same note

✗ Gordon Brown UK Prime Minister had a strange jaw-dropping, back of the throat, breathy thing before he said key items

✗ Bill Gates Microsoft founder is often highly nasal sounding, which can be perceived as 'whiney' – defo for me!

And all these men have succeeded to the top of their field.

So vocal distractions don't mean that you can't succeed, simply that you may succeed faster, better, more easily and get more people to understand and like you when you work to improve your voice – the core aim when we're talking business video online!

Who are your Vocal Pet Peeve, Distracting Voices and Why?

_____

_____

_____

STAGE 3: Confident Vocal Variety

Voices of the World

Now we may all like different voices from different places in the world, but we must understand one big thing:

Different nationalities also like and expect different things in a voice - in volume, clarity, variety and tone

The Chinese Government in Hong Kong always wanted my documentary VOs to be with a 'light' voice, as their ideal for an 'English lady voice' is a higher pitched, articulate, trippingly light voice – a nightmare for a non-Chinese speaker when you have ten tongue-twisting officials' names that must be pronounced perfectly, all in a row!

Different languages also have different mouth positions for the lips, the jaw and the tongue – often all too easy for an inarticulate Westerner to miss or confuse! Mandarin, for example, is very much at the front of your mouth, using lots of lips and tongue tip; Cantonese, more nasal at the back of your mouth and tongue, but each only has limited vocal pattern tones, so you have to be very careful how you pronounce certain things. You will know what delivers clarity in your native tongue and the need for vocal variety, clarity and flexibility is more than likely the same.

I love and appreciate the clarity of people I've seen on stage or met who have that rich gravitas, controlled power and can express real or raw emotion just by using their voice. Anthony Hopkins, in *M Butterfly* in the West End in 1986 – my first night on the stage crew and just as he swept on stage, all he said was, "Hello, please do call me Tony." Tongue-tied, SWOOOON!

The Awesomeness of Accents

Mr Hopkins is a Welshman and proud of it; Sean Connery, Christopher Walken and Michael Caine never change their accent no matter which role they play, and you don't have to either! Accents can actually enhance a voice, as long as the diction is clear, we can hear the words and it easy for us to understand through appropriate pause and emphasis on key words we need to hear.

Once you really start listening you may even notice how often people in your life often adapt their voice to fit in! It's part of our arsenal for creating empathy – it can work in your own language, but not so often picking up accents when you travel.

Funny how on arriving in Dublin, the Australian inflection 'twaaang' I'd developed on purpose for some TV jobs wasn't fooling any real 'Stralian, but had me pegged by the Irish as an Aussie! And at the time my Irish accent – I thought acceptably developed from Brian Friel plays during my drama days – was suddenly dashed and ridiculed by the people who have that accent for real. It's taught me a valuable lesson about *trying* to do accents. In that country – don't! As a foreigner, accept it is probably going to sound wrong and it can be perceived as insulting. So please native English speakers, stop putting on accents or shouting when you travel abroad – it doesn't really help. But one day people WILL believe I'm Irish in Australia!

Obviously, with global business connections growing online, nearly everywhere is getting much more international and we're hearing more voices, languages and accents. Differences don't matter anywhere near as much as they used to, but clarity still does. I always encourage clients to use their accent as part of their Unique Selling Point (USP) and personal charisma, as long as the words are clearly spoken and understandable.

Attitudes to an Accent

Because of ear-tuning training and travel, I can usually understand even strong accents in English, but many people can't and we have preconceived judgements about certain regional inflections, pronunciation or ways of saying things. So if your spoken English has a strong accent, you need to slow down, practise pronunciation for clear articulation and good diction – i.e. how clearly you say the words. And if you're native English, you need to be aware of colloquial phrases that can easily be misunderstood!

From Ireland…

A few of my favourite Irish phrases are:

"Go on so…" – meaning anything from "just do it" to "you go first"

"Come here till I tell ya…" – as in "come and hear this…"

"Get away with ya!" – in the context "you are having a laugh/joking!"

When you think the last one means 'go away' and they're all said in the same sentence, very fast, it can be superconfusing!

Voice coaching an Irish politician when I first arrived, his aim was to get to represent Ireland in the European Parliament, but he felt his accent was a huge drawback to being understood. It wasn't, he had a lovely tone of voice. His only issue for being understood in Europe was the Irish TH which can be pronounced as D – so he would say "dis, dat and dose" instead of "this, that and those."

Some countries have a stereotypical, negative perception, 'country bumpkin' type judgement about this Irish habit. It's often actually perpetuated by other Irish accented English speakers around the world, so he felt this could be holding him back from being taken seriously. But it was actually *only* preventing him from being clearly understood.

Perception can be – if you don't take time to speak clearly with your accent, to make an effort to be understood – that you're lazy, so why should we work to hear you?

To Asia…

All across Asia many people from China, Thailand, Indonesia and the Philippines called me Nottie or Rottie because they didn't hear the L at the start. It never mattered to me, it was always fun, but they always apologised as if it was *their* incompetence, rather than *my* language being difficult for some nationalities to hear or say! So I learned to articulate the L in my name more.

Any vocal habit you may have that you find is distracting and want to improve can have a solution. Or choose to make a thing of it – as English TV presenter Jonathan Ross who has a speech impediment to say R as W; he makes a joke of his own name *"Wossie"* and gets on with it!

The main point is to stop judging how your accent may be perceived and start focusing on **how clearly you are understood** and what, if any, part of your speaking may need some work. And it will take work, so here's an example…

A quick solution to the 'TH thing'

Some of my Japanese students also found saying "TH" difficult and they found it very stressful and distracting for them and their listeners. So I found a fairly simple solution to fix up by learning proper tongue placement…

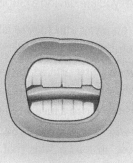 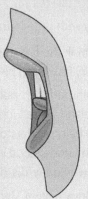

1. Relax your jaw with your lips just open.
2. Place the very tip of your tongue just between your teeth, with the end on to the edge of your two upper teeth.
3. Gently press your tongue up into the top teeth.
4. Blow air out gently – you'll hear a hissing sound and should feel the air blowing gently on both sides, against the inside of your top lip.
5. Then all you have to do is add the "THhhhhhhhhh" voice sound.
6. If you're hearing a "Sssssss" sound, the tip of your tongue is too far behind your top two teeth.
7. There is no need to stick your tongue right out between your teeth like you see in films!

Did you have a go?

Now have another go, but add more voice to really feel the sound vibrating and the tingle in your lips – apologies if you almost ended up spraying the book when blowing a bit too hard, I almost did the same to the laptop while writing it!

Did you notice the difference between the softer *"th"* and stronger *"TH"* with voice?

Notice which words in English you use which for:

"th" – is soft for words like thing and thought

"TH" – is with a vibrating voice sound, a little harder for the "TH" of this, that and those

It really is *THHH*at simple!

Yet it can take some practice and some work to get it.

You never need to push the voice – you simply learn to control it, project it and breathe with it.

～～～～～～～～～

YES! Voice control comes down to our old friend Breathing!

～～～～～～～～～

How does the Power of my Voice work on Camera?

The best thing is there are a myriad of things that work vocally on camera – remember, within reason, almost anything goes!

Because of its impact, good sound is imperative when you record.

With the recording quality of most cameras and smartphones these days, you can often get away without a microphone, but using one does provide a more professional, cleaner sounding voice. If it's noisy you must use one; if you're interviewing someone, you may get away with a mic between you; check if your camera mic makes your voice sound tinny, tiny or echoey.

No matter what or where you are filming, **always do a sound check before you start and check the sound is recording** *(been there oops!)* – that's The Power of your Voice 101!

Whether you have a microphone or not, you still need to project your voice appropriately, use vocal variety and make it congruent to the message you want to portray.

You also need to breathe properly, have good breath control and breathe without it getting in the way. Without your good breath control you will find it hard to exercise and control your voice and it *will* break down at some point. So go back and remind yourself of the breathing exercises and how to breathe with confidence if you need, before you start doing any voice exercises in this chapter.

We're going to keep your Vocal Impact fairly simple – it's a separate 20 years of performing and coaching experience book in itself *(and yes, The Power of Your Voice e-book is available!)*. So now let's get specific and break down your voice into a few specific areas, so you can see which, if any, of the key parts of your voice need work to improve.

Then we'll look at the Voice 3 Ps: Pacing, Pausing and Vocal Performance and how to look after your voice and avoid wear and tear… plus a couple of bonus pointers as always!

Your vocal variety and colour all help boost that 30% extra energy you need to achieve to maintain interest on camera and often even a small shift in one area can do just that.

STAGE 4: *The Power of the 4 PART Voice*

One of my actor/trainer colleagues at Maura Faye Workshops came up with the 4 P.A.R.T.s of the Voice, so thanks to them for such a great acronym. I thought of the Vocal TRAP – but that sounds too limiting to me and it could just as easily be what makes us RAPT in your voice, so I don't think it's a hard copyright! Thanks to MFW anyway. The PARTs of your voice are a simple breakdown of the core elements that can affect us when we listen to you and enable us to hear you.

The 4 PARTs of your Voice are:

✓ **POWER**

✓ **ARTICULATION**

✓ **RANGE**

✓ **TONE**

POWER	This Power is how loud you can actually speak, without shouting!
	How you **Project** your Voice: the volume you use, the variety of that volume, being heard in a larger room.
	We can use Power to impact an Actional Connection and create congruence – say the words as they mean.
	Low volume can be hard to hear or used as secretive or exciting; loud volume can deafen – or wake people up! Shouting is not Vocal Power, it is straining your voice. Vocal Power must be used but never forced.
	Projection with a clear, strong voice is a confident voice
ARTICULATION	Is how clearly you speak in terms of your pronunciation and clarity of diction; how you get your mouth around the words; how you enunciate (announce) the words you say; how you ensure accents and vocal habits are clearly understood. Poor articulation can be perceived as laziness, so we need to move our mouths to speak clearly. You must articulate to be understood.
	A clear, understandable voice = a clear and confident mind!
RANGE	Vocal Range = the variety of notes you use and the patterns you use them in. Think of singing, it is the sing-song-ability quality of your voice.
	High and low notes are the musicality in your voice – your pitch.
	We use a variety of notes, inflections, emphasis and vocal patterns to demonstrate our interest and keep the audience engaged.
	Listen to your vocal patterns, watch for ending on the same note or when high notes make you sound a bit strange!
	No variety = monotone – hence the word *monotonous*.
	Develop your bass notes, they equal Credibility.
	Vocal Range holds viewer interest
TONE	Many people ask me *"What do you mean by Tone?"*
	It's that part of the voice we put a description to, the quality of the voice you hear. Or as singers might describe it, your timbre, texture, colour or quality. It's what makes a voice sound different, even when talking at the same pitch or loudness as another.
	You might describe a voice as smooth, warm, rich or friendly, or harsh, rough or raspy, or possibly nasal, throaty or chesty.
	It's where we naturally speak from.
	It is directly linked to our breathing and it can be adapted and changed to impart a mood or feeling for greater congruence.
	Only voice exercises can help you change your Vocal Tone.
	Vocal Tone sets the tone!

The 4 PARTs of your voice *must* work together to produce a fully rounded, easily understandable, animated, congruent voice that viewers want to listen to and take action because of.

The Power of Your 4 P.A.R.T. Voice A&E

The full 4 P.A.R.T. Power of your Voice breakdown online takes you through each of the four sections looking at:

- ⊥ what works for each PART of your voice and how to make it work for you
- ⊥ potential vocal pitfalls and solutions to help
- ⊥ exercises to practise and improve each PART to come across well on camera

Plus a bonus tip to help you with your warm, friendly tone of voice – what do you think that is? ☺

Before absorbing that online and testing out your vocal skills as you do, fill in the form for your gut instinct assessment of what you think are your voice PARTs:

1. Voice Powers
2. Pitfall Habits
3. Solution Focus

The form looks like this or jot down here:

My Voice P.A.R.T.s				▶
What PARTs of your voice need work?	POWER	ARTICULATION	RANGE	TONE
My Voice: What Works?				
My Pitfall Habit				
My Solution Focus				
My Practice Exercises				

Make the Demand with your 4 PART Vocal Command!

Hold on to those first perceptions of the PARTs of your voice, what strengths and potential habits you *may* have, and how you can adapt and shift your voice to have a positive Vocal Impact. Let's look at how you can easily bring even more vocal variety to grab and hold interest using the **Voice 3 Ps: Pacing, Pausing and Vocal Performance** and how to look after your voice and avoid wear and tear + a couple of bonus pointers.

STAGE 5:   The Extra PPP Parts of your Voice

Once we understand the Power of our Voice through its PARTs and trust our confident voice to deliver for us, we can free up our focus for the 3 key Ps of vocal delivery:

1. **Pace**
2. **Pause**
3. **Presenter Performance**

1. Pace depends a lot on the mood of the subject matter and can be affected by the subject matter itself. We have to be congruent with speed of speaking too!

Delivering detailed facts and figures or tragic stories demands a slower pace. However, the pace would lift somewhat if talking about something uplifting or exciting.

So your pace is relative to the choice of subject matter. Think how a newsreader changes pace from one story to the next – notice how it is usually tied in with a possible body shift, change of tone, range and power too.

Changing topic from chat to fact also requires a pace change – play and see what works for you because pace is also heavily dependent on individual presenter personality. I tend to talk fast, to get a lot of info in, so have to consciously slooooow down to deliver killer facts or leave spaces for rhetorical questions (see Pause below).

Pace holds interest too and the 3-7" Rule also applies to vocal pace and variety.

If you chat naturally your pace will be natural – we can skip through in-between chat and slooow right down to hit... the key... points. You can also write your scripts like that to designate when you want to slow... or Pause/or Stop for a conscious break //.

Pace creates momentum, but sometimes the momentum created by one presenter at one pace is so different from another, even if they're saying the same thing. Both of them can sound right because they are each speaking within their own pace comfort range, using their own 4 PART voice.

If you feel yourself dragging slow or rushing fast, you probably are – so simple: take your time:

~~~~~~~~~~~~~~~~~~

Change your pace to suit your Pace = Confidence

~~~~~~~~~~~~~~~~~~

2. **Pauses** are very deliberate. A pause gives us time to absorb your information and to think about what you have said or a question you may have posed. Pauses are put into your script deliberately, so need to be timed accurately.

Use Visual Impact to back up a pause – back up your congruent credibility! e.g. pause after a question with a query look on your face…?

If you ask a question of your viewer, count 1… 2… this will probably be long enough for them to engage. Obviously count in your head, not mouthing the words! Give us that moment before you rush on, even if you feel you've got a lot to get through in your one-minute piece; an extra few seconds of time for us to contemplate and absorb is worth it.

And enable your viewer to understand by seeing your reaction to what you said – let us see it's a pause with a reason, instead of a stuff-up, with an expression on your face! Make us think it's worth your while taking the time to find the RIGHT way to say what you want to – take us on your journey through your pause.

Pausing naturally in the right places: breaking up your script with commas, / breaks / and full stops …   also gives you enough time to breathe, collect your thoughts and deliver your presentation with ease. Pauses allow you time to remember too.

A pause that is too long can be very obvious or sound awkward – especially if it is because you have forgotten what you want to say and your face or eyes show your panic. However, a pause in that moment of panic is NEVER as long as you think, so find ways to cover your pregnant pauses, with a concentrated look, a gesture, a smile.

And remember to breathe – your words will come back. An easy breath in is usually the right length for a pause. Do be aware:

If you gasp in for breath too fast it can be very loud.

A gasp of air like Gordon Brown at the start or end of each section can be very distracting!

So pause and smile and allow yourself to breathe naturally.

This will also to ensure your lips or mouth avoid the lip-smacking sound that can also come with gasping in air.

A video piece without the necessary pauses for us to absorb the information can sound rushed and insincere. We are far more likely to turn that off halfway through if it's all at one speed, with no space to think for ourselves.

Making pauses in the right place is an art and does take practice, but once you have acquired your Pause technique, your presentation will feel and sound far more confident.

~~~~~~~~~~~~~~

**A Pause is your Power to connect both for you
and your viewer = Credibility**

~~~~~~~~~~~~~~

3. Performance. This is your personal style – it's unique to you and how you bring even more interest and understanding to your words to engage and impact the viewer.

Performance can be broken into two main areas: **Intonation** and **Inflection**.

Vocal intonation is the *colour* that our voices add to the text – literally how you add the appropriate variety that helps give tone to your voice. Do you chant, drone, croon, sing or say?

It is the chosen mood behind the actual word that gives meaning and allows correct understanding. The wrong intonation can create immediate incongruence.

We need our voice to work *with* the thought behind the words so our tone depicts the picture in the form of sound. The congruent Emotional Connection again!

Think back to that child being told a bedtime story, painting imaginary pictures from the way the words are said. Good intonation animates and colours the sound to give the story depth and dimension.

~~~~~~~~~~~~~~

Correct intonation enables us to engage in your story

~~~~~~~~~~~~~~

Vocal inflection is slightly different from intonation. It's when we inflect **em**phasis on a word, or part of a word, for a reason. It's how we highlight certain sounds of a word to add different dimensions to it.

Intentional inflection draws attention to the *importance* of a word or issue.

We like to know the HOW, WHAT, WHY of something – we stress the **key words** to designate their importance.

The meaning and understanding of a simple sentence such as *"I love tea"* can totally change by emphasising a different word. Say these out loud – what's the meaning to you?

> *I* love tea = ...
> I *LOVE* tea = ...
> I love *TEA* = ...

So we have to be careful we em**pha**sise the right word or part of the word to avoid misunderstandings. This is very important online, as you are speaking to a global market and want to avoid mixed messages, misrepresentations or muck-ups!

Inflection can be a distracting habit we may not notice in the moment – like the Aussie upward inflection or stress at the end of sent-**unce!**

Do write your scripts in CAPITALS, **bold**, *italics* or underline them so you know what keywords to stress. Highlighting these will also allow you to remember your script more easily, which we'll hear more about in next Step 5: The Verbal Impact.

As long as the inflection is not overdone – with FAAAR too MANY, or **the** wrong key word OR **sec**tions **of** words high**lighted** – it is a very effective technique that adds strength, authority and clearer understanding to your presenter performance.

Use emphasis for emphatic understanding – always avoid excess!

So performance is the combination of both appropriate and adaptable intonation and inflection, which can totally alter the meaning of your text. Your performance can make it mean so many different things or moods: real, fake, sarcastic, overdone, true.

Performance can not only change the meaning of the words, it can change how and what we understand and therefore what we do as a reaction to your words – or whether we DO understand them or not! It can instil the Emotional and Actional Connection that causes us to react and take action, so never underestimate the power of your vocal performance – get us talking about you through how you talk.

Performance = engagement + understanding + YOU = Charisma

3 Ps Queries to help your Vocal Power

1. PACE – do you need to slow down, can you speed up anywhere, how can you make it chatty/ more hard-hitting/relaxed? How/where can you vary pace and volume to hold our attention and keep our interest more? When can you link it to your variety in range?

2. PAUSE – Pause before or after a key word or point to give it greater emphasis or importance. Where can you pause to breathe? When does it feel natural to pause for a better understanding of the piece? Write and mark your script with:

N.P. = new paragraphs, full stops, slashes // and/or commas – find the natural places you can pause and breathe, even in a 'chat' script.

Choose your annotation meaning: a comma is usually a short pause, a slash or full stop = longer!

3. PERFORMANCE – think when and how you stress the words and put the congruent intonation meaning into them – all about variety! Where will you **stress** key words or phrases you have identified for more performance style? Where, when and how will you:

1. Identify your key words you need to stress?
2. Know your M^3 for each specific part of your script?
3. Increase or decrease volume?
4. Streeeeetch out the key word for strong emphasis?
5. Chat at a faster pace, or suddenly S..L..O..W.. then pick up the pace again?
6. Choose which key points to EM-PHA-SISE the key word?
7. Give it some Welly for Performance sake!

Give your 3 Ps your 3 Cs – Confidence, Credibility and Charisma!
Pace = Confidence to say it in your own time
Pause = Credibility to take your time,
your way and allowing us time to understand
Performance = Charisma to show us the Power of your Personality
– to be Connected and REAL

STAGE 6: The Power of Your Voice

THE POWER OF MY VOICE SELF A&E

Right, you've guessed it – it's now that time for some actual performance with your full Vocal A&E to work out exactly what, if any, your real vocal powers and pitfalls may be.

Get your *Power of My Voice Self-Assessment* form and instructions online and what we're going to do is record your voice step by step – no leaping ahead and trying too hard to be perfect, or you won't hear the real you and how you naturally sound. You're going to need about 30-60 minutes in total.

You're going to need and do:

1. Some means of recording your voice: whether a smartphone, dictaphone, webcam, video camera, record via a PowerPoint slide on your computer.

2. Any piece of text that is about one minute long – something from the newspaper or a magazine will do, as long as it reflects your style you want to portray.

   If you want to use your own text, that is great – one minute will be about half an A4 page.

3. To record your voice and do a 10-20 minute Vocal Assessment: what PARTs works, what could be better?

4. Focus also on Pace, Pause and Performance – the other 3 P-P-P-PARTs of your voice including intonation and inflection.

5. Think how you could better support your voice – what would you need?

6. Think how to play with your voice in a fun way, for continual improvement.

7. Time now to plan and create your personal 10-minute voice self-coaching plan; you can practise whenever you need and use the form to readjust your Self Vocal Coaching as you improve.

HOW TO VOICE 3 STEP A&E

1. Record yourself for up to 1 minute reading text in a straight read i.e. how you'd normally do it.

2. Review your first vocal recording at least twice, making 4 PARTs self-assessment notes below or in your workbook – what works and what could be better…

The Power of My Voice Self-Assessment & Exercises

Focus on your overall Vocal impact
- what works / what could be better? BE KIND!

1. What I like MOST about my Voice is:

2. Power – projection + volume + variety:

3. Articulation – clarity + diction + mouth movement + accent:

4. Range – vocal variety + note patterns, highs & lows, 'musicality':

5. Tone – nasal, bass, credibility, warmth, matching the mood:

6. My Potential Pitfalls or Distracting Verbal Habits to Improve?
 -E.g. vocal patterns, enunciation, laziness, difficulty understanding, lack of
 variety, incongruence to words in empathy, emotion or energy, etc.:

7. How I can improve my Vocal habits?

Your Vocal impact can influence as much as Visual – develop your Vocal skills!

3. Then re-record your voice reading focusing on the 3 PPPs and what you could do better.

3 Ps: Vocal Pace, Pause and Performance Assessment		
Now have another go! Re-record 1 minute and focus on the 3 Ps when you talk… **PACE** - reading speed for ease of listening + variety **PAUSE** - where to pause for understanding + reflection; **PERFORMANCE** - vocal variety, colour, intonation, inflection, interest…		
	What Works?	What could be better?
PACE:		
PAUSE:		
PERFORMANCE: Intonation Inflection		
Proper Performance requires Pace and Pause – Play with your Vocal 3 Ps!		

Be Vocally Ruthless but Kind

Be ruthlessly honest with yourself, but also as always be open, be kind – starts with what works, what you like first.

Once again, if you really can't do this without picking on your faults first, ask a supportive, trusted person to help you. Ask them to pick out what you are **Good at** first. They'll spot it far quicker than you often can!

But please ensure when you ask them for feedback, you always ask:

1. What works? FIRST – at least three things that do.
2. Only then ask about anything you could improve.
3. How would they best describe what they like about your voice? How do you sound?

So how did you do?

OK/better than expected/wanting to do better?

You've heard yourself back once now, so go review your PARTs notes for potential solutions to what you could improve on. Have another go and this time REALLY focus on the 3 Ps, especially boosting your performance – go for it!

Play with your Voice!

It has come as a shock to many clients on hearing their own voice how much they have to adapt it and how much more inflection, vocal variety and power is required to sound like a pro.

Radio DJs are often joked about going to extremes, but when all you've got is your voice, you'll see exactly why: it's too easy to get bored by a voice with no visual stimulus!

But radio performance is the oldest and still one of the most effective mass communication forums in the world. We may be more focused on podcast for business now, but radio is never going to go away – and if you don't learn how to use your voice for radio and VO for your videos, webinars and training online, you'll miss out on business in years to come.

PLAY with the presenting, go over the top, have some fun with it and boost that 30% extra energy with all 4+3 = 7 PPP-PARTs of your voice!

STAGE 7:   A Voice Needs Support too!

Doing vocal exercises helps give your voice greater dexterity. By supporting your voice sensibly without pushing it and with exercises, warm-ups and recognising when you need a break, your voice will have more flexibility, variety and interest.

**Vocal Confidence + Congruence = always say the words
as they actually Feel to be Real!**

As you increase your awareness and strengthen your vocal muscles through voice assessment exercises and vocal warm-ups, and develop your breathing, breath control and vocal flexibility, you will be far less likely to damage your voice from overuse.

If you are a person who has to talk for a living – teacher, trainer, barrister, lawyer, doctor, lecturer, professional speaker or VO artist – then you MUST hone your vocal skills to prevent straining your vocal chords or future damage from incorrect use.

The Actor Steps up to Support your Voice

It's usually not until you've damaged your voice as a pro actor that you *really* bother to pay attention to protection advice from your voice coach – there's no teacher like the personal experience of pain! While I'm not a voice-chord expert, my experience is your gain as these are **seven common voice care tips** you can read in many an article online, brought together as my favourite tips to pay attention to, to support your voice pre, during and post any time you have to present in public or on film.

7 Common Acting Voice Care Tips:

1. ALWAYS warm up – your voice is a muscle too.
2. Avoid shouting – project from your diaphragm.
3. Drink water – your own bottle please!
4. Avoid milky drinks – they clag your throat.
5. Sorry chocolate fiends – avoid it, it makes your mouth sticky.
6. Listen to your voice and your body – if your throat is sore or overworked, give it a rest.
7. Naturally, smoking is not good for you or for your voice.

BONUS: if you are very interested in your voice there are a couple of books you MUST buy.

The best old actors' voice bible is by the queen of voice Cicely Berry who wrote *Voice and the Actor* – still used in drama schools across the world today. And of course, my *Power of Your Voice* e-book!

Remember Vocal Warm Ups A&E

When you present, get into the habit of doing your vocal warm-ups, mouth stretches, humming, tongue twisters and the exercises you pick from the lists online, to get your throat muscles working in a relaxed and unrestricted way with full support of your breathing and confidence in all P-P-P-Parts of your voice

Like any muscle in your body and your M³ – once you connect to and know how to use your vocal power and breath control you can more easily turn it on when you need it. Like I do at Scotland rugby matches… but that's another story! Here's your Warm Up A&E table…

My Vocal Warm Ups A&E

MY VOCAL EXERCISES:

E.g. light humming, low + high; mouth & tongue stretching; Open Body Position and Breathe control counting + Range + Power counts; Laughs + Smiles;

_____

_____

_____

MY TONGUE TWISTER LIST (pick ones you have difficulty saying!):

_____

_____

_____

MY VOCAL COMMITMENT:

I WILL do my Voice Exercises Daily @ _____ for _____ mins

Like any muscle in your body and your M³ – once you connect to and know how to use your vocal power and breathe control, you can more easily turn it on when you need it.

M³ Vocal impact always connects when you say it like you mean it!

STEP FOUR:

My 7 Steps Vocal Impact
Review A&E

My Playlist Learnings for a Confident on Camera Me!

Now you know what your voice sounds like, you have completed your Vocal Assessment and know how you can support your voice, let's create your powerful 7 Step Vocal Impact A&E plan of what specifically you CAN and WILL commit to create the improvement you want for yourself...

My Learning Stage Notes:

To make an Impact with the Power of your Voice – create your I'M-PACT!

VOCAL AREA:	WHAT WORKS – I AM	I CAN IMPROVE...	I WILL IMPROVE BY...
1. Power			
2. Articulation			
3. Range			
4. Tone			
5. Pace			
6. Pause			
7. Performance			

Empower and Enhance your Vocal Impact to 'Give eyes to the blind'!

Note that not all boxes have to be filled in on your table, if you are happy with that aspect of your voice. Focus on what needs work right now and do each step by step. Write them in pencil if you want so you can change the table as you improve each specific area and gain great vocal strength and confidence.

So now we've covered the Vocal Impact let's move on to the words you actually say, how to write them and how to remember them, so you CAN say them successfully.

STEP FIVE

The Verbal Impact

It's extraordinary how self-obsessed human beings are. The things that people always go on about are: 'tell us about us,' 'tell us about the first human being.' We are so self-obsessed with our own history. There is so much more out there than what connects to us.

David Attenborough

Confident Verbal Impact – where do you start?

The Verbal Impact is all about **the words** you choose to use to tell your story when you present.

Confident Verbal Impact – starter for 7…

1. Have a think about the last times you've had to write a presentation or a video script.
2. How long did you spend pondering over the text to get what you're telling us just right?
3. Did you ever practise telling it out loud?
4. Did you then spend more time later rewriting what you wrote?
5. Did you spend just as long or more time rehearsing how you would tell it?
6. Did you just do one run-through and present it cold on the day?
7. How did that work for you?

Divide the percentage of time spent between writing, editing, re-editing and actually rehearsing – saying it out loud…

Which side won?

I bet you spent a lot more time writing than you did on rehearsing the performance side of it!

You may know exactly what you want to tell us – but how happy are you saying it and do we listen to you when you do? How can you do it faster, more effectively, make the verbal writing process easier and remember your stories too?

You've actually already learned how – stop telling and get more involved in connecting to more than just your words! This being the Verbal Power chapter there's *loads* to write about, and so many different PoVs about what makes good copy (text or script as journos call it – hence copywriter). So my main points will be here, but you've got access to loads more background information online from each of the 7 Stages and sub-steps here – see, even saying that sounds scary, but you know how to negate that fear now!

According to Adult Learning stats, we remember up to over 90% of what we say and do *and* teach, so along the way always share your ideal script with others and make sure they understand it before you invest your time to get it down on film. Or film everything and teach it by sharing!

Confident Verbal Impact – let's go!

So let's have a look at how you script, how you can script better and improve the power of *your* Verbal Impact by releasing distracting habits and remembering what to say. Time to prime yourself with credible content for verbal success!

STAGE 1: What Works When Scripting Verbal Impact?
Why Focusing on Script First won't Work!

Think about it: why did I start with coaching you about mindsets and performing and voice *before we even got to your preferred most important bit* – the stuff you write about how great you are, the *'all about me'* bits?!

So many people will fret and worry about whether they have a script exactly right, word for word. They spent soooo long writing the darn thing, to get it text perfect, that when it comes to presenting, they become desperate to say it *exactly* as it is written, with their perfect words…

Which we now know doesn't work.

Especially in just a minute or two on video!

Then they get panicky and nervous, as they start to fear they won't remember and perfect it all.

But all this does is actually prime us for perfect failure in the first place!

We now know how much easier it is to simply chat around a core message and theme, because you now know what you want to say AND how you want to say it.

So this is why I start with all the other Confidence on Camera not-so-secret steps to on-screen success first – so you can get your head around the fact that, in the end…

~~~~~~~~~~~~~~~~

as long as you know exactly what you're talking about, who for and why…

**when you know how to connect with us on screen
and ask for what you want…**

you CAN say anything in your video you want!

~~~~~~~~~~~~~~~~

Surely your busy time is better spent learning how to grab our attention on screen and connect with us personally, rather than hours on a sticking-point script?

We could have turned off before you've even opened your mouth!

Watching clients spend hours and hours, planning and writing the 'perfect' text, then losing confidence as they struggle to get it out *exactly* as they wrote it down, is heart-breaking to see. Even more so when I'd heard them tell their story and heard their passion and expertise just minutes before!

So flipping the power of your Visual, Vocal, Verbal Impact chapters here reflects that – the Verbal Impact *has to* come last after building up your confidence in earlier chapters of the book.

Yes, your choice of words is hugely important – words are what influence us, but we do know good videos, great TV and films are also made without them!

So how can we quickly create and write scripts that will have an impact on our viewers?

How can we sell ideas without actually selling? How can our words influence action?

By getting our viewers involved – by creating an image of how we can help their lives improve. And we know what that is because of our own research and listening to what our clients actually want from us – this is the starting idea for all of your video scripts.

What Scripts Do Work?

You need to write talking scripts with Confidence, Credibility and Charisma too!

And how do we do that? By working out what is the core of our message.

What, Why, How, Who for, When, Where? You don't have to cover every W? in the script, but you must know the answers for planning your brilliant video idea!

And trust in your brilliant idea – and if you're not sure, have the confidence to ask – clients, family, friends. Find out what they want to know about your business and you.

Writing great words we want to read and absorb is something totally different from working out what we actually say. On camera we have limited time, words must mean something or they are waffle. For videos online we need clear words aimed at first-time understanding; our viewers probably only hear it once, so make your chat words count instead of complex discussion. So any time I say "chat" on screen, I actually mean a very planned chat on one specific theme! You spend as long on this as you need and you will get quicker fast.

> For your script to work you will:
> 1. Plan your chat to connect with whom?
> 2. Know exactly how you will start and (more importantly) the exact words to end.
> 3. Write and learn great congruent lines.
> 4. Choose congruent impactful words.
> 5. Pick your business facts that cut through.
> 6. Have series of 'sound-bite statements'.
> 7. Know who you need to be to serve me!

Sound-bite Statements + Taglines

Sound-bite statements are lines you will start jotting down in your notebook from now on in!

Quotes people say about your business and you, testimonial lines from clients, killer facts, promotional pitch phrases, lines the sales team use, fun facts and a **tagline** – that 10 words or fewer killer line that *could* become your catchphrase way to end every video…

> *"See you soon on screen for more Confidence on Camera!"*

And so much more you'll look into with the ideas you'll pick up here.

Remember you need great lines we can 'quote, tweet and repeat' from you!

What could your tagline be?

Cutting Through: Writing vs Scripting Copy

If pictures paint a thousand words, then great video words paint a thousand pictures in the shortest possible time!

Face it – writing is written for people to read.

We can afford to glorify our ideas, embellish for greater interest, use more colourful language, use expansive vocabulary. Our readers can re-read to garner greater understanding and feel smarter by discovering your secret message or perceived hidden gem that only their brain has noticed – even when there isn't one to find!

Clever wordplay makes for better reading and reading expands our minds.

To quote Nassim Taleb (#lovelyhubby's No. 1 modern thinker!) "

A good book gives you more when you read it a second time.
But a great book you get more every time you read it."

But **Scripting Copy is how we talk** – it's how we tell a story and needs to give the 'more' first time! To throw in another Taleb concept, *Via Negativa* – we need to:

"Remove or omit that which is not required, rather than
adding as a way to improve things."

And reminder for actor self – that's *improve*, not improv.

I keep this on my wall as ad-libbing is the actor's excuse when we lose our lines!

Scripting Copy is – simple language, clearly spoken to enable clarity and instil confidence and trust. Converting a relevant story with congruent presenting, so our viewer gets the point.

These days watching online usually includes an internal conversation and multi-tasking, so viewers may not be paying 100% attention. We listen out for our WIIFM that benefits us; to learn how we need to interact to get something; or maybe we're not listening at all!

Our brains self-edit so fast – we filter to hear what we want for ourselves, adding or taking away for clearer understanding. Or if we're confused, for misunderstanding!

Humans have a phenomenal M^3 clever ear to hear.

It's why alliteration, rhyming and triple word groupings can work so well – it sounds lyrical, musical and fun in our minds. It's also why jokes and double entendres often don't. It's not just cultural. Use humour by all means, but steer clear of jokes unless for a very good reason.

It's also why I write some of this the way I do – it's chat speak on the page – some sentences are longer, sometimes snappy and short.

Mostly – they're easy to say out loud!

Speaking Scripts Engage Us

Great speakers and presenters edit and adapt language for their audience superfast too.

But they've always rehearsed – to make it look like they've never said this before! They may not have said it in that order, but bet your bottom dollar, they've said the key phrases out loud over and over to check what works on an audience.

They practise out loud; test with mastermind audiences; add targeted, emotional stories to engage; involve the audience with rhetoric; and know when to stop…//

A cliffhanger is a cliffhanger for a reason: they've given just enough information and we leave wanting more. Then they make another video, or prep another talk while we talk about them ☺

Engage Us With Easy Words!

The human listening capacity for hearing and understanding unusual vocabulary is far smaller than our reading vocabulary, because we can't check words we don't hear or understand. We rarely want to expend this effort and energy when watching online – we expect the information to all be there for us these days.

- ✓ The Verbal Impact must be congruent, clear and concise.
- ✓ We must make messaging precise and take out what we don't need.
- ✓ In general, if you must use words such as multi-faceted, bi-partisan, disparage, condone, stigma, dogma etc. you may need to clarify their meaning in context.

To make the best Verbal Impact we can on camera we need to adapt Taleb's *Via Negativa* a bit more. In the statement:

You read: 'remove or omit that which is not required'

I say: *"take out what we don't need"*

One you'd need to read; the other you'd hear – it really IS that simple!

So what's my point here?

Complicated Copy can confuse us when we watch online, so…

Target your Language for the Greatest Understanding

It's great to be the expert that you are and know all the right words to say and language to use. But remember, some of us might be new to it all, if you go too highbrow, industry lingo *(slang for language ☺)* or techy-type overkill you'll lose us – no matter what your industry is.

Not every viewer is highly educated, so keep things simple, use everyday TV words rather than TV intellectual debate words!

Unless you're doing a specific 'how to' promo or training video for your own industry, or an acronym-laden in-house marketing VC *(Coke talk for video conference, see!),* choosing a less formal 'chat' script is what makes you, and us, more comfortable right from the start.

Not everyone will understand us or like our message all of the time – and yep, that's OK!

Emulate the News Online

In most countries we do tend to trust our own newsreaders, documentary, lifestyle, panel/chat show or online TV presenters. So again, find what you like about your favourite presenters' choice of words and emulate them. A lot of them got the job on TV or followers on YouTube because people preferred them and their way with words, over tens of thousands of others.

How can you have that draw with your news/docco/lifestyle/chat show/promo story?

The news is still on TV as our daily catch-up because it succinctly delivers in a minute what takes many more to read. Congruent presenting allows the message to be heard and understood far faster and in an interactive, connecting way. Emulate this to empower and enable your viewer to be confident and relaxed watching you, because they understand you as easily and like you as much as those folks they see on TV.

Your Verbal Impact is never writing a webpage – focus on the news of you!

How Long is a Piece of String?

A bit like asking a production house, "How much is this video going to cost?" it depends on what you want.

So how long you want your video to be is totally up to you too.

Marketing timings and viewing stats suggest viewing focus is getting shorter, hence:

- ✓ One to two minutes (1-2') is good for chats, tips, intros and promos.
- ✓ Showreel style self-promotions should be this short too, but will need different examples of your work – like a TV presenter.
- ✓ 'How to' product demos and mini-trainings can be longer, between four and seven minutes, but are less likely to get away with a simple PTC (Piece to Camera). You will need to involve editing with added visual stimulus.
- ✓ An interview can cut back and forth between you and your guest(s) for three to seven minutes

✓ Long-form video, 10-18 minutes, will be for TED Talk (Technology, Entertainment, Design) style webinars, skill demos or Q&A instruction. TED's Chris Anderson proved 18 mins is the ideal max for the human brain to listen to serious stuff, but absorb, retain and gain from it!

Quick TV/Video PTC A&E

How long are you happy watching a presenter talking direct to you?

_____

Watch those news presenters on TV, especially the ones on location with only one camera and time how long we see one shot of a presenter talking direct to us in a PTC = Piece To Camera.

PTCs are often longer than you think – because they are quick, easy, cheap and efficient to produce. Yet online people seem to think we'll always be bored after five seconds of your face and flash off to another image or fly in some natty device with edits galore. I find that irritating myself, but I am Gen X! No matter what generation you are, come back to the fact:

YOU ARE YOUR NO. 1 PRODUCTION VALUE!

Spend more time working on being a better presenter that people will like paying attention to and stop wasting so much time getting the perfect whizz-bang edit effects *please!*

Seeing for yourself how long you're happy to watch your favourite presenter on screen may show you that you really don't need too many edits in a one-minute video story.

Learn from the TV pros – take the best, for you, forget the rest!

Know Who You're Talking to

We know there are *sooo* many things that can influence the viewing habits, choices, understanding, reaction and action of a viewer, so know who your target viewer is and appeal to their potential tastes, to what they might like to see.

Talk their language, address them in their style.

OK this may take a bit of whizz-bang for Gen Z and screenagers, but still…!

Different tribes and age groups do talk in different ways, so talk the lingo of your target tribe. Target your word choice, match their style, get down with their riff vibes, slick suit style or groovy granny chat! Again, more time researching this than editing, watching what they watch, will stand you in good stead too.

Proviso here – ONLY ever do this if you can ☺

There is nothing more cringe-worthy than a dressed-up business person *trying too hard* to be hip, because they've been told they have to be. Sometimes your smile can be enough. Yes, adapt your words, adapt your style, but it does inherently have to be from inside you.

Be Verbally Flawsome

If you have to do or say something and you hate it – turn that into something included in the script. Be brilliantly Verbally Flawsome and you could have an online video hit!

NB. Yes you… *please* bring in that side of you that no one else at work has seen – that side of you that can surprise us all on screen: the secret surfer, princess storyteller, nerdy coder, chic make-up stylist, help-the-aged volunteer, yummy mummy or dopey, doting dad.

Are you a super sailing, mountain-climbing adventurer at home and 'boring' auditor by day? Why not adventure-up your auditing script then?!

Kiss Your Credible Content

Whether you're a strict script rememberer or an ad-libber, interpretation is subjective, so keep it simple.

But it must be credible – structure your content, make it easy for yourself and **KISS** it!

KISS stands for **Keep It Simple Stupid** – an age-old business acronym that utterly applies to video scripting and presenting. Plus it sets you up for actually LIKING the words or lines you write, rather than stressing on getting it perfect word for word.

Kiss and Tell

While we can't set out to create a viral video (more on *that* topic later!), we can influence the like-ability factor by coming back to my old favourite: the simple storytelling.

The more you KISS the storytelling, the better story you'll have, so think of:

- ⋏ your core theme as the story title – not necessarily the video title
- ⋏ your Call to Action as the moral of the story
- ⋏ and you as the story teller – all you have to do is KISS and Tell!

Why complicate a story when all you are really there to do is what Attenborough said:

1. Tell us about what you want to tell.
2. Tell us what issues we may have without it/you.
3. Tell us why we need it from you.
4. Tell us how much easier or better we will be with it/you.
5. Tell us who you are to be telling us about it (optional).
6. Tell us how we can get hold of it, or grab the chance to get it NOW!
7. Tell us what to do next!

Watchers like simple instructions – lead us sheep to (your) pastures green, my friend!

That is a very basic way of structuring your script and you'll find many videos online that do exactly that. Many of them work extremely well but others can miss the mark – mostly because the presenting isn't connected to the story, they're not congruent, untrustworthy, not real.

Invest in your Idea and we'll Invest in You

Some company video presenters don't appear at all invested in their idea, or in helping us with our pain – it seems to be all about them.

Often they don't even suggest their USP solution to serve the viewer.

Often they just look flash, *"Look how great we are! Look at what we do!"* basic show-offs, with loads of the whizz-bang images and edits.

The presenters never seem real and the animations + VOs sound disingenuous, no matter how hard the VO person is trying. There's no excitement or engagement. Or the CEO or team leader presenting is just so dull and lifeless, you wouldn't want to connect with them for fear you'd be asleep in the meeting with their team, never mind listening to or actually hearing what they say on screen…

OK – total judgement OTT rant there, but we've all seen those videos and I know those companies have probably invested thousands of euros/pounds/dollars on a beautifully produced, bells and whistles video!

But what's the point for you unless you invest this time and effort to present a more powerful you on screen?

STAGE 2: Plan Confident Copy with Credible Content

So talking of investment, let's focus now on the actual process of how you plan that credible content to give you the power to look like you do care.

Again, this takes time to start with, but as with everything else, the more you practise, the better you become and the faster your M^3 brain kicks into creative mode each time. Even if you don't consider yourself to be a creative person, these steps will help you get more simple structure behind your message – and then you never know what you can do!

Soon you'll only need a couple of sheets to get creative: my Video Planning Sheet + Scripting with Impact sheets free for you online because you bought my book ☺ will be your starting point to prepare any video.

Research, Plan, Prepare and Practise = NO WORRIES

Talking to the converted, I'm assuming you do know you have to gather information and do some planning before you actually sit down to write what you want to say, right?

But it is amazing the number of people who make it hard for themselves when writing a short video script, because they don't bother to identify *WHY* this video is important, right now today and *HOW* that will actually affect what they need to say! They often leap to writing a script before bothering to check what goes behind that copy.

So here's my Content Planning Process you can follow every time.

Every client uses it, I hand this out to anyone for free; it's common sense, practical, shifts your focus away from anything to do with nerves, and works and each time it gets quicker, I promise! I can get video planning down to 10 minutes by starting with these simple questions I now know I need to know, to get to my video core.

Video Content Planning

Every video MUST start with knowing the core reasons you are eager and willing to create THIS video, right here, right now. If you do nothing else because you're 'just' doing a vlog update – DO at least answer this section – it will clarify everything you want to say:

1. WHAT is this video? – a promo, product, web intro, training, vlog etc.
2. WHY is it important WIIFM for you? – "I want…" sign-ups, sales, network growth etc.

3. WHO is it for? – target viewer.
4. WHY is it important WIIFM for viewer? – "Why bother watching?"
5. HOW you are going to do it? – Pro/DIY/PTC/VO/animation/length etc.
6. WHO are you to 'be' doing it now? – Emotional Connection presenter style.
7. What end results? – Call to Action?

And before you grab my Video Planning Sheet you may need to think for each video re: **No. 3-4 – who's it for and what's in it for them!**

Review Client Research

If you've done your research, you will know what your clients want from you, like about you and how you best serve them. And how that can be turned into marketing joy too!

So you do already know what potential new clients want to hear…

What do existing and potential clients want to know?

Quick Client Connection A&E

1. You know what your product or service can offer.

2. You know their pains and can see that you can help (walk away or you'll waste time if not!).

3. You know what might be missing for them from previous successful experience.

4. You can identify how, with you, they can ease their pains and get to where they want to be.

5. You can show the gaps between where they are now and that place they want to be.

6. You know how to help them identify those pains and present your solution as simple chat without the hard sell, because you're truly coming from a place of really wanting to help/empower/invigorate/ regenerate/stimulate or inspire your new viewers.

7. You know others who have their pain, whom you really want to help out; you've just got to let them know you're here to serve them… so share the news – via video!

If you don't know, that's OK.

Why not send out a survey asking what are the top 10 things your clients want to know about?

Share these as your 10 *WOW!* facts about you – the amazing things you help others do, what you do, how you succeed and ask which ones impact them most.

Ask how you best serve them or could serve them even better.

Ask how they felt at the start of working with you and what's the biggest improvement in their business and life since working with you/using your product or service.

These could even be the ideas for your first 10 Top Tip Free Vlogs on social media!

Which of course you could DIY + PIY film over a couple of video shoots or organise as interviews – see, easy credible content already!

How to set that up later in Step 7: Confidence in Planning, Production and Promotion.

As I've said, if you're not sure what angle to take – simply ask.

If you're not sure what might interest people – simply ask.

We do like to help those who appeal to our altruistic better nature, when they ask in a nice, polite, friendly or fun way. Once we can see how what they'll do will help others from our success story statements too, it's amazing how many people will go on video or as a voice recording if you simply ask – and especially if you offer them a wee word of *WOW!* promo with their business details in the video and VSEO too!

And there's a promo series title, instead of **Testimonials** – sooo bored of that business video buzz-word – we've got to find some more words:

Words of WOW! / Success Stories / Client Quotes / Winning Words of Wisdom / Supporters Spirit / Awesome Acknowledgements / Rocking References / Tales from Others Like You!

(…ideas on a post card ☺ OK, email link to your videos please – I'll be sure to quote you, as I do!)

Video Planning Sheet Online A&E

So here's your ultimate tool for video planning – go print one off and with your research information, fill one in for your next video idea:

Video Planning Sheet

Before you start any video creation you must KNOW your video strategy W ?...

1. **WHAT** is the purpose of this video?

2. **WHY** am I doing this video? What's the main point?
   - WIIFM 1 – for me, what will I get?
   _____

   - WIIFM 2 – for my viewer MOST important – why will they bother to watch me?!
   _____

3. **HOW** will I help / serve / ease the viewer?

4. **WHO** am I targeting?

5. **WHAT** is my Call to Action? What will they feel/say/do after watching?

6. **WHEN** will I plan/produce/promote this by?

7. **WHERE** will I promote/share this video? Link to my current social media plan...

BONUS ACTIONS I need to check?
   - set up/re-brand my YouTube or Vimeo Channel
   - learn Video SEO my Channels and/or Video promotion
   - my current video VSEO success?

Get brownie points with search engines – use a public video host service!
You need a Branded Channel with properly linked Channel & Video SEO

~~~~~~~~~~~~~~

**ONLY IN KNOWING THIS INFORMATION will you see clearly why
it is worth your time and effort and whether
the video idea will work**

WILL YOUR CONTENT BE CREDIBLE?

Credibility comes from a REAL Connection to Content!

~~~~~~~~~~~~~~

Plan your Video to go On Screen

With your research and your planning sheet you'll be able to work out what type of video would be most appropriate to tell this relevant story.

⋏ What type of video will best show what I want to
    show the viewer?

⋏ What kind of video will work for me?

Basically, after your research, make the decision what kind of video you want to produce within the time and budget you have available to do it.

Video Types – do you need a:

Company PromoWebsite	Welcome Intro*	Personal Intro*
Company Interview	Product or Service Demo*	Help Request
Quick Tip Giveaway*	Factual Stats Service	Informal Chat
Information Update	Instructional Demo	Funding Appeal
Training or Coaching Clip	Pre-record/Live Webinar	Skype Interview
Q&A Discussion	Expert Interview*	Client Testimonial*
Client Success Story*	Virtual Meeting	Conference Recording

Live Presenter Promo or Showreel* - for Pro speakers it's a *must*

The ones with the asterisks are the videos you really should have on your website – a mix of personal and what you do. The others you can create for social media and for your YouTube Channel VSEO to improve Google rankings. There are other types of videos – it depends how creative you can be!

What Kind of Video will Work for You? A&E

Each style of video can deliver totally different perceptions of you, your company, your business – so like your Emotional Connection for you "I am..." you need to decide who your company needs to be.

Sometimes you may want to shift perceptions – from pompous to down to earth; from home business to networking queen; from boring bank to real people financial helpers etc.

You also need to decide:

1. **How you're going to make it** – film, animation, presentations etc.

2. **Who's going to make it?** – pro or DIY

3. **Who's on camera?** – PIY/guest/client

4. **What's on screen?** – straight PTC/edit options e.g. with pop-ups/captions/B-roll edits.

5. **How long** – the ideal length for you? Test it: if it feels too long, it is – cut stuff out!

The aim with all styles is to help the viewer, help the viewer, help the viewer – their WIIFM!

Planning the *structure* you prefer instills the Confidence you will require on Camera.

Long-Form vs Short Form Video Writing

Long-form (10 minutes +) webinars and training videos are usually aimed at developing learning, to enable and encourage slower thinking and give time for mental absorption, so can use more contextual language. Remember these are not lectures though – you still need to chat and be likeable!

In general, you can use more detailed, complex language in sections, but you may need to clarify their meaning in context. You do also need to break up the 'telling' instructional bits with some interactive moments and pauses for thought. Just like I keep asking you questions here to get you thinking while you read, or asking you to say things, do things = effective adult learning and imperative for long-form webinar, demonstrational or training videos.

Is Storyboarding Necessary?

Storyboarding is something that production companies do to plan out your video visually so the camera person knows exactly what to film. This saves time and money in the video shoot and ensures you won't miss a shot. If you are working with one, you need to know what they entail – see Step 7 – but if you're DIY + PIY you can keep it simple with just one or two shots, pop-up captions or cutaways to B-roll or images you have on file.

What you DO need to know is your TV style copy must be written for the ear, matching what appeals to the eye.

Words must go with the visuals and at the same time make sense to the ear – if there is any competition between the two, what we see wins every time.

Paid Videos or Give them Away for Free?

When people pay for something they expect more, but they are happy to have the video you also gave away for free in there too. Paid video programmes online need to be planned as a video series with most of the videos in the list included somewhere.

We will want to watch slightly longer videos when we have paid – they don't all have to be an hour long though!

Remember, even if we've bought in to you, we may still need an intro video to you and what you do and how you're going to help us, at the start.

Please DO still give video information away for free – do some social media top tips or connect and grow your fan base by hosting interviews or virtual meetings via video. That way you keep viewers coming back to you with an abundance attitude.

The more you give, the more likely people are to like you and want to work with you.

Keep the in-depth detail for the training videos you charge for.

Marketers say it takes seven points of contact before people take action – make engaging video strong points of contact for your viewers, for free, and you might be able to do it in less!

What you give away for free can never be replaced by your one-to-one interactions with a client on their individual issues, so you're not giving away all your information, you are sharing and demonstrating why you're the best person they need to work with.

Planning Wrap Up

Right – so enough of the planning.

As we're on the Verbal Impact chapter, do a quick notes reminder review of what you've got to do here and then we'll move on to the actual writing. These are general rules to abide by for writing in English *(probably work for many other languages too!)*

Planning Notes:

_____

_____

_____

_____

STAGE 3: Know Your Writing Rules for TV Style Copy

There are so many tips and rules on how to write, but our key focus here, once again, is:

you are writing for a vocal medium, not a verbal one

i.e. write what you say, not what we'll read

Scriptwriting TV Style

Writing for TV requires a scripting technique that gets to the point fast and delivers all the key info within a tightly constrained time frame.

Think of that news report or the intro or segment link in your favourite documentary style TV show. I always think of nature reporters – my dream TV job – one day!

1. Start to notice how TV presenters introduce ideas, themselves, people, places, things.
2. See how they top and tail stories, coming back to a theme.
3. Hear how they keep over-complicated facts to a minimum.
4. Notice how they keep things brief, concise, specific, to the point.
5. Pick your favourite and really listen to the words they say.
6. Note how their performance subtly shifts between fact and chat.
7. Spot if they have words written for them, which they read on autocue – the best present their own words.

Now watch online and see how the TV style has crossed to the good presenters – they may well have been in TV in the first place or they've presented so much by now they're confident on camera under any circumstance. Gen Y and Gen Z grew up watching this all online, so they've had a head start remember!

Empower and enable your viewer to be confident and relaxed watching you because they hear your news as easily and like you as much as those folks they see on TV. And be heartened by the fact that even if viewers don't really like the presenter, they still watch the news every day because they know it's good to know!

~~~~~~~~~~~~~~~~~

The Power of your Verbal Impact is to never write a webpage – focus on the news of you!

~~~~~~~~~~~~~~~~~

TV Talk is Quicker

On camera we need to adapt the spoken word for easy auditory absorption and fast thinking understanding. Using the modern idiom with conversational form enables this.

Now say that sentence out loud and you'll get exactly what I mean by 'write as we speak'.

It's *way* too hard to say in a short space of time, you'd be over-enunciating, intoning, inflecting and explaining nearly every section!

So how could you adapt it for Short Form <1-2' video script?

Try it here:

_____

_____

_____

OK here's mine – it's not much shorter, but can you understand it more easily when you say it out loud?

When we've only got a few seconds to speak,

we've gotta use words you can easily hear and understand.

So I'm just gonna chat to you!

I can say that version clearly in seven seconds (7"), but the first version I'd need double the time! I'd normally write 'got to' and 'going to', but slang is how I'd say it.

If I was presenting long-form over 10 minutes and I was introducing a whole concept, I could probably use the original sentence as is, as long as I clarified what I meant at the end.

NB. Note how I've written the text double line spaced and in the centre of the page. That's how they do it in the movies to leave loads of space for your annotations, quick rewrite and notes. You don't have to centre, but DO type double spaced for your scripts.

3 V Congruence is Still Key!

Again, while we can say succinctly in a minute what takes many more to read, your congruent presenting allows your message to be heard and understood far faster and in an interactive, connecting way. Ideal in the fast-paced, short attention span world modern technology has delivered to us today.

Scripting Key Objective – write, clarify, write, clarify

Scriptwriting and editing takes practice. When you learn you'll basically write, edit and rewrite and re-edit, then finally break your written text down to the keywords and phrases that enable you to remember your script. As you do it more, you get better.

Once you find a script format that works for you, you'll get much quicker at writing copy and will develop the skill to improvise on the fly.

Your key and first objective is to set out information clearly, simply and to the point.

DO:

1. Write on one core theme, with one intent, in chat language.
2. Edit + re-write + edit – do this by hand for writing M^3 – associate action with memory.
3. Tell the story with enticement, excitement, flair, occasion.
4. When possible bring in your sense of enjoyment or fun!
5. Never assume your viewer knows all the info you know.
6. Be accurate, clear and to the point.
7. KISS your copy!!

Script structuring is coming up in a moment after a look at some bonus background TV writing rules to abide by...

Bonus Background TV Writing Rules

So I've condensed seven pages of our TVPro TV presenter copywriting notes from 2003 into short headings and a story here. But as TV and on-camera presenting doesn't really change, it's simply what works and what distracts, these notes are as relevant today as they were then.

Make 'em Laugh!

Remember just because your business is serious, it doesn't have to all be serious, so if humour is not your thing, you must at least find the moments to be a human connector and smile!

KISS your Word Choice

Be kind to yourself – write for easy articulation and correct pronunciation – always check!

Simple or classic mispronunciations can cause an immediate 'STOP!' reaction!

BTW – we never 'preform' – pet-hate-AAAAARGH! It's pronounced '**PER-form**!

To pre-form is something totally different and not cultural like 'arks' and it's so not 'nucular' ☺

Why Waste your Words?

| **Why say:** | terminate | **When you mean:** | end |
| **Why say:** | came under discussion... | **Simply say:** | talked about |

Colloquialisms – beware of using them too freely!

Unless you're doing it for a specific reason, steer clear of local slang and idioms i.e. colloquialisms – words that you can trip over.

Clichés to Avoid

Avoid common TV corny clichés and feel free to add your own pet peeves!

It goes without saying...

To be honest…

Overly Expressive or Negative Clichés

Not all action is 'drastic' or criticism 'bitter'…

Dependent Clauses

'Which', 'who', 'whom', 'whose', 'that' clauses can confuse a story if used in a clumsy style.

Statistics, Numbers and Dates

The ear can be confused by too much spoken data.

Keep them simple and easy to say, stick to one style e.g. fractions or percent.

Names and Titles

ALWAYS make an effort to get names and titles right!

Naming Acronyms and Places

Avoid local, regional or country nicknames – non-local viewers may not know what or where you are talking about, so clarify.

Get to the Point!

Never leave the viewer hanging to find out for too long – grab our attention from the start and give us the point. Dragging out "we'll get to it soon" annoys by the second time!

Tell Stories

Telling a story can be an immediate connector between you and your viewer, especially if you divulge something personal. So I'm going to tell you a favourite story from a lovely Irish friend, which she kindly agreed for me to share *(thank you, you know who you are!)*.

And this is about how it went:

> *"When we were little my sister and I used to have to walk to church with Dad very early each Sunday morning. We hated it, so to make it more interesting we used to look for different things to find. One Sunday we found some coins... Wow! And best thing – we didn't have to put them in the offering plate, Dad let us to keep them to buy sweets after church!*
>
> *We were SO excited that we started looking for and discovering coins every Sunday – it was brilliant and made us love the walk to church with Dad.*
>
> *When I was 16 I had to write about my 'Happiest Childhood Memory' and remembering this made me smile...*
>
> *Suddenly, as I was writing I had a revelation.*
>
> *I ran downstairs and shouted at Dad, "It was YOU!"*
>
> *He smiled but didn't say a word.*
>
> *It took me years to I realise he must have dropped the coins on Saturday night while walking the dog as our reward for walking to church.*
>
> *His reward was time with very happy kids.*
>
> *Our lesson – to always be on the lookout for a wonderful thing!"*

That is a minute to say, but if you were doing a Service Video, it could be a wonderful 'moral of' story with a 30" addition of how it relates to your business and what your viewer can find 'wonderful' too!

The other thing to note is how much more interesting the story sequence is with the big reveal at the end, rather than starting with "*My Dad used to leave us coins to find on the way to church.*" Stories must have an emotional input from within you from the start or the audience cannot expect to be interested either – USE STORIES YOU CARE ABOUT!

7 Verbal Impact Writing Rules Wrap Up

DO:

1. Use simple crisp English.
2. Make clarity your objective.
3. Shun big words and involved sentences.
4. Don't exaggerate.
5. Be wary of adjectives.
6. Make fewer words – especially for headlines.
7. Write it so you can enjoy saying it – you're allowed to have fun!!!

STAGE 4: Structure Your Script to Remember

Structuring Your Script – whether you want to Remember or Improvise

When it comes to the actual scriptwriting, the common questions clients ask are:

- How will I make the video interesting?
- What will I do to grab viewers' attention?
- What stories or *WOW!* facts can I tell to add interest?
- How do I tell them?
- How do I remember the sequence?

Strangely very few ask about the actual Script **Structure**...

Now you've looked through scripting rules for TV, you can choose which structures and presentations planning you prefer with some more step-by-step styles and a couple more impromptu, more fluid, flowing options to create scripts.

They all do work, it totally depends on which way of working you like best.

Easy Scripting

Simple script structure allows us to break our script into chunks and make it easier to remember with keywords – to **Chunk + Keyword** a script. So I'm going to start with the quick scripting and get into the more detailed methods of how to write and edit after.

Most of us know that we need to have an Introduction, a Body and a Close, but there are actually more defined structures that add more clarity, allow you to expand or condense information and flow in such a way that it is easier for your brain to remember the sequence you want. So now we're going to look at:

1. What structures work? What goes first + then what + how do you finish?
2. How can you make your videos a little bit different from the rest?
3. What skills will allow you to improvise and still stay credible with your content?

Short Video Script Copy

In short videos, when we want to remember the script to flow as one chat PTC, our brains only remember between five to nine items at any one moment, so make it easy for yourself! It's why so much of the Confidence on Camera power is 7...7...7!

Simple Script Structure

Working with clients over the years helped me devise the simplest method of structuring a business video that also helps you remember what you want to say – because it's three sections and your key points all fit on one hand!

1. Intro – Icebreaker + Intro you
2. Body x 3-6 key points answering key Ws – why, what, how, who for, where, when?
3. Close – Linked to Intro with Call to Action

1. INTROS

Most people start with "Hi… I'm… and I'm here to tell you about…"– so what's wrong with that? Nothing, it's easy! But how interesting/exciting/attention grabbing is that?

It may absolutely suit what you do, so I'm not saying don't do it, simply that there could be a better way for you to start to get more creative with your video content.

So that's why so many people do it. My challenge for you here is to get more creative, so how could you start in a different way?

Grab Attention from the Start

Relevant in any video, but especially in a short-form video where you only have one to two minutes total and ideally less than three minutes!

What can you do or say within the first three to seven seconds that will grab the viewer's attention, spark their interest and cause them to keep watching and do what you want them to do?

So start in a thought-provoking way....

... your *WOW!* fact, your story, your challenge, questions or a truth. It's totally up to you. Here are some ways that work:

---

7 Ways to Impact from the Start

1. Set the scene – "Picture yourself on the most beautiful beach in the world..."
2. Use rhetorical questions – "Have you always wanted to write your book?"
3. Share WOW! statements – "Mobile phone theft is the largest petty crime in the UK today."
4. Intrigue or shock – "Dolphins like sex as much as humans do."
5. Statement + direct personal challenge – "Many people today waste too much time online. Are you one of them?"
6. Question or challenge the audience, often in threes – "How many of you here find it hard to listen? Is it because you're lacking focus? Or is because your brain is not letting you hear?"
7. Always make it strong and relevant to your theme.

You will be coming back to this theme at the end as you **Top & Tail** the script – referring back to this intro in your close, so make it strong. @MattRudd and @KatieGlassSF both write for the SundayTimes.co.uk Magazine and have fantastic examples of video length Top & Tail themed articles.

2. BODY

Always remember – in its most basic format you are simply answering a selection or all of the six W questions + your Call to Action:

1. **What** I'm here for/offering is...

2. **Why** it's important for you – answer viewer WIIFM?

3. **How** it/we can help /inspire/empower you.

> The Essential W?
> to answer in your
> own preferred order

4. **Who** we are to be telling you. OR Who it's for.

5. **Where** do you get this/me?

6. **When** you can get more...?

> Optional W?
> to answer in your
> own preferred order

7. **+ CTA**: what you will do right now viewer!

You can answer your key questions in any order you choose, but always answer the viewer WIIFM: *"What's in it for me?/what am I going to learn/why should I watch you?"*

3. Close + Calls to Action and Taglines

In a short clip, you don't have to do a formal summary of what you've covered, like you would in a long presentation. But DO remember to link back to your core theme or first line at the end of your clip, Top & Tail and always include your Call to Action – CTA.

Some people prefer to deliver their CTA then finish with a company tagline (or strapline), it is totally up to you. Remember, your tagline is your own personal creative catchphrase and may include a Call to Action. These can take a while to come up with, so get creative and get feedback – you'll know what you like because it flows, it's easy and a fun thing for you to say! e.g.: "When you want to Press Play to empower your Confidence on Camera, call or Vmail The Video Coach today!"

The screen would have a visual cue with pop-up captions with the number and video email address. I could even point to it on screen, if I'm clever with my planning and have chosen where the pop-ups are going to be.

Pop-up text or caption

Vmail The Video Coach

Always avoid ending with "Thank you" – unless you are doing a video appeal for money or donations it can smack of desperation as it often lacks confidence and conviction.

"Thank you for…" **doing** something can work, like "thank you for your time/ donating now/ joining us" etc., but "thanks for watching" is another old TV cliché, so be corny if using it!

Video Scripts in a Flash – 3 x 7 Ways to Improvise Videos on the Fly

If you're confident in your content and know what you want to say, or you prefer a less formal structure, not got much time to plan or you like to improvise for authentic conversational connection, then here are three ways you can do that fast.

Because they are fast, on your feet quick thinking, instinctive techniques, these methods also help you remember what you want to say. You can make them linear, cyclical or mind-map layout, whichever works for you. They are KISS simple structures that work.

1. 7 Steps to Newspaper Headlines!

Start your planning with knowing your Newspaper Headline – your one-line catchphrase.

It's your key to excitement about your video – if this excites you, you'll remember it and perform it with gusto too! As an improviser, this may be enough for you to stand up and present a video off the cuff.

To create it, think:
1. I need a Newspaper Headline for every video that I do!
2. What is the core message of your video?
3. How can you say that in a fun and interesting way?
4. What words will grab attention WOW! with a great one-line?!
5. Make it easy to remember – it may end up as the title.
6. Make it lyrical, make it fun, make it stand out – like you!
7. Make it make you happy, make you smile ☺
   If you Plan with a Smile, you'll probably present with one too!

Lottie's Newspaper Headline Story:

When I was in Jamaica first writing this book we went to Goldeneye, Ian Fleming's writing bolt-hole in Jamaica *(yes, I was visualising James Bond size success!).* I took some stunning photos the team loved, and to show them how, I made a video for them, using Videolicious on my iPhone and my monopod, in less than 10 minutes.

I had no script, just the photos to make a story…

But I did create a Newspaper Headline theme:

'Sun, rum and fun – a Goldeneye holiday haven'

It's still online - Press Play Video Coach at Goldeneye Jamaica when you want to get jealous!

It's not perfect, but it's so quick and so easy to do with your Headline.

2. Improv. Style with the 7 Steps from Intro to Close

Confident beginnings and confident endings make the biggest impact.

When you know where you're going to, the script has a flow. Any time you lose track in the middle of the script, pause, breathe and simply go to your close with confidence. You can always film another video with the content that you missed if it's that important!

Intro to Close Script Rules:

1. Always know exactly how you are going to start a video – include the viewer in the first line.
2. Always know how you're going to end – include what you want from them CTA!
3. Plan, write and learn your first line word for word – keep it simple, easy.
4. Plan, write and know your confident last line – direct me what to do.
5. Your last lines may be a final product plug + Call to Action or CTA + Close tagline.
6. Know as the expert you can say anything in between.
7. Rehearse your Intro and Close only and let the rest of your story flow.

   For example:

> **Intro:** *"Confidence on Camera – what does that mean to you? If you're a presenter that has to do this… and the thought fills you with fear, then I'm Lottie the Video Coach and I've got an easy solution for you…"*
>
> **Close:** *"Register for your free chapter of my e-book with loads of tips to help you overcome your fears and discover your… Confidence on Camera – go on click below right now!"*
>
> **KNOW your first line. Know your last line.**
> **Anything can happen in between!**

3. 7 Steps to Working A to B: Theme your Top & Tail

Building on the steps from Intro to Close – it is extremely effective to:

Top & Tail your video with the **same theme**

✓ Have killer Intro + Close lines

✓ Know your killer facts in between

✓ Make your A to B video make a scene!

I call this video scripting Working A to B

One of the best ways to demonstrate this is to show you how. So if you go online you can see how I've broken down a hugely powerful road safety awareness talk I saw in Australia back in 2003, when I was speaking about presenter confidence in schools.

Cars Kill You, Seat Belts Help Stop Them

There was just the right amount of guts and glory in the story coming from a police sergeant, non-pro speaker, to appeal to the kids with his shock factor of Icebreaker Intro and Call to Action Close. His talk was designed to have the maximum stun, fear and drive impact on teenage drivers. He had no visuals, pictures or slides, just the power of his story, his key lines and congruent delivery. He said he delivered it slightly differently every time, but always started and ended the same way, because it had the desired effect. And success: 'Buckling up' was all the kids could talk about for the rest of the day!

In fact they were such vividly *'WOOOW!'* fact Intro and Close lines, I've still remembered them to this day. But – artistic licence – OK I am making up the stats and lines in between for you!

So let's turn this Road Safety Seat Belt story into a potential video script by simply following the Video script **Working A to B 7 step process** = Easy!

Quick Video Scripting with Impact A&E

Think of an idea like this that you could create using these quick script techniques.

⅄ How could you start and end with impact?

⅄ How could you play with what you could say in between?

Print out my full Video Scripting with Impact script instructions to use any time. Create quick scripts, following the basic structure of Intro, Body, Call to Action + Close, but add your **Newspaper Headline** to make it easier to remember your core theme.

Quick Video Scripting with Impact:
Working A To B + Newspaper Headline

My Newspaper Headline: exciting core theme = easy to remember!

_____

INTRO: My First Line A…

_____

BODY: answer what the viewer wants to know?
E.g. WHY? WHAT? HOW HELP VIEWER? WHO FOR? WHERE/WHEN?

_____

CALL TO ACTION (CTA) + TAG LINE Close: CTA = I want my audience to…/My Tagline = a catch phrase for me…/Close = Last Line B… - Link back to Line A to 'Top & Tail' the story…

_____

TIP: KNOW your Newspaper Headline, create an appealing story, then work Intro line A to Close line B. As the script-writer + expert in your field, you CAN say anything appropriate in between!

Be #Flawsome with your story - excite, entice, entreat me, in sharing it!

Practise by asking people at work which of your stories/skills/tools has had a powerful effect on them and re-work it for video like I did with my seat belt story. It's fun and you'll have another video to film straight away!

Top Tips for Newspaper Headline + Intro to Close + Working A to B Videos

A themed, keyword connected, Newspaper Headline can work as a YouTube title – this gives just enough intrigue to work + 'How to drive safe teens' on the end.

The first Line A can appeal to a broader market than just your target viewer.

Challenging, naming and shaming from the start, with three *"you"s* in the first line dramatically increases the Verbal Impact.

Once you've introduced yourself – with your name and what you do *(not necessarily for every video)* you can go in to the Body text and say anything you choose.

Last Line B uses a triple word, rhyming ending, which is aurally appealing. It also repeated the viewer WIIFM + CTA making it even stronger.

So now it's your turn…

> ### Quick Video Scripts in a Flash A&E
> Think of an idea like this that you could create using these quick script techniques.
>
> How could you play with what you could say in between?
>
> If you're someone who loves to improvise, then this is a guaranteed method for you if you feel yourself losing it. Any time you feel yourself going off track you can simply jump to that Last Line B: to Close with your Call to Action.

You can see now how easy it can be to come up with an idea when you're passionate about it and have a good base for a story. Once your scripts are final with first and last lines down on the page and in your head, you can simply use keywords to present the rest to deliver real spontaneity.

What about if you're doing a long-form video, webinar or presentation – how can you plan that?

When you're creating a live or long-form presentation you need to structure your presentation to have a logical sequence and flow.

The 5 Stage Long-Form Presentations Structure

1. **Icebreaker**
2. **Intro: Your Credentials + Aims + Objectives**
3. **Body**
4. **Wrap Up: Summary Conclusion**
5. **CLOSE – your wrap up to include: CTA + Tagline**

To present a formal talk, you will follow this five-stage sequence – it is a very commonly trained presentation structure that works. The five stages help you remember and refocus on where you are – you know you've got to cover off five areas, which you break down by themes. The Body can still simply be answering your W questions, but now you can answer all of them because you have time! The five stages become your keyword section titles.

You will Chunk + Keyword each section down as reminders and print them on separate pages. Whenever you present, never be afraid to have these notes to hand – on the table, on the wall, somewhere you can easily refer to them. In long-form video recording you are doing your viewer a service to take a moment to check you are on track, you can mention it "right, where are we?" You are checking you have it right for them, demonstrating that you value them and they're worth getting it right for, taking time over. And it gives them time to check in their listening brains too. So you have no need to panic when you lose your way. A confident check is easily forgiven as they'd probably be doing the same!

STAGE 5: *From the Head to the Page to Performance*

So what happens if you're someone who really likes to get everything word perfect on paper?

What if you've got no video ideas?! How do you find 'em and get 'em out?

What easy steps can you follow to write your scripts?

Well, to get set to perform all you need to do is get it from your head to the page and back into your head! Pick out ideas that jump out at you – use whatever you need to help you create a story.

The following editing steps will help to expand the idea, focus it into a story, find the emotional reason for it, structure the script, pinpoint important areas and focus your ideas.

- **Brainstorm Video Ideas**
- **Draft your Script – by hand**
- **Write + Review + Re-edit – quick step creativity**
- **Set your Mind for Success**
- **Ensure you Add M³ Connections along the way**

How to Get the Words from your Head…

Brainstorm Video Ideas:

1. Brainstorm topics with lots of blank paper.

2. Think of the initial topic and jot down every single phrase and any word associations that pop up even if they may seem silly.

3. Have fun brainstorming – these are simply ideas and themes, what you could do. You don't have to do them all.

4. Once you see a pattern of ideas, start putting them into groups – they could be a series.

5. Then compare them with the feedback you've got from clients – what do they want to know?

6. Separate the short-form ideas from long-form – look at the quick and easy first!

7. Make sure to capture all the ideas in different groups before someone clears them away!

Remember no idea on that topic is a bad idea – not yet!

Brainstorming is always great to do with a team – make an event with it – it's the creative process after all. If you're stuck for ideas in the office, take yourself out for inspiration, speak to clients, ask your friends – you DO have great ideas or you wouldn't be in business in the first place.

To the Page…

When you get to writing, there are many ways you can do the same thing, i.e. get it down on the page. You can write your draft, edit it, check and re-edit over and over. My 7 Step Write + Review + Re-edit process gives similar results, but is more performance based. When you plan and say it more while you write, you prep your script and mind ready to present it in a shorter time.

Choose what works for you. You may need to edit a number of times to start off with but you will get quicker with practice. When you reach the point where my Video Planning Sheet and Scripting with Impact Sheet are all you need, you're on the improv roll!

But for those detail writers out there, here is how you start…

Top Tip: Use M³ – always write your scripts by hand first, leaving spaces for edits…

1. **Plan your core theme – what are you saying?**
   - Think what could be your Newspaper Headline to write about?
   - Choose attention grabbers to include.

2. **Draft 1 – write by hand, double line space**
   - Write free flow as a stream of consciousness, no thinking, just write until you end.
   - Forget punctuation.

3. **Read your text out loud and mark up text changes by hand**
   - Is it how you'd say it, is it how <u>you</u> speak?
   - Highlight your core themes – make sure you've covered what your viewer needs.
   - Check the questions + answers + themes you must say for you – CTA?

4. **Draft 2 - re-write script as you'd actually say it**
   - Write by hand again, then type it up, to further trigger the memory bank.
   - Change the language to what you'd <u>actually</u> SAY.
   - Say it out loud as you write to check!
   - Check your logical sequence - 'chunk' your script in to segments to remember.

5. **Final draft - type up + re-read your script and when happy, space words so they are easy to read**
   - Add in punctuation where you'd normally breathe…
   - <u>Underline</u>, *italic* or **bold** key words to stress.
   - Add full stops for a long pause, commas for a breathe.

6. **Print + Highlight key words that are THE MOST IMPORTANT by hand**
   - These are what you need to remember.
   - Ensure your Call to Action (CTA) is there!

7. **Write out only 'chunk' titles + highlighted keywords to remember (e.g. Why? + answer)**
   - Print 1 pager big so you can easily refer to notes - use a clipboard (no paper rustling).
   - Enlarge on to flipchart on the wall – use colour, write up keywords only!

Writing, saying + colour trigger Mind Muscle Memory M³ Connection

These steps are also useful when you want to create longer scripts, or if you prefer to remember your lines word for word and stick to it more than ad-lib.

The more you write a script out, the easier it is to remember.

These writing processes also remind you all the way that:

〰〰〰〰〰〰〰

You are not writing for you – you're writing for who…!?

〰〰〰〰〰〰〰

Whatever way of writing you prefer, we all also have different styles and ways of remembering things. It's highly unlikely outside a pro studio that you'll have an autocue, unless you have the set-up or studio budget for it – so learn what helps you when you come to perform.

To Performance…

A big part of your verbal power of your performance is your confidence in trusting your own brain and M³. If you have to remember lines, you'd better get into the habit of doing so.

If you don't like it, then don't! Use some of the other improv scripting styles you've learned here. However you bring your script to life, you *have* to commit to your Verbal Impact in performance.

STAGE 6:   Ways + WOWs! to Remember your Lines

Set your Mind for Success

Only you know how best you remember things – whether you need to learn things line by line or are an improviser to a plan like me. Here are a few thoughts you may not have had to help your confidence in your own memory – you are not alone!

Repetition to Remember – Play with your Lines!

When I had to learn lines, I had to know them so well I could say them any which way my director told me. So I learned them by saying them over and over during the dull moments in life – always when I was actually doing something else to train my mind to do more than say the lines. When it came time to perform there would be so much more to think about instinctively, in the moment, than fear of not remembering lines!

I often turned learning into a game. Anytime I went wrong, I re-read that one line out loud, over and over at least 10 times, each time in different ways or singing the line to make it fun. THEN I went back to the start of the scene and said the whole lot again. I'd repeat this exercise again and again until I could get through the lines word perfect at least three times. Then I'd ask someone to give me an Emotional Connection mood to perform and start the playing!

You can always record the lines to listen to while walking, washing up, cooking, in the bath. Leave spaces in the recording for you to say the lines back – a classic old acting technique.

Or my *absolute* favourite, superlazy method – listen to your lines while going to sleep. Honestly, when you listen to your own voice it's like hypnosis and they sink into your brain as you do! Then you just gotta trust your brain you know!

Repetition cements exact lines – so you must make time to Rehearse...

Remember... to remember, you MUST...

1. **Rehearse to Remember and Remember to Rehearse!** – connect Visual M^3 by doing.
2. **Read your script out loud** – connect Vocal M^3 by saying.
3. **Play with your emotions involved – get emotionally involved!** – connect Verbal M^3 by hearing.

Performance practice allows your M^3 mental and physical muscle memory to connect the 3 Vs together. So when you rehearse, plan and work in your performance energy, pace it, use pauses, add movements, gestures, facial expression and FIND YOUR MOMENTS TO SMILE!

Do this in front of a mirror and you'll get to see what your viewer might see and adapt your presenting to project your power and energy accordingly.

Rehearsal also gives you the freedom to be spontaneous, to ad-lib, say it differently and be *REAL*. You can look like you're saying it for the first time in your video, because you actually are! So the more you can DO, the more likely you are to remember. This is some of the easiest yet most important marketing you will ever do of and for yourself, so make the effort!

~~~~~~~~~~

Rehearsal re-sets the physical and mental M^3 effort in your mind

~~~~~~~~~~

If you really don't have time to rehearse, then read, read and re-read your script out loud. Focus on how you will say the words, where to put in meaning and write on the script what, when, where and how you will use your Visual and Vocal Impact. See how far you can play in rehearsal and have fun doing it.

Stuff up with Confidence – and get over it! = LAUGH

VIDEO COACH SECRET TIP here: if you're rehearsing on set, on camera, film *every* rehearsal when you PIY. You could be that one-take wonder or hit a perfect performance far quicker than you expect. Especially if you are an ad-libber and repetition makes you stale.

BONUS – you can catch some great bloopers for the out-takes!

> ### Quick Memory Games Playlist A&E!
>
> Your mind is a muscle – exercise it to get into the habit of remembering!
>
> A good game to play to help remind you that you ARE the EXPERT and you CAN say whatever you want is an old BBC Radio 4 and television game that's been on for years – *Just a Minute*. It's also another way to get your one-minute timing ingrained to your brain!
>
> **Just a Minute Rules:**
>
> Talk on your Topic for one minute exactly – time yourself.
>
> You are not allowed:
>
> ⅄ Repetition
>
> ⅄ Hesitation
>
> ⅄ Deviation
>
> ⅄ You have to stop and start all over again if you do!
>
> Obviously this is better with someone else to play too, but if you don't have a partner or team, record yourself on camera or just your voice and see/hear how you do. Otherwise do it with the family – it could be a way to get the screenagers off the screen!

Prime Yourself for Verbal Success

Priming ourselves for Verbal Impact success prepares the mind to work for us – to know and recall our core message, to be happy and willing to give it a go and to *Stuff up with Confidence and get over it* if and when we don't!

Create your 'I am… I can… I will…' I'MPACT Power Priming Statements to say out loud when you need a verbal confidence boost. They are to help you **free your brain to say what you want to say**, releasing the pressure of *trying to remember* what you wrote!

✓ I am the expert in my field
✓ I can change my script as I choose
✓ I will remember what I want to say!

Actors Press Play

And if you 'go wrong' in your script you can never let it show!

Not even on stage in a one-woman show with an audience of 200 people... Yep, that was me!

Had to ad-lib for three minutes to get myself back on track, but I did and no one but the director had a heart attack, as far as I know ☺

You *have* to ad-lib your way out of it, which is actually far easier to do *on your own stage*, and even easier when you've written the script!

We can improvise on camera if things go wrong because we know we can be *Flawsome*!

THAT should give you the confidence to remember what you want to say and not have to worry if and when you 'lose' your lines and give yourself away.

When scripting your text to make it easy to remember – test it out to hear what works.

> Write free-flow, read it out loud... is that *really* how you'd say it?
>
> Are your words easy to understand? – say them out loud.
>
> Does your sentence structure flow easily? – say it out loud.
>
> Could it be more interesting to hear? – ask someone else if you're not sure!

The Actor's Improv Scripting Skills A&E

Right, quick example A&E – write down a promo of what you do or take the text from your web page...

- ⅄ Now SAY IT out loud...
- ⅄ Have you answered what you do?
- ⅄ How does it sound?

Now think off the top of your head – you're talking to an old friend in a café or bar who says: "Intrigue me – what do you do?"

- ⅄ What would you say in *that* casual conversation?

You Know Best

You know better than anyone else what *needs* to go in a script, because you are promoting *your* business or some product or service where you're invested in the success.

If it's not your company and you 'just work there', you still know your job, right, or you wouldn't have been asked to present the video. So you're still the expert in that field!

You already know the business or product or service story: what it is, why it's important and how we will benefit from it as a result. So that's all you have to tell us!

If you've found a conversational way to tell your story with style, a touch of excitement, humour or occasion, with facts set out clearly, simply, to the point and using any words like help/you/easy/easier/easiest – you're hitting key marketing appeal language that connects with impact. Resonate with me the viewer enough to make me want some of what you're offering!

I call it *'How to W.O.W.'* your audience, by choosing to trust your body and brain…

Only you can choose to use your **W.O.W. = Wisdom Over Worry!**

Wisdom over Worry – WOW your Viewer

Trust in credible, confident you – the expert to write and present your video.

Who knows why you are presenting and what you want to do to benefit every viewer? **YOU DO…** So now choose to use your W.O.W. to *WOW!*

Choose W.O.W.

Wisdom here is the experience and knowledge together with the power of applying it for a successful outcome. Keep your focus on your Wisdom rather than your Worries – let your confident brain work *for* you rather than against you.

1. When you write video script yourself why worry?
2. Never try to remember every single word.
3. You can always shoot a short video again.
4. Word for word perfect is irrelevant when you've written your own script.
5. Only you know if you forget something.
6. Stuff up your lines and laugh – at yourself, smile, relax your muscles and mind.
7. Get to the end and choose your own W.O.W.!

WOW Facts Factor too!

Of course, actual *WOW!* facts actually add *real* W.O.W. factor to your scripts!

Exciting examples or fun facts, mountainous challenges overcome, success stories, juicy titbits or historical truths always add interest and intrigue, and make lines easier to remember using W.O.W! So see which WOW! facts you feel most comfortable to use in the moment. You know what they are, you've probably said them hundreds of times - so step up from thinking they're just banal comments about what you do, boost that energy and make them *fascinating*!

My WOW Fact Playlist: ▶

Which WOW facts make the most powerful/exciting/enthralling/intriguing/challenging argument for my viewer to commit to doing/using/buying/sharing/getting involved?

1. _____

2. _____

3. _____

One-liner W.O.W. data fascinates you, your colleagues, mates and family (especially teens!) over coffee or out on the town!

NEED to Know your Lines?

If you're an ad-libber like me, you're sorted on how to write and remember your script.

If you are highly task and details focused in your script that you want to completely KNOW, then here are some more reminders online to help you de-stress about your lines.

They are YOUR lines, so no... one... else... knows – if you go wrong!

Only You Know it's Not Perfect!

Never struggle through a video shoot – we're all human and know it can be hard.

This is meant to be fun for us all, so forgive yourself in the moment and let your worries go...

Watching someone struggle on screen to be 100% correct on their words in a video is very hard to see. It looks like lack of confidence, it makes us uncomfortable, so we turn the video off. Never neglect the power of your smile that can cover a multitude of fears!

There are lots of ways to *Get Over It* when your mind goes to mush – it happens to us all!

So work out here and now what can help release you from those worries and get you back to *W.O.W.!*

BONUS: *3 Memory Tools to Help You Not Lose!*

1. Chunk and Keyword A to B

1st Line – Learn first line A

Keyword Body – 3-5 points max

1. Keyword
2. Keyword
3. Keyword

Keyword – Call to Action?

LEARN LAST LINE B – CLOSE.

> **Intro: 1st Line A**
>
> **BODY:**
> 1. Point e.g. why?
> 2. Point e.g. what?
> 3. Point e.g. how?
>
> **CTA + Close: Last Line B**

2. A Video in One Hand

Simply answer the questions in any order:

1. Intro Line
2. + Why?
3. + What?
4. + How?
5. CTA/Tagline – Close

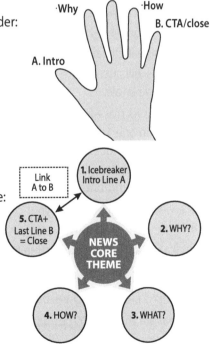

3. Memory Map Circle

Simple mind maps with News Headline core theme in centre:

⅄ Each branch is a section of your talk

⅄ 5-7 branches max

⅄ Use different colours for each branch

⅄ Write Keywords on by hand

My Call to Action to you = Your mind is a muscle – exercise your memory

STAGE 7: What Verbal Performance Habits Distract?

After that you'll be very glad to hear there are far fewer distracting verbal habits than visual or vocal ones that give you away on camera. Sadly though, the ones there are, are usually annoyingly noticeable and far more relevant to the filming process.

If you fall apart, filming has to stop and you may mess up the best take you've done yet...

Good news is an editor can help you hide them.

Bad news is too many edits can often be a distraction in themselves as we've discussed!

Do Edits Distract You?

Think for yourself – now when you see someone talking on screen:

- Do you now like one-shot PTCs?
- Do you prefer it with lots of cuts between sentences, or does one take give you more confidence in the presenter?
- Do you perceive editing as saving time, or covering mistakes?
- If the cutaways are to other images, does that work better for you?
- Are you happy with one-shot PTC + pop-ups + captions for you now?
- This will dictate your storyboard and how many shots you want to use.
- This will also dictate the time and cost investment required, as we know.

Editing has its place for sure, but learn the ability to create 15", 30", 45", 1' PTCs in one shot, in one **Take** *(one Action to Cut filming moment),* and not only will your confidence sky-rocket any time you're on camera, but your production crews and media friends will appreciate and value your skills to give brilliant, quotable, repeatable sound-bites *any time you're on air.*

As a viewer we already feel your confidence, because you got through it all in one go!

You'll also save yourself a fortune too, as you can now film these DIY + PIY with just your smartphone – yes, tips to come!

The Top 3 Distracting Verbal Habits (DVHs)

So what are the irritating or potentially Distracting Verbal Habits? *(the DVH that could cause GBH!)*

There are **three main Verbal Distractions** that can stop your connection dead in its tracks.

And guess what – they're M³ based and *breathing* is the only solution again!

So here they are – some of them reminders you already know…

DVH No. 1: Stopping because you've 'gone wrong'

As I've said, it can be extremely frustrating when a client comes in so doggedly determined to say *every* line exactly as they wrote it. They start brilliantly, then lose track and as they desperately *try* to remember the exact words, panic shows all over their face.

In a split second they stop breathing, the brain stops, focus stops… they just **STOP**…

They usually get embarrassed, frustrated or even angry at themselves, sometimes me…

Trying too hard only causes frustration – we need to know this is normal.

Improv takes time to develop and it's totally OK to stuff up!

Even if you do 'go wrong', we viewers never know until you give the game away.

Remember our subconscious brain notices way before we do and we appreciate seeing someone get out of their stuff-ups *Flawsomely*.

If you mess up the words, or trip over a line, get over it – apologise, say it again, laugh, whatever it takes. But for the filming process – ALWAYS… KEEP… GOING!

Breeeeeeeaaathe…

We don't know what you wrote, we don't know if you missed something out – so let your expertise and confident delivery get you through to the end you chose.

When you focus on your 3 Ps of Pace, Pause and Performance your brain kicks into gear for you and you WILL come up with the next thing to say, that fits in with your core message, and you WILL get back on track. You know what your last line is, so just smile and say it.

PERFORMER SOLUTIONS:

No matter what happens on camera, you always get to an end and hold that camera lens with the laugh in your head or a smile and maintain the focus; use your *"I love you"*s until the CAMERA STOPS rolling, not you.

AND THE NUMBER ONE SOLUTION TO COVER DEAD STOPS…

PAUSE AND BREATHE!

✓ Add an expression and breathe…

✓ Keep going, say your last line with confidence, and with practice, we'll never know you've gone wrong!

DVH No. 2: Overuse of Crutch Words or Phrases

Your **crutch words** are the words you may repeat without even noticing you say them.

Mine used to be *"I mean..." "It's like..."* until someone pointed it out, RAS kicked in and I couldn't stop hearing me using the phrase. Then I heard myself say it three times within 10 seconds recording my next show and I stopped it that day!

We add crutch words to fill in our self-perceived 'gaps' – we think we're filling, but actually crutch words only undermine our credibility and confidence.

Verbal crutch words might be:

Crutch Word > Solution

1. Uuhms/Aahs > use one, then the other!

2. Mmmmmms noises > add these to your uhms + ahs.

3. Overly breathy delivery to cover lack of words > use some uhms and ahs!

4. Word repetition, often at the start, so mine is often "So…" > find alternative too!

5. Cliché line repetition – "At the end of the day…" "you know what I mean…" > are classic, use once!

6. Lip or tongue smacking or popping – often with breath in, sound like "Tchaaaa…" or "Dtaaa…" > try Vaseline on your lips, drink water.

7. Once you start stopping habits, you may do a mouth movement to cover the old habit > Again, this is OK! Notice it and it will go! Stay aware and make sure your mouth is not dry.

Crutch words are simply a safety habit mechanism when we are unsure – and they **are** OK!

The distraction can be because they are often accompanied by a visual and/or vocal discomfort clue that adds to the distracting power. They can often be waste words, so replace them with words that deliver and add to your content.

Stop wasting your words – kick your *"but"*s; change *"if"*s to *"when"*s; make *"stuff"* and *"things"* into specific words!

You do need to be aware when you use them, especially when you are creating a video series.

No worries – you'll notice after you see the first three takes, so when you use one of your habits simply notice and use something else next time!

DVH No. 3: Hesitant Rambling!

Losing the plot because you're not breathing is often covered by two opposite ends of the spectrum and you never know which one you're going to go for until it happens to you!

1. The Slows = Hesitation for no apparent reason.
2. Rambling or waffling = Deviation away from the core message.

1. Hesitating is different from a Pause

Hesitating is when you slow right down, you may even use crutch words or DVH 1, stop with that blank, disconnected stare – the rabbit in the headlights or the eye flick away from the camera showing us you've stuffed up. You *can* recover, but we've already seen it and you know we know that! That's when it's time to pause the panic, breathe and have another go – say it right this time with a smile!

A **Pause** is when you stop for a specific reason, to enable understanding, to give the viewer thinking time and increase comprehension. We can tell from your guiding body language and expressions that you've done it for us, so we know you know that too, and we appreciate you giving us time to think or ponder what you said.

2. Deviation from your core theme

When you deviate because you've lost it, you can often speed up the pace without realising – to try to gallop through. You can lose articulation, clarity and our understanding.

Breathe, pause and pace yourself through memory blocks…

Or you might ramble or waffle to cover your 'mistake'!

This can result in the video going too long.

Going off topic is fine – but make it for a reason to help the viewer – be excited to add bonus info and cover script mishaps at the same time!

Deviations can also lead you to be careless with adjectives. Use adjectives like you mean them! 'Interesting', 'brilliant', 'exciting', 'unique' are matters of opinion unless you encourage your audience to believe from your face. BE CONGRUENT!

PERFORMER SOLUTIONS:
AND THE NUMBER ONE SOLUTION TO COVER HESITATIONS
AND DEVIATIONS...
You guessed it…
PAUSE AND BREATHE!

✓ Taking a moment to gather your thoughts is far more impressive on camera than carrying on regardless and ending in a waffling mess. When you need a moment to think on camera, a purposeful look away with the Thinking Expression we spoke of in the Visual Impact Tool gives you that moment to breathe and gives your brain the oxygen to remember and get back on track.

✓ Look like you're coming up with something important and we'll believe you have.

✓ Only include bonus information that will benefit the viewer, and if it can be in another video, let it be and leave it out!

✓ Finish in the present tense, it heightens the sense of immediacy – today/now!

✓ Never strive too hard to be clever when it all goes out of your mind! A confident and coherent presenter plays with words for effect, but they let the simple facts speak for themselves.

Script Rememberers vs Improvisers Note:

You should know now – which are you?

If you prefer to learn word for word, you need to build in the pause moments when you write, because you'll be more inclined towards DVH No. 1! Ensure your scripts are read out loud and timed to fit with pauses *before* you learn them. Check you can say the whole sentence out loud in one easy breath. If not, break it in two. Practise improv with the *Just a Minute* game.

Improvisers like me have to work on DVH No. 3, as most of our scripts will be improvised around a core theme. Practise timing exercises and you'll start to know instinctively when you've spoken for 30 seconds, one minute, two minutes, three minutes etc. and you wrap up to the end!

Avoiding these three key DVH is easy with Awareness and Exercise A&E.

Remember **they are all OK to do, when you do them for a reason!**

You can always cover them with your Flawsomeness and a smile to include us in your stuff-up!

If they're happening without you noticing and creating discomfort in you, that's when you need to reassess your Confidence on Camera, review these three V Steps 3-5, practise and get more aware – pay attention and prime your mindset for verbal success.

STEP FIVE:

The Power of my Verbal Impact
A&E

My Playlist for a Confident on Camera Me!

Here's your chapter A&E review so you can know what to say, how to write it and how to remember it.

My Learning Stage Notes:

1. Scripting for Verbal Impact…

2. My Planning Notes…

3. Writing Rules to remember…

4. My Structure to use…

5. Stop thinking, start performing!…

6. How will I remember scripts?…

7. My Verbal Distractions – DVH improvements…

USE POWER PRIMERS:
"I Am The Flawsome Expert In My Field!"

Remember all you really gotta do is take what's in your head and get it out in a chatty way we can and will want to remember!

My Playlist for a Confident on Camera Me!

Online

STEP SIX

Sharing *with* **Confidence**

> *I think you should take your job seriously,*
> *but not yourself - that is the best combination.*
>
> **Judi Dench**

The greatest Human Desire is to be Accepted
- we are pack animals and most of us want to be part of the crowd.

The greatest Human Fear is Rejection
- we take it as failure that we haven't been accepted,
whether it's our actions, our ideas or ourselves.

Yet, you're reading this book and planning to create your own videos that will put you out there to be judged. Interesting decision a lot of people regularly run from, for fear of that rejection – but you are not, I applaud your choice. And before you reject me in this chapter – there are not 7 Stages because you *can* cope with just three to know the power of confidence you need when it comes to sharing your video work with the world.

STAGE 1: *Accept Acceptance – your Desire and YOU*

Video can be perceived as a 'show off' arena – so some people *(our troll friends under their bridges!)* feel justified in leaving unconstructive negative comments. It's OK for anyone to not like what you do, it's not OK for people to write destructive, personal or potentially damaging comments, but they may and do!

It's because most of those people are simply too scared, lack the drive, lack the creativity and completely lack the confidence to make their own videos, so it's easy for them to knock it when others do.

As humans, we already know it's easier to identify what we don't like, instead of what we do like, so keep shifting your own mindset to more positive day by day!

Think what your denigrators, sledgers or potential competitors might say about your videos when they come out…

Could there be negativity?

Could there be jealousy?

Could they then scramble to try and create something 'better' than you?

Yes, yes and yes – but they will probably never sledge you as much as you could do to yourself could they?!

Anyway, you're already a step ahead in the game with your Confidence on Camera knowledge and skills now, so they're going to take a while to catch you up. By which stage you'll be presenting even more powerful things and boosting your business success online to the stars!

It reminds me of this *Peter Pan* quote from JM Barrie I love, for the mindset of needing belief in the power of your confidence to put yourself on show for the world:

"All the world is made of faith, and trust, and pixie dust."

Like an actor's dream of being a star really!

Main point is – at some point you're going to have to show your videos to the world to share your genius, expertise and help serve success around the world.

Simply trust you're good enough and believe in what you feel is good, real and true.

So in this chapter I want to work with you on how to arm yourself against video rejection and embrace and ask for acceptance. But most of all we're going to learn how to share our videos with confidence, ask for positive feedback and cope with criticism when it knocks you down.

How to Share without Showing Off

Now we do all love a good 'show off' every now and again – when you've worked really hard on something and you're superproud of it, it's very normal to want to shout about it a bit, even if you do so quietly. You might be a person who likes to tell everyone or you may simply smile at your achievements and move on – we are all very different. But by nature of the expression 'show off' we all know that showing off can be perceived as both negative, flaunty, in-your-face, loud-mouthed or cockiness.

But it can also be perceived as positive: proud, successful, instructional, sharing. And guess which we're going for? Of course – the showing off of your knowledge and skills with the world to make this world a better place – and thank you very much, it means a lot to me that you make the effort to do so! I couldn't and wouldn't be where I am today without amazing people like you who thought of showing off as a brilliantly positive thing – done without arrogance it has phenomenal impact!

First thing when you are looking for feedback is to shift off that negative mindset.

You never 'show off' your video, you simply SHARE or 'Pitch your Video Idea'.

First thing when you are looking for feedback is to shift off that negative mindset.

You never 'show off' your video, you simply *SHARE* or '*Pitch your Video Idea*'.

This takes out your emotional involvement and allows you to step back from any overly zealous or negative feedback. You allow yourself to cope mentally with any perceived rejection and accept it as help to gain a better understanding from your viewer. You can then see more easily what could be missing from your content or confusing how you present this specific story. You can also see if you've nailed your CTA or not.

Or you can realise that you are really happy with what you've produced and maybe that negative reviewer is having a bad, rejection-filled day and taking it out on you.

Pause, breathe, smile – that's OK too!

People project their moods, good or bad, and you have a choice to take their positive or negative energy on board and use it or not. Or just say thanks and move on.

So when your Video is 'Finished and Fabulous' in your mind and you're ready to show it off, you probably want to receive a similar response back... but maybe you won't and that's OK!

Whether you are Introverted, Extroverted, Task or People focused or Visual, Auditory or Kinaesthetic minded, you present your video in your own special way!

- ⊥ If they didn't like the video idea, simply ask did your presenting work?
- ⊥ If they didn't like your presenting, did the story work?

You can always find something to learn from any feedback, whether you perceive it as 'good' or 'bad'.

Remember to be accepting of yourself and tell them it is OK for viewers NOT to like it!

Tell them before they watch that it's OK for them not to – you'll ask them what you want to know from them. We all like specific task instruction, as I keep pushing home with CTAs!

They probably still like you, so might desperately need you to let them off the hook if they didn't. So ask for specifics of what they liked or didn't like/learn or didn't learn/understand or didn't understand and so on.

It's all about you knowing and trusting you've done the job you wanted, you've created and told your story and now it's about sharing it with the world in a way that empowers your confidence, focuses your self-awareness and helps you do better next time. It's showing off in an acceptable manner!

What if I'm scared to share?

Some clients do get scared just before they share their videos with the world, it's normal to reject your videos when you first start out. Others just accept, post, promote and move on. You're ultimately aiming for the point where you almost have so much footage you can pick and choose what to use because any of it can work for a viewer, and you know what you want to work best today. This is the beginnings of your Video Strategy Plan or Video Training Online Course – the internet is your video limit!

If you're waiting to release your video publicly from lack of confidence or waiting for exactly the feedback you want, it will sit in your channel Unlisted or Private for months, so bite the bullet – post it as Public and either ask for feedback or don't!

There really is no point making a video, investing time, effort, money and then making up an excuse to not use it because 'it's just not quite right'. If it's not good enough quality for your web page, at least get it on YouTube and start making it work for you to improve your search ranking and brand SEO. Share it as a vlog on social media, use it as an email newsletter – but DO something with it.

You'll probably be amazed by how many people watch it, enjoy it, benefit from it and act on it and they don't even notice that niggle that you see. I've got hours of raw unedited footage I've done nothing with, but anything I invest time to edit goes Public as soon as it's done and the rest can come out another time or go to a paid programme. So practise, film loads, accept your best efforts and move on – and do 'even better' next time!

STAGE 2: Asking for Feedback

So how do you ask for feedback that might give you answers in a way you want?

You simply ASK!

Nicely, politely, specifically and please do say please and thank you!

Now we've learned how to negate the knock-back impact of negative comments, the next key is to avoid getting overloaded with **loads** of different ideas of what/ where/how you could now change it all to be even better!

People do mean well and anyone who has agreed to review something for you probably wants to be positive to help you. But without specific instruction reviewers are more likely to take their own tangents, focus on negatives, forget to tell you what they like and throw in the feedback kitchen sink, when all you want is a simple answer to *"do I smile enough?"*!

So let's go through the when, who, how to help you ask and get positive, valid and useable feedback and what to do with it once you have it.

When to Ask for Feedback

To prevent confusion, too many opinions and delays, there are two main times you can ask for positive feedback to give you useful advice:

1. When you are still editing.
2. When you've finished.

1. When = with last edits still to do

This is feedback on specific items you want to check. It is about the Visual Impact of the edit, not your presenting style. Does the edit look good and is the core message clear?

If not can you re-edit or add captions to help?

Only ever show a couple of key people before a final edit, be clear with what will not change, what you are keeping and what specific things you want their advice on. Stick to fewer than three key items you want opinion about, or you will have a confusing list! Ask for very specific details.

For example:

1. You may have two different edit versions – which do they prefer?
2. You have two different Intros/Closes – which is best?
3. You need to cut 10/20″ – which 10 seconds to remove/ which lines to remove?
4. Which music is better suited to your style/business?
5. Which In/Out visual slide design do they prefer? Does it fit your branding/designs etc.?
6. Do you need captions to clarify or quantify your message?
7. Did they get your core message/service/CTA? Does it fit your aims?

Edit Advice Form Example

You can even create an Edit Advice form to help them:
– it's online of course!

Edit Advice Form Example				
Time Code	Line From	Line To	Your Notes	Query to Editor
00:30 – 00:35	Do when you feel the need…	Call me today	PTC + zoom. Use version 1	Better to zoom in or out?
00:35	Call me today		Add phone no.	Confirm font?

Important Note!

Only ask about items that CAN be changed in a final re-edit – there is no re-filming or re-ordering feedback unless you are prepared to do so. When you've taken the time to get it this far, they haven't seen how much work you've put in, so if someone gets overly picky…thank them for their time and walk away!

2. When = after edits are complete

When you have finished your video completely and you want specific feedback on what works for you as a presenter and to assess viewer feedback to the message. Make it clear this is the FINAL edit and you are unlikely to change it from this point. You are asking generally for the video and specifically for you, according to the 3 Vs for your presenter development:

✓ The more specific you can get the better!

✓ Ideally ask three to seven people to give you visual and vocal specific presenting style feedback – this will give you a broad enough spectrum to work on – not all will like you on screen!

✓ If you want feedback on your Verbal Impact and clarity of message, CTA and ease of understanding, aim for getting three to five similar opinions and you're doing very well!

When you are ultimately happy with what you have done and feel it will work for you, just go for it! Get your video out there in Public and ask for the feedback after. Have confidence in your gut instinct that you have finished and are happy.

Who to ask

1. People you trust will give you constructive and useable feedback.
2. People who are in your target viewer profile.
3. People who will respect the way you ask for feedback and not just tell you to change it all!

Avoid asking well-known Rejectors – those people you know who will make negative comments just for the sake of argument or to bully you.

Reject Rejectors!

While it's easy to ask easy targets for opinions – the like-minded Acceptor people who give you the response or the feedback you *want* to get – challenge yourself to learn! Look for positive, target market colleagues and friends who will give you an honest and true appraisal.

You may want to show it to a loved one, a friend, a partner face-to-face, especially when you need an immediate response. This can be tricky if you put a live viewer on the spot, they really may not like it! So you must give them instructions.

How much feedback works?

'Too many cooks spoil the broth' is an old saying that works for video too. The more people you ask, the more different opinions you will get. This is another reason for creating a specific feedback guide for your three to seven test viewers to follow.

When and where to view you?

It is easier for viewers to watch and give you constructive feedback when you are not there, so emails with links are easiest. Top tips on asking face-to-face and via email are up in a moment.

Please only ask for live feedback IF the viewer is truly supportive of your efforts and will not use this as an excuse to put you down.

Live F2F Feedback Tips:

1. Ask them to help you as a bit of fun on a good day – not when they get back from work tired or drunk!

2. Tell them they may not be your target market, so tell them who is and ask them to put themselves in their shoes – does it make sense then?

3. Ask them to wait until the end before saying anything.

4. Ask them to follow the positive format of how you are asking for feedback from everyone else (see How? on the next page).

5. Ask them what they like first – before they start wading in with what they don't!

6. Ask if you are giving yourself away at any moment – did they notice if you felt nerves, if so what habit was it? Loved ones will probably recognise if you do because they know you well! And if they miss it, great – you're faking it good!

7. As colleagues, friends or loved ones, they'll also probably know when you are being your most real and natural you, so ask about that too.

This sets you up to succeed and helps avoid judgement, especially with a partner, friend or loved one. Trust me – it's all too easy to get emotionally involved and react to feedback because they know you, and can press your emotional buttons both up and down if they feel like it!

So step back from emotional involvement in this moment and accept:

✓ You asked for the help – maybe at a bad time for them, so they may take it out on you... simply thank them and step away – it's OK!

✓ Everyone is allowed their own personal opinion and perception, even if it isn't in line with yours and you disagree with them – it's OK!

✓ And you can't please everyone all of the time – especially your mates – IT'S O…K…!

How to do it

Ask for Confidence Fuelling Feedback

Positive feedback needs to be structured so it is:

1. An easy to follow feedback guide to help whoever you ask.
2. In the same three-step format, so it's easy for you to take action on.

When you are not in a rush the main way to get constructive positive feedback is to ask via email. You need to advise your research viewers exactly *HOW* you want them to give you the feedback. Remember to advise exactly what you can and can't change and that you're looking for specific feedback on the overall feel, does the message come across, your presenting etc., not necessarily the editing or shot choice, which may be beyond your control.

If something mildly irritates you, ask if they notice any irritations without saying what it is – they may not even notice! But they may highlight something you can easily change, especially in YouTube, such as 'it's a bit dark', 'it needs a phone number' – both can be improved direct in YouTube using their YT Editor tools.

You can use the format of feedback you have been giving yourself in the book so far:
1. What did you like?
2. What could be better?
3. Overall what worked best?

The Specific Email Feedback Process

Upload the video to your preferred video host (YouTube, Vimeo, Dropbox, iCloud, Slideshare etc.) and share a private or unlisted link (not Public yet) then ask them to respond to the specific questions in your email.

Set up WHO the video is for – your ideal client – and ask them to think with that perspective. Also let them know how long it will take, that you are happy to receive any feedback in your ideal format and to keep the video private!

On the next page is a positive feedback request example I've created for you.

My Positive Feedback Request Form

Subject: Video Feedback

Video Link: _____
(video is not public yet, so please keep this link to yourself)

What?:   Website Intro

Who for?: 30-50yo business women

My Aim: To get sign up – is this clear?

How long?: Video = 1 min, so this should take you less than 10 minutes to review

How?:   Please respond with format below

1.   What did you like about the Video?

_____

_____

2.   What could I have done better?

_____

_____

**3.   Overall, what did you see and hear that worked for you
       as a client / potential client?**

_____

_____

BONUS PLEASE:

What 3-5 words you would use to describe me as presenter?

_____

Any other Specific comments are gratefully accepted...

_____

_____

_____

_____

What to do with Feedback when you've got it?

A great piece of advice that I received from my book coach Mindy Gibbins-Klein, The Book Midwife, is to actually **wait until you have received all feedback** and open it together. Then you can compare comments, see any patterns and decide whether it might be worth a small re-edit or addition of captions, enhancements or music before putting the video out live in Public.

Or whether you may need to start again! If that is the consensus of your first DIY video, it's OK to accept it. Simply review your notes from here and start again, but maybe this time invest in some help with research, planning or coaching for a better result. You know where I am!

The huge benefit of opening feedback all at one time is you can choose what you want to do with all that feedback ONCE. You can spot common themes and therefore urgent changes.

You will also avoid the temptation to look at each suggestion, then start fiddling with re-edits over and over after each opinion. I've been there and it can waste SOOOO much time and money – so file feedback and diarise one time to review it all and make action notes for later.

Set Yourself Up for Feedback Success

Before you open the feedback, sit for a moment and breathe… set yourself up for success.

You asked for your viewer feedback, so whether they accept or reject this video, accept their opinion gracefully, gratefully first… then later choose what you thankfully want to do about it.

7 Successful Feedback Receivers:

1. Breathe and smile! – no matter what you read, positive people want to help you!
2. Be open to accepting opinions and perception instead of judgement.
3. Accept your emotional responses and let them go – smile and breathe again.
4. Be willing to listen, acknowledge and say thank you for any comments.
5. Accept that you can learn from comments for next time, both bad and good.
6. Accept that no matter what, your video is YOURS, you CAN leave it all as it is!
7. Accept your confidence in you – trust your final instincts.

Changes Without Changing

The feedback may lead you to leave your video as is, but simply change some of the Video Search Engine Optimisation (VSEO) write-up that goes with it online; in YouTube that's the Description, Title and Tags they use to assess your page rankings for YouTube and Google. You may change the design of an Intro or Outro end slide, add or change music, make light, sound and caption enhancements. All of them are very easy to do in YouTube too.

But if you are happy with the edit, step back from fiddling or changing it all or you could ruin it.

Always save each version of your edit in case you change your mind again and always keep the original footage – you may want to use parts for another video as B-roll. Files are huge, so invest in an external drive for storage whether you're on Mac or PC. Remember your iCloud deletes your videos when you delete them from your phone, so back them up elsewhere too!

Finally – never make changes straight away.

Let the ideas sit with you, then react and act. Otherwise you'll jump on the edit/re-edit/shoot/re-shoot confusion train to huge time, cost and loss of video love!

STAGE 3: How to Cope with Criticism

What happens if you receive a piece of feedback that really knocks you for six? When all you can spiral into is self-rejection, self-pity, fear…

Coping with Perceived Negative Criticism:

"After all the effort and hard work I've put in, all they can do is sledge me. They don't like me, they don't like what I do, everything is wrong, I have to change it all…oh woe is meeeeeeee…!"

Any of that ring a bell? I've been there over time for sure. I've been in super-streaming tears over something someone has said; stuck in rejection fear-fuelled emotional reactions; forgetting my wisdom, simply worrying; feeling hopelessly at a total confidence low.

WOW – downer eh?

So I do know that when you reach a point of either low self-worth or confidence crisis, you can simply say *"enough is enough – I'm good enough!"* and get over it!

Now think back to the Actor's First Night Review – we could follow the path above, but would we ever get back up to perform again? Why would we bother? Well, we have to!

We have to find a way to take the good with the bad as a practical learning experience. We absorb what can help us and go back to rehearsal to work on what we need to improve for the next performance. Or we get over the judgement and don't change what works for us, our director, the company and what gives us our audience applause! Reviewers can have bad days too. And if we took every review to heart we'd never act again!

We're back to my old doozie favourite: Judgement vs Perception.

Now with added Rejection vs Acceptance!

If you allow yourself to be knocked back by others' opinions *(aka accepting the judgements as true fact)* you'll probably never do another video again. Video will become a painful memory of a huge effort, time and cost investment or business experiment that took too much effort or didn't work.

In the meantime your competitors will have the guts to reject judgement and simply accept perception. They'll believe in presenting their power and they'll put their videos out because they have the confidence to do so and reap the benefits of their VSEO = better search rankings, and expanded audience that could have been yours...

We simply MUST step away from our emotional involvement judge at this stage, and allow comments both good and bad to be stated as preferences, not facts.

With our business babies it can be tough to step back from the emotions and personal feelings, but we can stop… breathe… physically step back from the spot where the emotions and feelings took control… breathe and think…

✓ IT IS **ONLY** YOUR VIEWER'S PERCEPTION

✓ IT IS NOT A JUDGEMENT **AGAINST** YOU

✓ ULTIMATELY **YOU ARE IN CONTROL OF ACCEPTING**, THANKING AND DOING WHAT YOU FEEL IS RIGHT FOR YOUR BUSINESS AND YOU

Reject the Rejector, buddy!

Sometimes the person who gives you all this negative feedback that may cause you to leap to judgement mode may be a highly trusted friend, a mentor, a loved one – someone who thinks that you can 'take it all'. They may or may not be 'trying to make you feel rejected' (no one can *make* you feel, remember – you always have a choice). They may feel that their opinion is better and more valid than yours, in their world. They may want to overprotect you from their negative fears for you or just project that on to you.

But remember – that is THEIR world.

You are in YOUR world.

You know what you set out to do and what you want your video to achieve.

You have done all of this work. You've bought and read my book *(thank you very much indeed!)*, and you've absorbed these confidence gifts for you. I truly love it when I can help, empower and inspire you. But even if you've read to here, you still might not like or believe or act on what I say, no matter how much I and my clients believe and trust in it ourselves – and I have to accept that… It's OK!

And when you've invested your heart and soul in your video and someone dismisses or sledges you in a totally derogatory, dismissive manner – STOP… BREATHE… STEP BACK… THINK…

In your perception…

(which may have led to an emotionally charged negative reaction from you…)

- X Have they done anything similar or are they taking their own lack of confidence out on you?
- X Are they projecting things they see, because that's how they feel about themselves?

Each piece of feedback needs to be put into context; maybe they were just in a bad mood the day they wrote those things down – you never know unless you politely, gently ask!

If they are simply in bullying mode, give inappropriate responses or you get comments like my video sledging troll, simply let it go. Something is going on in their world that is causing them to lash out; if you have to feel, feel sorry for them, rather than for yourself.

Simply say thank you, smile and choose to reject what they say!

There is nothing quite so quietly rudeness shaming than responding with a thank you and a smile!

If it is someone you know, next time don't ask this person for feedback again.

If they ask you why, you simply say:

"…while your comments may have been valid and appreciated last time, they did knock my confidence a little, so I've chosen to trust my own instincts this time. I really don't want to waste your time, but thank you very much for your kind offer!"… something along those lines ☺

Or tell them you don't need it, thank you – you know exactly what you're looking for now!

Where does your confidence come from?

Chumbawumba may get knocked down and get back up again, but it came from Fred Astaire and Ginger Rogers singing in *Swing Time,* when things knock you right down, all you can do is…

> *"Pick yourself up, brush yourself off and start all over again!"*
> **Jerome Kern and Dorothy Fields**

Pick Up Pointers

1. No one can make you feel anything – only you do!
2. Only you can let someone else's opinion knock you down.
3. Only you get emotionally involved with what they say so far that you allow it to affect your confidence.
4. Only you know where your confidence comes from: in you!
5. Only you know how to build it back again when it droops.
6. Only you can stop, blow your nose, breathe, smile and stand for your OBE empowerment to let these comments wash over you and…
7. YOU CAN SIMPLY GET OVER IT!

Ah you #Supergreat #Flawsome #Superstar #VideoStar you!

POP the negative bubble!

Choose:

✓ Perception vs Judgement

✓ Opinion vs Fact

✓ Perspective vs Reality

Accept every person is entitled to their own opinion, objective and subjective, and they may be different from yours. That's life! Because of all manner of things from nature to nurture, social influences, education, learning ability, knowledge, skills... YOU just keep sight of:

"With the knowledge and skills that I have right now, I'm doing the best that I can."

And if they sledge any of your presenting skills, tell them to come buy my book to find out how hard you've worked to be better. This is pro-presenter level knowledge, so your skills WILL improve when you put the effort in! And there's always support at our Confidence on Camera Club!

Make Negativity Nice

When you've had a moment to release any negative thoughts negative feedback can bring on... you guessed it!

Pause... *breathe...* **smile... laugh... and** *breeeathe!*

Do something nice for you – you may realise that *some* of what they say may be pertinent and useful next time round.

It's that light bulb moment, M^3 connection and realisation that they *may be right*... WOW!

People do know you and do want to help, so it can be worth listening to their opinions even when it's hard to hear and often even harder to act on. You know we are our own worst enemies and can lash out ourselves at times too, so you need to make nice with the negativity folks!

Whenever negativity strikes, go back to your Confidence on Camera notes.

Or come back to the section that is relevant in this book, read it over and work out how you could do even better next time round.

Remember, if the feedback isn't exactly what you want, you are probably in judgement and rejection mode! If information is missed, film another video, but when your gut disagrees, and you're happy with your production values, USE THIS VIDEO ONLINE NOW!

THEN learn what you can do better next time.

Give me a call, do a reassessment – as a Fred and Ginger romantic, I'm here to help build that confidence back up and love to support you to get going, to pick yourself up and start all over again!

Accept the Power of Your Confidence

~~~~~~~~~~~~

FEEDBACK REALITY CHECK PLEASE:

**If you can't cope with perceived negative feedback,
you shouldn't be coping with the praise that comes to you either.**

Accept them both with grace and ease.

~~~~~~~~~~~~

We have all got other people to agree with our opinion, to do something for us at some point in our life and most of us do it every day: from getting someone to make us a cup of tea, to putting someone down through mental agility or physical bullying, to convincing people to trust and believe in our business proposal. We can use our confidence to build others and ourselves up, or we use it to knock them down. Recognise that and accept the power of your influence, then believe what you have to share via video IS worth sharing with the world, no matter what others may say.

Accept it – we were all born with confidence.

Most of us learned to smile and luckily found someone who wanted to nurture us.

Sadly, we may have just lost, forgotten or been misusing our confidence – withholding our success through F.E.A.R.

You CAN influence others to get what you want with confidence; it's how you share that confidence that counts.

STEP SIX

Sharing *with* **Confidence**
Review A&E

My I'MPACT Playlist for a Confident on Camera Me

So now make another I'M-PACT and choose to use it for the greater good and you can also find a special inspiration message for you online that I like to use at the front of my live one-day to three-day workshops – enjoy!

My Learning Stage Notes:

My Feedback Confidence I'MPACT + Playlist Mantra:

On receiving feedback I AM...

When receiving feedback I CAN...

To ask for feedback I WILL...

My negative to positive thoughts Playlist Coping Mantra:

Start positive before reviewing feedback – it's only an opinion and you're in control!

Now write your own Playlist Coping Mantras that will help you cope with negative feedback and allow you to turn it into ways to improve:

I will ask _____

I will accept _____

Choose to share with Confidence!

My mantra is a life-changer thanks to my #SuperChamp World Champ Shelley Taylor-Smith www.championmindset.com.au - #Legend! Whenever negative thoughts or worries appear I say out loud...

"Thank you for that thought and dismiss it."

Presenting You... Inspiration

Before I leave you accepting your confidence with clarity, ease and grace I would love you to please…

Today choose never to fear rejection…

Choose acceptance, to learn from failures, accept the things you cannot change, because they are beyond your control and focus and work on the things you can.

Reject rejectors.

Accept yourself.

Cry, scream, laugh, cry, breathe – notice what you want, what is good and know you have the power to choose to **be** and to change (or not!) what you **can** and that that **will** make you even better than what you see today.

Confidence is our own creation, just like our fear and we *can* influence others to take action with it whether we know it or not. Even someone who says they have NO confidence can still convince us – they just have, by convincing us they have none so we might feel sorry for them! Think about that!

Possibilities are only out there because somebody has the guts to dream them.

Make that someone you…

STEP SEVEN

Confidence *in* Production *and* Promotion

"Technology can be our best friend, and technology can also be the biggest party pooper of our lives."

Steven Speilberg

"Men have become the tools of their tools."

Henry David Thoreau

Technology is often what holds us back from getting involved with video production.

My research **'Top three fears about making video'** survey always results in:

1. Fear of the camera.
2. It's too expensive.
3. Don't know where to start and how to 'do' them…

And in that order too. We've shown these fears can be overcome with a bit of know-how, but there's still a lack of confidence over the techy lingo, the actual film and edit process, how that works and how to promote those videos online, so let's have a look at some stats from what should be your first point of upload – YouTube.

Videos are Viral!

OK – here are seven of my favourite YouTube quotes* as I write and *my thoughts…*

1. Over one billion users = vast video market!
2. Hundreds of hours of video are uploaded every minute = how much is business vs fun?

3. 60%+ of views come from outside home country = 75 lands, 61 languages = new markets.

4. Over half of YouTube views are on mobile devices = small screen editing!

5. Mobile revenue on YouTube is up over 100% y/y = mobile optimise website w video.

6. Advertisers using Google ad platforms are mostly SMEs = we can react fast i.e. LEAD!

7. Top YouTube creators were found to be more popular than mainstream celebrities among US teenagers = get your YouTube Channel now – screenagers are growing up!

*YouTube Stats webpage

Those are some pretty staggering stats when you think about it – they could overwhelm you or inspire you to make more of your YouTube Channel. Which will it be?

Most of the vlogging stars I've mentioned are under 40, but there are more and more Gen X-ers creating channels day by day and big business knows that YouTube and social media video ads are the way to go. But there are still a few misconceptions we need to clear up and decisions on whether to Go Pro or DIY; what gear you need to film; how you need to look on camera; set up a shoot; edit and then share it all online at the end… Phew! Loads more background info and industry lingo, so again, highlights are here with tons more details online. Please do forgive me for keeping sending you there, but otherwise this would be twice the length and I don't think you'd have got to this – the final act of production and promotion power!

STAGE 1: Dispelling some Video Myths

The Viral Video Myth

The main thing is – you never have to go too far out of your comfort zone with the text or try to be crazy, push whacky ideas or aim to make a 'Viral Video'.

No matter how many people talk about them, YOU CANNOT MAKE A VIRAL VIDEO!

Only viewers can make your video viral and how many unique views are considered to be 'viral' changes all the time. In the late 2010s it was one million views, but then big marketing companies said it's when they hit 100,000 views, because it suited their marketing recommendations to their clients! Others think a video is viral at 50,000 views. And YouTube, Facebook and Twitter all have different ways of measuring what a 'view' actually is. So never get too hung up on them.

It's How Long Viewers Watch that counts!

It's far more important to check and see how much of your videos people are actually watching. You can either post and ask for feedback or simply check your YouTube/Vimeo/video viewing stats to see how long viewers watch and when they click off. YouTube say 30% retention after 30 seconds is considered good by them and this is a great retention-tracking tool.

If most of your viewers are stopping after 10 seconds (10") of a one minute (1') video, then you're going to need to look at why. What's happening? Is your visual Intro too long? Do you not get to the point fast enough? That video isn't working for you.

It could mean a simple edit to take something out and you can have that clip back up online, successfully finding full view viewers in no time.

Klout Counts with Sharing

You *can* influence how many views you get on YouTube and Facebook via proper Video SEO (VSEO) and paid ads, but *only* other people can make it viral for you. It's all word of mouth recommendations and social media sharing that determines how much clout and influence your video has.

As my good buddies Terry Brock and Gina Carr would advise – **Klout Matters!** It's your personal social media signal of success score, how much people are interacting with you and what you do. So keep it simple and make your video and VSEO links really easy to share – name them on a theme, use your name if need to boost business awareness, use W?s in the title: YouTube loves that!

Top Terry and Gina link sharing tip was use Bitly.com to shorten and personalise any long URL links. Very useful and free to start.

Quick Kiss 'n' Tell Video Styles

So here's my kiss and tell study of video production style from the early 2010s.

Outside the USA, people were slow to catch on, but business videos started to become a bit more popular by 2013. And also a bit formulaic. Most execs and SMEs followed the *'Tell 'em, Tell 'em, Tell 'em'* advertising pattern in the rush to get into video and webinars. Long-form videos still fall into that trap – hence the interest in Virtual Meeting podcasts, interviews and collaborative videos. Short 'How to…' videos often don't tell you what you actually need to do, but are useful to find out that you need to 'buy the series' to get more info – great marketing ploy eh? No, seriously DO give some specific answers if doing a 'How to' video!

The early videos were expensive as not many quality low-cost options were available.

But they spawned the beginning of fresh young business people making their own hugely successful DIY and PIY videos. The tech savvy millenials, Gen Z and the screenage generation started the online video revolution and the Gen X 'oldies' took a while to catch up! And they may not have had such viewer success with ROI because their focus was on production style and selling, not presenter style and viewer service.

Also not many serious business people wanted to show their flaws on camera, so many businesses looked for alternatives to a PTC video with a presenter to still 'do video, but more creative'! Animations, quick draws and specially designed screen shots were hot in 2014. Creative and fun, but still expensive. Video animations became cheaper with stock DIY apps in 2014/15, but are still time-consuming and the DIY VO stories still aren't that well done!

As smartphone cameras started to be good enough quality for online, GoPro images appeared all over TV. Great simple video creation apps became readily available (see page 209) and suddenly snappy PTCs, quick and easy social media videos started to really boom.

You know that when politicians start trying to use social media video too…

Did that work for you? Did you get on board? Did it work for you then?

SMEs started to realise they didn't have to spend a fortune and could react far quicker than big business to the trend. Google brought out Hang Outs on Air (GHOAs) and everyone started Skyping for meetings, rather than the previously corporate-price-range-restrictive Video Conferencing (VC). Everyone started promoting and pitching via video, offering free webinars and one-minute experts and TEDx talks became the video length of choice.

So on screen, all these recordings may look and sound vastly better than early DIY clips, but how many still suffer from poor simple set-up, disconnected content and presenter performance?

Low-cost in-house DIY or PIY videos still take time and energy to make.

And if you're going to make video an ongoing marketing tool, surely they need and deserve this early effort to get better? That's *why* this book is here, to help you be the face that drives ROI and boost business, increase social media interaction or awareness, by presenting your service with the power of the real, Confident, Credible, Charismatic, Connected you on screen.

You need to conquer all the Video Presenter Steps that will enable and empower your video confidence and ROI, whether you choose to webinar or animate with VO, DIY + PIY or PIY + Go Pro *(that's go Professional with your Production, not the GoPro Hero camera. Though they are a **must** for action videos, travel companies and any wide angle event shots you want to make. Not great for DIY PTCs, but as a scuba diver – they're the bomb!).*

What Helps Videos WOW?

Videos can be produced in so many different formats: as animations, quick-draw sketches, or photo series with VOs, PowerPoint slide shows or Prezzi, recordings of Skype calls or GHOAs – all very creative. But if you don't have the time or budget to do those then the quickest video you can make is *still* your PTC face on film, telling us about what you offer/want to help us with in a natural and real connected way.

And when you get practised at creating a script with a basic structure that you can repeat, adapt, flex to suit different needs, you will find you can easily create an interesting, impromptu video that pays back for you, whether financially, with new client reach or with customer loyalty, at any time you need.

A lot of people think that the number one way to 'WOW!' is through editing.

Personally, I think that is often doing your viewers a disservice or even insulting their intelligence! Come on – you've watched your presenters – can we *really* not focus on one person talking for 30-60 seconds? Are we really so fickle and lacking in concentration that we need a constant stream of visual stimulus to hold our interest? If they are likeable, no!

I still watch presenters talking for longer than that and I still enjoy it and learn! And actually, if someone is trying to sell me themselves or their service as their business online, I'm less likely to trust them if they can't talk to me for more than 10 seconds at a time and have to hide behind lots of whizz-bang flashy images!

Now, I'm not knocking editing – I know it is an amazing tool and am very thankful it has saved my bacon on TV many a time when I stuffed up far too much to leave it in. A good editor and good editing *can* make or break a video and it is a professional skill that takes years to learn. So what you need to decide again is: **what is your No. 1 Production Value**?

It's Got to be You!

If you want lots of shots, special effects, loads of images, fast changes, visual variety to create an interesting story from your script, that's great, go for it. OR you can believe you and your script and message stand up well enough to create an impact with you simply telling it.

What I'm getting at is that in my Confidence on Camera World YOU are *always* your most valuable asset and production value.

And when your message is strong enough, the visual extras can even become a distraction themselves. When you present, you can enable us to like you and want to watch you. Then just like our favourite TV presenters, we're happy watching just you. We enjoy the journey you take us on, the experience of watching you in your world and the stories you share with us and gems you impart are our bonus learning.

Now, I do know plenty of people want to know about the 'flashy' style of vids too! So here's my pro-Pro take on this!

STAGE 2: Confidence in Production Planning – Go Pro or No?

You now know what you need to do to mentally and physically prepare for your video production and you are in control of that. You know you want to present it yourself – PIY.

But what about some of those things that, unless you DIY produce your own videos, may be beyond your control?

That starts with the choice of *Go Pro or no*?

Why Go Pro?

I'm not a professional film maker, but my time on shoots with professional TV production crews, video crews, expert coaches, producers, editors, interns, camera and lighting experts, and from both making and teaching how to DIY HD quality video, has taught me more than just a few production basics.

To help you save time and money when making this decision, you need to be armed with some of the perceptions, judgements and expectations to expect… because the ONLY person who can make this choice, with confidence, is you.

How the Pros can help

You *can* easily learn to film PTCs in one take and top and tail **'Trim'** edit yourself with basic editing tools or in YouTube. But when you want more, my advice if you know nothing about editing is to Go Pro. You can waste hours seeing what works (or days when learning!) when a pro instinctively knows as they have done so many times before.

A pro video producer and editor can:

1. Provide filming gear, storyboard, filming skills – they fit the storyboard edit as they film and know what shots and best framing, what 'extra background' B-roll shots to film to make a better 'montage' in edit to create the complete video story, etc.

2. Give you ideas of what shots to use, help you add all the extra images, captions, titles, text, logos, Intro and Outro/End slides. Some even design visual graphics for you.

3. Source and add copyright-free music or buy it for you, and edit in time to that music.

4. Edit out any 'hiccups' with cutaway B-roll – changing the visual on screen to cover where you didn't look so confident, while keeping your original audio.

5. Help you save or recycle footage you may have thrown and record a new VO.

6. Spot the things you visually miss – most editors are visual, attention to detail people.

7. Save you time and effort – editing can be painstakingly slow.

Go Pro!

As I've been saying all along, if you have the production budget to hire a professional camera crew and editor, you **will** get a better quality look and feel for your video than DIY when you first start out. The pros also take away concerns of how to frame the shot, best angles, lighting, sound and how to mix that all together to create a fantastic looking montage.

But do they know how to get you producing the best you on film?

They are usually selling you their services for a specific time. And because post-production editing is a highly time-intensive process, they have to get through the production filming asap or they'll blow your budget! Often they don't know you or have time or focus to help you during filming. You need to know what you are doing as the presenter – hence me writing this book for you! Never get ripped off – know what you're doing from the start – plan and price it all.

How Can the Pros Help YOU? A&E

Use my pro-Pros and Cons sheet to help you decide: with the kind of video you want, is it best to Go Pro or DIY?

GO PRO VIDEO? The Pros + Cons Playlist

PLAN…

✔ What video style? What is it for?

✔ Pros and Cons for hiring a Pro Production team?

✔ What will you still need to provide/do? Assess how much time you still need?

My Video Style:	PRO Pros:	PRO Cons:	I will need to Do:
1. E.g. Montage for company promo	Save me time, they have gear, can do green screen…	Expensive, disruptive…	Plan, script, storyboard, shoot day, edit form, visuals, music, etc.
2. E.g. Testimonial interview	May be able to get better client reaction without me	Client might prefer less formal/more private?	Invite + liaise w client, check contact info they want to use?

So that's the 'Pro or No?' Montage moment, now back to your scriptwriting…

Make a Montage?

If you want more 'flash' you may have to go for a **Full Montage** or **Mini-Montage** video – this has a number of edits with different images to set the scene. Montage videos take skill, proper planning and deserve pro help. But time and costs will increase exponentially. They are tricky to DIY unless you know what you are doing.

Or Simple PTC?

Piece to Camera – PTCs help you connect as you talk directly to the viewer.

✓ You can film with a simple but effective **one-shot** *(just you on screen)* with **Top & Tail edit** *(trim the start and end only)*.

✓ Or you can film a one-shot **wide** *(you at a distance)* and then cut to a **close-up zoom** in shot – all done in your editing software.

✓ You may just choose different shots and settings for interest – in the office, outside on **OB** *(TV talk for an Outside Broadcast i.e. anything you film out of an actual studio or your office)*.

Or you may, like Marie Forleo online, become known for your version of her red brick wall backdrop. Whatever and wherever the lighting and sound work best for you.

So do you really need to invest in a montage video?

James Wedmore, US video marketing megastar, advises you ought to have five key videos on your website – welcome, a stats, success story, Q&A, tutorial.

James also advocates DIY production!

You've already picked out the top video styles for your plan.

Did they match his common sense video marketing advice?

Make sure You're in Control, but Let What You Can't Go!

You now know what you need to do to mentally and physically prepare for your video production and you are in control of that.

That usually starts with the choice of do you Go Pro or do you DIY?

But what about some things that are beyond your control?

A pro team will have to make artistic decisions without you – so once you have planned and clarified *exactly* what you want to produce, trust the process, trust them and let it go.

This info will help you understand the Pro Production process…

The Pro Production Process

When you opt to Go Pro with a production house you need to understand the production process so you can have an influence on all aspects of the production – *before the editing starts!*

It's broken down into three key areas:

The Video Process = Pre-production + Production + Post-Production

or

Pre + Production + Post for short

Some people see those three steps and wonder…

'It's not much work in a three-step process, so why is it so expensive to create an online video?'

Because there are actually *loads* of different steps and stages that have to happen in a specific sequence to plan, create and produce your video!

OK, there's also a lot of confusing repetition to keep it all in-house within 'the biz' – i.e. show business, TV and film jargon lingo. But the work entailed is a simple yet very detailed plan, so indulge and go online for full clarity of exactly what each step entails – Going Pro, you need to know…

The Pro Production Process

1. PRE-PRODUCTION is planning the whole process.

2. PRODUCTION is everything DURING filming.

3. POST-PRODUCTION is everything after the shoot – from downloads, raw footage processing and importing; to reviewing, editing, timing, sharing, you reviewing; rerecording, final edits and adding features from visuals to music; then rendering, saving, converting, uploading, VSEO and analytics if you want!

You Need to Stay Pro too…

Do remember:

In Pre – always be clear on what you want. Never waste a pro team's time by making them guess – they'll find a way to make you pay later!

In Production – when you are presenting and filming on your shoot day – come prepared with all you need, wardrobe, make-up, scripts, props etc. Rehearse what you need and want to do the week before.

Your camera person doesn't know you or necessarily know how to get the best from you on the day – so ultimately your performance level is up to you. That is why clients come to me to get coached *before* a pro-video shoot or superspecial clients and top-level production partners take me with them for a confidence boost or to enable changes on the fly when things don't work out as expected. I look after you, 'the talent', while the crew sort the nitty-gritty of the shoot.

In Post – leave them to get on with it! Agree a deadline for first edit + re-edits + final video upload and how you will view/share/post the video. They are unlikely to know about hosting, but they should know about YouTube and Vimeo.

Check with your web team about hosting and confirm what format you need to see your video. Mac and PC will be different – if they edit on Mac, you want to be able to see it on PC.

What Format Works?

Your pro editor can also advise on what format to save the final clip –AVCHD, HTML5, .mp4, .mp3 or .wmv are most common. Note that .mov is the Quicktime version and if you don't have the software you will not be able to play them. Any video format MUST be mobile compatible!

If saving in your own editing software yourself, you can usually 'save as a YouTube' or Vimeo version either:

SD = Standard Definition lower resolution – good for social media or

HD = High Definition like on TV – good for business promos.
These are formatted for faster upload to YouTube and Vimeo.

Note: any time you convert the video format from the **RAW footage** *(the original clips direct from your camera)* it will lose some quality, so **always** edit from the original footage if you can, rather than the new formatted version.

~~~~~~~~~~

Pro = Time = Quality = Investment

Save yourself some angst – never think of videos as a cost…
Videos are an investment in your brand awareness and reach.

~~~~~~~~~~

Pro Dos for You:

1. **Save** yourself **time** by going pro – but let go of artistic control.

2. **Get involved** in the Pre + Production – save money with very clear outcome expectations.

3. **Step back** once you've done the shoot – if you start changing your mind during the Post-Production process, you might as well start all over again!

4. **Be branding prepared** – with low-cost production teams, have everything ready for them at the start: your additional visuals, logos, slides, your captions, music, VSEO etc.

5. **Track** how they are doing on **budget** plan before asking for re-edit changes – then they have little excuse to go over time and over budget, unless you start changing your mind!

6. **Make confident choices** and accept what you choose.

7. Check if the project has any success tracking **follow up...**

Post-Production Follow-Up

Some production projects do include VSEO, online analytics, effectiveness tracking and re-edits down the line, so ask about these. They are companies you take on retainer projects to produce videos as an ongoing process as you cannot track VSEO otherwise.

Good teams will be able to set up your properly branded YouTube Channel, create playlists and create copy for your VSEO – if they do not know the YouTube/Google VSEO advice, coming for you in a bit, or can't show you brand aware client copy on YouTube, don't use them!

Other Things to Know to Help Go Pro

You need to find out if a production team offers the production service you want, with people you want to work with and that you'll get the help you need across all areas of the production.

You should and must ask for a Pre- Pre-production planning meeting to build the trust. I offer a complimentary Discovery Meeting or call, and live free webinars for my training and online courses, so you can *know* you want to work one-to-one with me. And if you don't that's fine! I need to feel I can empower, help you and inspire you to get the results you want, and if it's not right I can choose not to work with you too. My attitude to business relationships is co-preneurial – we need to like each other to start with. Because I know the work you need to put in, the challenges I'll have to throw up and the potential pitfalls you can blame me for when we hit the roadblocks that can pop up in our way.

When we like each other we collaborate, we are co-preneurs for you and we stay positive results focused – we'll spurn the negative nay-sayers, get through it to succeed and create videos you love to do!

See – once a drama queen always one! But you do know exactly what I mean…

So back to those Production Pros…

Always Ask Questions

Do your research, ask the right questions and see what help you'll be offered before committing. Ask for a project price rather than a by-the-hour cost if you can. You can spend anywhere from £/€/$ 500-50,000 to get one, one minute, pro-produced promo video all dependent on what you want. If you're not happy with the final edit, you need to know that the re-edit is included in the cost. You also need to know what follow up post-production is included.

Make sure you can get hold of the raw footage too. You may want to re-edit it much later, so unless you have 100% faith your production team are collaborating with your best interests first, that they won't have deleted it after three months, that they will give it to you later, never be held to ransom over your own footage – ask for your raw footage as a prerequisite. You have paid for it, so you ought to get access but often you won't.

Pro vs DIY Judgement vs Perception = What Cost to You?

Some people think DIY video can ruin your reputation and *all* videos ought to be professionally made – judgement call! It depends what your video is for, how you use it and how much effort you are willing to put in to make it look and sound as good as your M³ I'mPact-ful presenting.

Whichever you choose, 'claim your stage', be confident, on the ball and going for it with that 30% extra energy right from the start.

Make Going Pro Have the Impact You Want too!

So when you prefer leaving filming and editing to the experts – brilliant, it's so easy to outsource these days. Just make sure you've put your budget aside, you know exactly what you want and recognise this may be a limited option for you. You really DO need to plan your video production process and production time extremely well to get the most out of your pro-production team.

STAGE 3: Pre-Production DIY – Get Set, Get Gear, Get Video Tooled!

Remember pre-production is everything you need to plan and prepare prior to your video shoot. With your pro team they will do a lot for you, but there are still some things here you will need to take care of.

If you are going DIY, you will need to plan, provide and check it all yourself!

Why Go DIY?

When you choose DIY with your smartphone or own camera, keep it simple and pay attention to the details. With a simple set-up PTC in the appropriate spot, with natural lighting and a decent microphone, you can make a big enough impact to overcome other *perceived* possibly snobby pro-production values.

DIY You Can:

1. Create a video in a day – KISS it with your simple, effective, impactful PTC with confident process planning and organisation.

2. Get creative with your team who know you – get someone to help you when you can, bouncing ideas, decide the vision at the start to save hours at the end.

3. Film in your chosen environment – choose your backdrop and where, when and how to shoot in a quality that you and viewers are happy to watch.

4. Ensure all production aspects are congruent with your message and branding.

5. Access free web production and how to video info – or use our team/kids to learn!

6. Build your mini or portable studio with little but quality equipment – need to see you and hear you, so make sure the production quality doesn't distract!

7. React immediately! Film videos at events, record on-the-spot interviews and post-training buzzy testimonials that sell more courses – and get them up online and sharing across social media (SM) that day or even before the event has ended. How cool is that?!

No Budget = NO Excuse DIY!

The style and quality of video you want is totally up to you and what you can afford. However, no budget is no excuse not to do video. If you have a smartphone you have a mini-studio already and free apps can enable you to produce quality content when you've recorded the raw footage well. As long as we can see and hear you and your message without having to work too hard, we will forgive a slightly amateur shot, but why not invest in a tripod to make sure it's steady too?

DIY Production Distractions

Be *Flawsome* with your DIY production too.

After your equipment check, notice if it's windy/noisy/dark/too bright/shaky.

Either move where you are, or if it's an event or OB video with a clear reason for the set-up, film it but briefly draw attention to the possible production distraction by saying somewhere in the clip that you are: *"action filming"* / *"set it up that way"* / *"are grabbing an opportunity you don't want viewers to miss!"* etc., with *(you guessed it!)* CONFIDENCE in your DIY style!

DIY Tools to Use

Technology is changing SO fast and fantastic new DIY video tools come on the market all the time. DIY gear gets better and easier to use, so I wanted to share a few tools I love – I suppose their success will be apparent if they're still around when you read this!

I've learned from my pro advisors how to use the gear effectively, filming showreels and presentations both in studio and out. You only learn from practice, so it can be trial and error to find what suits you. Bad buys may be inevitable, but hopefully my years of stuffing up with cameras, lighting and sound can help you avoid total disasters.

Many thanks to all my pro helpers, you know who you are!

Get Set, Get Gear – Your Complete DIY Video Studio

A full list of recommendations, helpful links and where you can buy DIY gear online are all available by getting in touch with me or joining the Club.

Here are the headlines with a few of my #superfavouritevideotools.

You can set up a portable studio with the few key items, but my key tip is:

Always check any new gear is compatible with all the other gear and test microphones, cables etc. if you can.

You'll save a lot I've spent to find out it *doesn't* actually work with an iPhone or an extender jack. Because of this I'm now a bit stuck as an iPhone and Sony girl!

Cameras

Always bear in mind that the pros will have the best camera equipment and you get what you pay for – it may be obvious, but we all look for ways to cheat. With picture quality, it counts!

Unless your market is a country where internet speeds are superslow, go for a camera with:

1. Decent zoom lens with steady shot – higher pixels = higher resolution.
2. HDMI (High Definition Multimedia Interface i.e. what you want!)
   + Full HD 1920x1080p (.ppt 16:9 slide side ratio) or 1440x1080p widescreen recording.
3. Stereo sound with built-in microphone + external microphone jack = a must.
4. Standard 3.5mm 1/8" external headphone jack.
5. AVCHD (Sony and Panasonic), .AVI or .MOV (Apple) video format for matching to editing software – avoid .FLV Flash format, as they won't play on iOS.
6. Sturdy but lightweight if you're out and about.
7. A decent case to protect your gear – easy to carry with hands full + shockproof/ waterproof are sensible or a solid aluminium box if going all pro-reporter style.

What camera you use is personal preference and budget.

Quality cameras I've used or want are usually based around my Sony and iPhones for business videos, but I do covet the pro Blackmagic Pocket Cinema camera range! For ease, stick to your quality smartphone and ALWAYS download and backup your video footage on an external drive on shoot day to keep it safe.

I am avoiding DSRL cameras as feel they are for the pros – you need to invest time in learning how to use and edit with them. Handycams are easier to use and edit.

Bonus Tips here:

ALWAYS take an extension cable out filming – learned the hard way, plugging in from the start can save your day!

Ensure the battery is removable/rechargeable when you're out shooting for a few hours.

WebCams

If you're mostly filming webinars or virtual meetings, invest in an HD webcam you can set up on a tripod. I use my iPhone now for Skype and GHOAs and a Microsoft LifeCam with a tripod mount, so I can set them up where I want, with the backdrop I want.

If you must use your laptop, see the set up tips on page 262 and…

A Sit up straight and tidy up.

A **STOP LOOKING DOWN AT YOUR LAPTOP CAMERA – it looks terrible!**

A Raise it up so the camera is eye-level or higher and always test the image to check:

1. Sound quality – this must be clear (see desk mics).
2. Lighting – face the window, never have it behind you.
3. Backdrop – nothing sticking out of your head or a mess!

Tripods

You need a tripod! You do get what you pay for, but here are the key tips:

1. **Lightweight, aluminium 60 inch** tripod is standard –thick, retractable legs + spirit level + removable plate + carry bag are a good investment.
2. **Little desk tripods suck!** – they fall over with a phone on, so get a proper aluminium mini-tripod with removable plate – travel size works.

3. A tripod **Dolly** – tripod sits in it to wheel around and increase the tripod height.
4. **Articulating Magic Arm and Superclamp** – clamps on to the tripod or a mic stand or pole to hold my Kick light.
5. **Retractable Smartphone Tripod Mount** – low-cost smartphone holder + tripod mount that grips firmly on to your smartphone in landscape setting for filming and fits most brands except the larger phones.
6. **Wifi remote shutter** – record and stop recording without touching the phone. DO check they work for video and not just for the camera shutter.
7. **Monopod or 'Selfie-stick'** – avoid the skinny aluminium ones, get a sturdy solid one.

A few of my favourite brands are Hama.com, Manfrotto.com, Joby.com

Bonus Tips if Shooting Hand-Held

If you have to hold your camera to shoot, hold it firmly in the palm of one hand and steady your wrist or elbow with the other.

Tuck your elbows as tight as you can into your sides and turn your whole body to pan across for moving shots, instead of just your hands and arms.

If you can, lean your hands/arms against a wall, a table, a post or something sturdy to steady the camera – it really does make a huge difference.

For **smartphones** hold the phone in landscape to avoid black lines down the side of the portrait image and use both hands, firm on either end.

7 Steps to Master your Selfie-Stick

If you are filming with a **selfie-stick** with one hand:

1. Ideally only extend it approximately one metre from you *(or length of your SmarLav+ cable)* – enough for chest up one-shots – or waist up two/three-person interviews.

2. Tuck the stick under your elbow, firm along your forearm, with the end fixed into your side – you need to be able to breathe without moving it, so practise.

3. Never hold the stick out by the end – it will shake too much.

4. Hold the camera up and look up to it, with a slight angle to your face/upper body.

5. Make sure light is on your face, not behind you!

6. Turn your whole body, not your arm if you move – keep it tucked in tight.

7. Have a laugh with them – they're great fun and make you more approachable!

Microphones

Microphone = Mic musts are:

1. Sound is your number one concern after your presenting power – always check it!

2. Check you can plug a mic into your camera and avoid a camera you can't.

3. Always check mic connections and do a sound check and listen back before recording.

4. If using external mics using batteries, carry spares and check them regularly.

5. If the location makes it tricky to get good sound, mention it and tell us why it's relevant.

6. If your video is on 'how communication is difficult in this busy world we live in' it makes sense to film it on a busy road or street or at a noisy event – but speak up on purpose and ask any guests to do the same!

7. AND AVOID MY HUBBY'S MISTAKE! If you leave the studio/room with your mic on (e.g. for a toilet break and vocal warm-up) turn the mic to OFF or MUTE, otherwise everyone in the production room will hear exactly what you're up to...!!!

Even microphones have their own complex lingo, but here are some basic tips.

Mic Bonus Tips:

1. A lapel mic = LAV mic = lavelier mic – it clips on to your clothes.
2. Most plug into a receiver pack, but some can plug direct into your smartphone or camera, like the Røde smartLav+
3. Best brands: Sennheiser and Shure.
4. Hama do a 6m cable lapel mic, so you don't need a receiver.
5. A desk mic is a must for webinars and virtual meetings – the Blue Yeti is my baby.
6. Handheld mics are only for on stage or interviews – avoid if possible or learn how to use.
7. Wifi mics allow you to film from up to 30m away – my Sony EC4 has lapel mic plug in, or you can use it as a hand-held mic for an interview. Or leave it on the desk for sit-down chats or presenting.

Wearable Mic Musts – lapel + wifi:

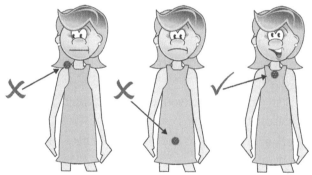

1. Always be aware of your microphone, wear clothes that will not interfere with scratchy sounds or static. Are your clothes suitable to attach a microphone to?
2. Keep hands away from your chest near your microphone as noises will be picked up.
3. Be aware that you are wearing a very sensitive piece of equipment and while you do need to project, you do not need to shout – sound technicians or you will check your mic levels at the start of the shoot.

Look for easy-to-use, plug and play mics that you can use across a variety of your devices – desk top, laptop, tablet, smartphone, camera – some mics do work across all tools. Research what's on the market at the time you read this. Obviously the better the quality, the higher the cost.

Lighting

Natural daylight on your face is always preferable and looks more natural than any lighting in studio can, but avoid bright sunlight direct on your face OB.

Film by a window – test light is on your face by turning the camera around.

Handheld Lights:

A handheld dimmable LED light with three colour filters is on Amazon for less than £20.

No. 1 BUY – the Kick light crowd-funded by Riftlabs.com – or buy direct from me, I love them so much I now stock them from Norway! Size of a smartphone, lightweight, USB rechargeable pocket size pro lighting system, it also works as some iPhones' tripod holder.

In Studio:

Softbox lighting set – worth investing in if you are setting up a studio to film DIY regularly. In studio a three-point lighting system is ideal = two side lights + one backdrop light to prevent shadows behind you.

Halogen builders' lights are the cheap alternative = low cost studio!

I'll go a bit more into how to set up the lights in the Production section.

FREE/LOW COST EDITING APPS

iPhone Video Apps – I use

Videolicious.com – turns photos into moving videos, with own VO + copyright-free music in App. Free = 10 pics + direct YT / FB / mail upload or save to camera.

YouTube Capture – owned by YouTube enables the fastest uploads direct to YT. Film different scene by scene, cam mix PTCs + B-roll w VO, trim + edit + VSEO in App for live Public YT upload.

Intro Designer – pre-designed movie style Intro/Outro animations, you simply change the text.

Android Video Apps – use in training

WeVideo.com – film, edit + upload quick and easy on the go.

VideoEditor: All in One – photos to video + video w VO + PTCs + edit and process in Cloud.

Most of these apps are free and so easy – if I can learn to use them, so can you!

Or ask the closest smartphone holding screenager what's best right now and get them to show you/do it for you ☺

Portable Studio I couldn't do without...

1. My iPhone.
2. Compatible microphone.
3. The Kick portable LED light.
4. Monopod/travel tripod.
5. 1TB external hard drive to back it all up in case of laptop loss or theft (*yes that happened to me in Venice, with no back up of work = grrrr*).

STAGE 4: *Looking Good on Screen*
Production Planning – Wardrobe

Aka what you wear, so it doesn't wear you!

Appearance and grooming give the first, impression viewers have of you – it's what they'll look at to make immediate judgement before you've even opened your mouth.

How you dress can influence initial reaction right from the first still thumbnail screen shot of you on YouTube or Vimeo. If they like the look of you, they'll click and watch. If you don't look so great, or appropriate, they won't. First impressions affect us even faster via video.

Make sure your clothes are CONGRUENT TO YOUR MESSAGE!

I really can't reiterate this enough. You *can* wear almost anything on camera if it is part of the story. But make sure what you wear is not a distraction in itself – your style choice should enhance your look rather than distract the viewer.

Remember, it's not a fashion show – appear well groomed, bother about your look and dress appropriately for a congruent style.

Theatre shows have whole wardrobe departments to make the clothes match the part, so make an effort to match the mood/image/value/net worth/colour meaning/perception you want. It doesn't have to be designer all the way – a well-placed high street necklace or jacket pocket square can lift a low-cost outfit to stylish glamour in a flash. If you're promoting something of high value, you need to dress expensive looking. Not saying it has to be expensive – simply fit well and look fantastic!

Experience, research and training TV presenters have taught me what clothes and colours work on camera, but I've also had image and subliminal colour meaning coaching from professionals myself. So these are the best wardrobe tips to share with you here to make sure you make the most of your look and look confident on camera.

You'll *feel* more confident with this knowledge too and it's relevant for any presenting platform and especially relevant when you're invited to go on TV – that's Sunday best, be bright, be bold, but know what suits you and will help you stand out from the crowd.

Wardrobe Planning

Plan your wardrobe well in advance, dry clean or wash and iron clothes and always take options with you to a video shoot. Change outfits if you're filming more than one clip and ladies, change your jewellery too, unless you always wear the same thing.

Backgrounds

Research and check the background you will be filming against – contrast your wardrobe colours to stand out from it i.e. wear dark or bright against a pale wall and pale against a dark background etc.

Top to Toe in Shot

The shot you will use – long shot, mid shot, close-up, head shot – will determine what clothes you need to bring. Why bother with your high heels or best dress shoes if we're not going to see them? Many a TV presenter has sat behind the desk wearing shorts below the suit jacket and tie and we're none the wiser! But if you're unsure what to expect at a shoot, DO come prepared to show all of you, top to toe, including your shoes, which MUST be shiny and clean. If you are only doing waist-up shots, kick your shoes off if that makes you feel more grounded, comfortable and confident! And if you have a long day shoot, wear shoes you can comfortably stand around in all day. Do what works for you to feel the best you can.

Avoid Clangers

Many a wardrobe item can clang, knock tables or make distracting noises – so be aware of what and where you are wearing them and be ready to remove them e.g. wedding rings, bracelets, necklaces, watches near a mic. Also be aware physically of any potentially distracting habit that may arise from a wardrobe choice – do you have to keep flicking something over your shoulder? Do you keep playing with a bracelet, necklace, ring or watch because you are not used to it? Either practise wearing it if it 'makes' the outfit or change to something else.

Screen Test

Test things out on camera, especially if it is new.

Always try your outfit on and make sure you are 100% comfortable in it, can move easily and freely and that the material doesn't make any strange squeaking or rustling noises when you move. Test things out on camera, with sound recording.

You are investing time and money in your video shoot, you've planned it meticulously, you've prepared yourself mentally so *make an effort* with planning your wardrobe for goodness sake, don't leave it until five minutes before! You could ruin it for yourself through an unwitting scruffy or unkempt image, so pay attention to details when you think of what to wear, your make-up, accessories and hair. Groom yourself as a VIP… AND TEST THINGS OUT ON CAMERA!!

Your Top to Toe Grooming Tips for VIP PTCs!

Top to toe tips will help at your shoots, interviews, auditions, TV appearances – actually any time you present.

Top 7 Wardrobe MUSTs:

1. ALWAYS be clean, have clean hands and nails.
2. Brush, comb and spray your hair off your face/away from your eyes – even the gents.
3. Take a mirror to check your look and ensure no food in your teeth!!!!
4. Use face powder if you are shiny, especially on a balding head ☺
5. Press or iron tops and jackets and make sure they're straight/neat/tidy on camera.
6. Hide the mic cable under your clothes – be ready to thread it up the back of a dress…
7. No marks on your clothing that would be visible on camera – if that top has a stain on it, even if it's your favourite, most confidence-inspiring look, WEAR SOMETHING ELSE!

Confident Clothes on Camera – colours, materials & styles that work
Colours

Colours change on camera – darks go darker, brights go brighter; reds can look orange under studio lights and certain pinks go a brighter scarlet red; navy and chocolate can look almost black; white is too bright. Colours also have subliminal meaning, so check online for that or to see if your company colours would work on camera as a uniform.

Most people equate business and work with dark sombre colours, which can actually come across as simply sad on camera. Spring and summer colours lift the mood on camera, too much dark winter colour can drop the mood like a stone.

Rule of thumb – if your skin is dark, stay away from too dark; if it's pale, stay away from too pale. Never wear the same colour on camera as your skin tone or the backdrop behind you – aim to stand out!

What Colours Work for You on Camera?

If you're not sure what colours suit you, go see an image consultant, style or colour specialist. Otherwise there are specific colouring tips online.

These are not definitive, so please do test any colour you want and see how you look on camera under studio lights and outside, as the lighting set-up will affect how they appear on camera.

Gents – the same colour choices work for you too. It depends on the look and feel you're after and your level of confidence for wearing colour! There are specific tips for men online too on your own wardrobe docs to download for your workbook.

Remember, match your M³ mood and image you want for your video – this can be a regular uniform, or a different look every time. If you've ever seen me online, you may have noticed I'm often in orange – the emotional balance colour ☺

7 Steps to Colour on Camera
1. Take clothing colour options – always take alternatives to a shoot so you stand out.
2. Change if you're the same colour as the background – or your host on TV!
3. Be a bit adventurous – the colour may perfectly match the mood you want to portray.
4. You can match/contrast the colours you wear with your company colours.
5. Busy patterns can 'strobe' or flare the camera when the lens can't focus properly.
6. Go bold with one main colour rather than a mixture.
7. Solid colours are smart, refined and defined – think of the congruent style you want to portray, e.g.
   - ✓ **Confident mood** = stronger colours + patterns
   - ✓ **Softer mood** = paler colours, little pattern
   - ✓ **Natural** = nature shades + soft patterns
   - ✓ **Fun** = 'brights', metallic, patterns

It's Black and White

Black – news flash! It's a myth that all black is more slimming on camera – it can make you appear dour, dull, potentially lifeless and really just not very approachable!

White flares the camera lens, especially under studio lights – we look at your white shirt not your face. Go cream if you must.

Always avoid white shirt under black jacket with solid, blood red tie or accessories on screen. This is a nature *Danger!* colour combo.

Materials

Smooth Quality

Iron clothes and look smooth and unruffled – that will be the impression you give off.

Think quality materials and styles…

1. **Natural materials** are best – cottons, wools, soft flowing fibres, cashmeres, tweeds – avoid material that rustles or scratches as this can interfere with the sound.
2. **Suits** suit the formal style, softer materials and casual tops your softer side. Ladies: add feminine touches please – we have no need to dress like a man to impress!
3. **Sports and leisure** wear must be crisp, fresh and ideally new, not faded.

---

7 WARDROBE ITEMS TO ALWAYS AVOID

1. New clothes you've never worn before – you don't know how they'll move or look on camera.
2. Tight clothes that restrict you or your breathing.
3. Floaty materials on a windy OB day that might blow up and expose you! Other times they're great.
4. Sheer materials without a chemise or vest top under.
5. Shiny reflective materials or high sheen – will flare lights.
6. Tight or busy patterns, especially on ties, gents – keep them smart and clean.
7. Houndstooth or tight checks and tight stripes – these all flare or strobe the camera lens.

These things don't work on camera and can be as much of a distraction as any body movement with Visual Impact.

Accessories

Jewellery – gold, silver or chunky bright jewellery on ears and necks works on camera.

Remove all watches and bangles if sitting at a table or desk – any tap is amplified by the microphone and can ruin a great take.

Ladies – bring a selection to filming and see what fits.

✓ Always dress your ears, but avoid OTT, large spangly or dangly earrings which will distract as you move your head. Likewise very delicate jewellery if you want to portray strength and confidence. Chunky necklaces can work, but make sure the mic is not near them.

✓ Always remove bangles, they will jangle and click as you move.

Gents – only wear jewellery if it is your image or is part of you.

✓ Always remove anything from your pockets that could jangle!

BONUS STYLING DOs:

Look at what good presenters wear on TV – if you think you have no sense of style, simply think congruent, simple, clear-cut and clean. Again, make your wardrobe congruent.

If you are conscious of a stomach and feel you want to hold your tummy in, wear a jacket or top that floats over your stomach. You MUST be able to breathe naturally and with confidence to empower your body, mind and voice, so choose clothes you are comfortable in.

Always mirror check your appearance before you do a PTC on video shoots. If you have to change your look during a shoot, start with your smartest look if possible. It's easier to get scruffy than it is to get smart.

Be BOLD with your choices, but be comfortable and follow these rules!

AVOID:

X A very low neckline that exposes the chest or cleavage – you are professionals here

X Being a fashion victim – unless of course that is the point of your video!

X Take everything, especially keys and coins, out of your pockets – remove the pocket jangle habit temptation!

LADIES

Make-up:

Please wear make-up, even if you don't normally. At a minimum use minerals face powder with a big brush to take off shine, highlight eyes with mascara, define eyebrows and use lipstick – they frame your face. If you enjoy your make-up do your 'normal' daytime look, with a little extra around the eyes and stronger lips for the camera – avoid over-glamour look unless for the story.

The three key things to highlight:

1. Appear natural.
2. Define eyebrows and use eye liner and mascara (if you can) on camera.
3. We **must** use lip colour – wear lipstick even if you don't normally:
    - go for a natural tone, matt look over too much gloss
    - check before filming it's not on your teeth!
    - you can match lip colour to accents in an outfit – have fun with it

Hair:

1. Always brush or comb to look tidy. Style it naturally, comfortably – never a new style!
2. If windy, move hair out of face smoothly, with grace, ease and a smile.
3. Use lots of hairspray, but never spray near a camera lens!

GENTS

Hair & Make-up:

1. Check your general appearance – no food in your teeth.
2. Carry a brush or comb for your hair and use hairspray as required, especially in the wind. If you have long hair or hair that falls across your face please follow the guidelines for ladies' hair.
3. Use face powder to stop shine, especially if it's hot and on bald heads – beg, borrow or steal from a #lovelylady friend!

Men in Suits – relevant for women in business suits also

1. When wearing a suit, shirt and tie make sure the shirt is smooth under the jacket and uncreased. TV tip = bulldog clips on the back make it sit flat and taught across your body at the front.
2. Sit on the back and sides of your jacket so it is pulled down tight – we want to avoid any puckering up at the front.

3. Always tuck shirts and tops in tight to trousers.

4. Do up buttons on jacket if you want a corporate look.

5. Clip mic on edge of jacket rather than tie and hide the cable.

6. Do not wear ties that clash or tight striped ties – they will strobe on camera.

7. Avoid ties if OB and windy or use a tie clip.

If in doubt take a photo, ideally a smartphone video of yourself in the outfit and see for yourself how it looks!

Make your Wardrobe work for you – dress to impress... subtly!

Wardrobe A&E Playlist

What will you wear on screen?

_____

_____

_____

_____

Use your online Wardrobe Playlist A&E form to plan your image and style to suit each video.

Confidence comes from comfort.
So dress for success and look the part!

STAGE 5: Production Planning

Production is everything that happens on or during the actual shoot – you need to have everything ready to bring and on top of your script and your performance, will have planned out what, where, when and how you will shoot.

These tips are now relevant to setting up on the day and what you may need to know to be confident with set-up or walking into a professional TV or video shoot with a production team.

Set the Scene with Confidence

Whether you are hiring a pro camera team or filming DIY you need to decide *where* you are going to film. Your set-up, background, lighting, props and wardrobe image all count towards making that good first impression.

Inside, outside, standing, sitting, at your desk, with a backdrop, in daylight, studio lights, with a microphone or not – so many things to consider, including what to wear! Many people ignore what's behind them when they shoot, but this can be one of the most important things to ensure your congruent message.

It's called setting the scene – and here's the list of what you need to do:

Locations:

- ⼂ Variety in backdrops and locations build interest for your viewers.
- ⼂ Ensure location is a place where you can easily, safely, legally film.
- ⼂ Ensure the location, background or backdrop and lighting suit your message.

OB = Outside Broadcast – aka outdoors, but can also mean 'out of your studio'

7 Checks Outside:

1. Ensure you can record good quality sound and in decent light; test at the time of day you will film.
2. In the sun, stand in the shade to avoid backdrop shadows. Film with sun in front of you, but not in direct sunlight – you will squint.
3. Check the sound for cars, machines, birds or any other loud distraction. If windy, check if it will be heard on the mic during filming. Use a mic windshield or use a lapel mic; if you can't, simply mention in passing how distracting it is for you too!
4. Check for silly signs or items behind you in shot = very distracting if not part of the story!
5. Use a tripod when possible or practise holding a monopod/smartphone steady; lean arms against something to steady yourself if you have to hand-hold.
6. ALWAYS do your test shot + playback.
7. Film indoors if the weather's really miserable!

Avoid:

- ✗ Messy or busy backgrounds, unless for a reason
- ✗ Outdoor things sticking out of the top or side of your head: a building, a machine, a lamp post or a plant or tree
- ✗ Missing the action you are talking about if filming OB – can you get it in the shot or 'frame' with you? Remember, the frame is what we see on screen
- ✗ A noisy spot where you will never be heard – unless you have a mic or it's part of the story; remember to use the Power of your Voice to be heard
- ✗ Something more interesting than you!

My one proviso on OBs in a busy area: only film OB when you are extremely confident you can keep going no matter what happens around you. The camera tends to bring out the voyeur and exhibitionist in others around you and it is amazing what can occur. Many a presenter has been scared off by getting embarrassed in front of total strangers – on OB you can have no shame!

So be prepared for possible interruptions, and no matter what happens, *YOU KEEP GOING.*

You may also get stopped by security guards, but have the courage of your convictions to keep going to the end as they come up and then say you're *"just packing up!"*

Always finish through to the end – you may have yourself an hilarious video distraction gem!

OB = But Inside?

7 Checks Inside or if you don't have a 'proper' studio set-up:

1. Film by a window if possible for best natural daylight – if not get lamps bouncing light off a bright wall. Never shine normal lamps direct on your face – use the Kick + diffuser.
2. Check sound for any background noise you don't hear – machine pings, mic reverb feedback.
3. Take a light with you in case of dark corners and if filming indoors.
4. Check lights don't shine directly down on your head – can cause reflection and put your face in shadow.
5. Check a wall light doesn't halo your head.
6. Check nothing sticks out of the top of your head in the background.
7. Check for silly signs, items or decorations behind you – especially if potentially rude – we all love a giggle at those distractions on video!

A five-minute backdrop, lighting and sound check can save a shoot, especially when you're interviewing someone and you only get one chance to do so.

Professionals check, so mimic that.

Suit Your Scene for You

When you can set up an actual scene for your video or film with the backdrop that suits your business.

CiaraConlon.com is my Productivity Queen of Ireland ☺ – regularly kicking my butt to get me organised – we did her first shoots with live coaching to create one of her online training courses. For the video on decluttering, my desk drawers of old were the 'before' shot, my wardrobe of colour arranged clothes the 'after' shot. (*Organised in the important places, see!*)

My Aussie world champ swimming mate Shelley Taylor-Smith films nearly all of her SM videos against the backdrop of the sea – obvious eh? – but… it's always a different sea… nice!

She whips the camera out wherever she is around the world and records fun clips or interviews with swimming legends at championship events. They are off the cuff, she doesn't worry too much about the details, just has fun with them herself and creates videos that inspire her tribe to action and make you smile. Check them out at Championmindset.com.au and OpenWaterSwimmingMastery.com.

So what kind of setting would best suit the videos you want to film?

Keep all RAW Footage from Every Shoot!

No matter what or where you film, a very important tip here before moving on to studio set-ups:

1. Remember you always have a choice to use or lose the RAW footage.
2. So always do a playback on location to check what you got – the camera or sound may have stopped! So always check you have what you need before you pack up a shoot.
3. Check for distractions on location and shoot another take just in case.
4. Even if the footage looks all wrong in playback, never delete it.
5. Sometimes footage with bad sound can be used as B-roll, so always keep it all just in case.
6. You may be able to do a VO over the visuals or use the audio as a VO with new visuals.
7. And of course there is always the Blooper roll you can add as a bit of fun at the end of your clip or make as its own Friday Funny clip!

Other times I'll bin it and chalk it up to experience! But I'm not so precious or worried by small things that might distract so much – I notice them because I'm looking, but others haven't.

Setting Your DIY Studio Stage

In Studio – aka inside in a designated 'studio' area, set up with lights and sound

7 Steps to a Confident Studio Set-up:
1. Simple backgrounds are best: move clutter and tidy up, straighten books, pictures, clean desks, check for cobwebs, marks on the wall etc.
2. Cream walls or light colour look cleaner and brighter than dark walls on camera, unless you opt for dark for a dramatic/funky/retro/specific reason. You can use a backdrop material – you can purchase frames, cotton, paper, patterned bricks or wood fairly cheaply online. Match your backdrop colour to your style and make sure your wardrobe stands out against it.
3. If filming against dark backdrop, check lighting levels to avoid looking dull or grey and avoid dark wardrobe choices.
4. Check your 'frame' – how much can you move backwards and forwards and side to side.
5. If possible stand or sit about four to six feet in front of walls to avoid casting shadows on the wall behind, otherwise see lighting note about back-lights.
6. Use a lapel or external microphone unless your camera is close up with decent sound quality; if the ceiling is low and the room is very quiet, you can get away using the camera's built-in mic. If it is cavernous, echoey or you can hear external noises you will need the external mic.
7. Always use a tripod for your camera – set up so you look slightly up to the camera to make your eyes pop open and avoid dreaded double chins, remember!

Some basic things to avoid are:

X Messy or busy shelves, walls or backdrops indoors
X Things sticking out of the top or side of your head
 – a plant, picture or lamp post
X An overly busy backdrop that will strobe on camera – be aware some backdrops look great for photos, but don't work for video. Use an interesting existing feature like a wall, stone, wood or you can buy backdrops in these patterns
X Avoid green screen unless you have professional help, editing or know-how
X Hand-held microphones unless you're doing an interview
 – looks too 'old school' TV

Not all studios are the same, so expect a different set-up and be prepared for different scenes. Your production planning for things that ARE within your control will give you greater confidence to cope with the set-up no matter where it is.

Webcam and Video Conferencing (VC) Set-up

It is imperative to adhere to these notes when using your webcam for virtual meetings, video conferencing or webinars. I've seen far too many global experts, gurus and professionals get caught out with very poor lighting, a totally incongruent backdrop and too many chins from looking down at the camera. I've also seen it in too many boardrooms and helped coach people in global mega-companies for their VCs. These are people who get paid thousands of pounds to present projects or to speak on stage, yet they don't bother with their own home studio or office – and what potential judgement message does that portray about them or the company they work for?

Check out the full Webcam + VC set-up doc online and how to set up p.205.

Again – PLEASE use your tripod to set the camera at eye-height or higher and test your backdrop, lights and sound before you go on air with VCs, Google Hangouts, webinars or Skype!

The 3 Point Lighting System

Again – a written instruction cheat sheet to set up your 3 Point Lighting System plus dos and don'ts are online, but you may find it easier to watch a video.

It is two lights in front on either side, one shining on your backdrop/wall behind to counteract shadows and light you from behind as a backlight.

3 Point Lighting Set-up

This is the basic diagram to set up:

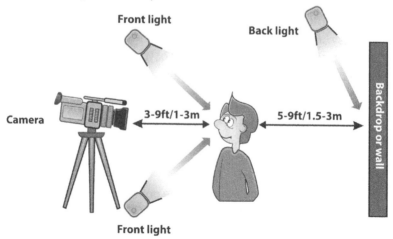

Front light

Back light

Camera

3-9ft/1-3m

5-9ft/1.5-3m

Backdrop or wall

Front light

Look on YouTube for 'How to set up 3 point lighting' or 'How to set up studio for video' with home lamps and shades – see the YouTube Creator Academy or James Wedmore for their simple instructions which are brilliantly explained by production experts. This is a prime example of where seeing it in video is so much easier than reading how to do it!

Use a soft box 3 point light system if it is within your budget; check the equipment listings for bargains online – some come with backdrops and all the lights you need!

Props

Props can be tricky – avoid them if you can. If you are doing a product demo and have to use props, ensure you get enough close-up shots you can cut between you on camera and the product.

DO:
- ✓ Avoid props unless they are for a specific reason – put all pens down!
- ✓ If showing a prop, show it and put it down or have on a table so you can demo it
- ✓ Hold props to one side, about shoulder height, close into your body, where you can tilt chin down to see it easily
- ✓ Move props slowly and hold for a viewing moment before moving again
- ✓ Hold with both hands – the hand crossing your body goes on the bottom
- ✓ Film close-up shots of props or still shots for editing crossover shots.
- ✓ Clean your hands and manicure nails!

AVOID:
- ✗ Keeping props in your hands – they distract and you can end up fiddling if nervous!
- ✗ Holding props in front of your face unless for a specific dramatic reason
- ✗ Moving props fast or waving props around = highly distracting

'Frame' your Shots

We have discussed Framing a bit already – what you want to see on the TV screen and therefore where you need to be, to be in the shot. This helps you choose where you have to stand or sit so we can see you.

⅄ How do you picture it in the final edit?

- Where will you be?
- Will you have captions or pop-ups?
- What will be your backdrop?

If you have no text captions or visuals, frame yourself dead centre of the shot in a close-up, head and shoulders or mid-shot to the waist. Remember your asymmetry visual image though – no hard square shoulders unless for a reason!

Draw What You Want to See on Screen

The Story Board Sheet online will help you design what shots you want and therefore how to frame them. It does make it much easier to draw, especially if you are not normally a visual person. It will remind you what to check on shoot day.

| Scene 1: PTC Intro Mid-shot | Sc 2: MS + Caption | Sc 3: PTC Zoom in To XCU | Sc 4: Image/slide +VO | Sc 5: PTC CU=Close |

Additional Visuals

Pop-ups

When you know you want additional visuals to show in the picture, you may want to be at one side so that you can leave room in the frame at the side. These are the **pop-up** items I've mentioned, which appear as a special effect to zoom, scroll or fly in as you talk about items, then fly or fade out.

Lower Thirds

You may also want to leave room at the bottom for a **lower third banner** – your name, text or titles – to scroll in and out.

Or across the top for text to appear, and/or your **branding logo** if required.

If so, stand further away from the camera for a slightly longer shot to leave room for the additional visuals.

Subliminal Messages – look to the past or future?

This is a very secret theatrical concept of subliminal messaging and mental misconnection, many pro speakers don't even know about.

As you watch yourself on screen, if you are standing on the left side of the shot with pop-ups or captions coming up on the right side, this looks like you are looking 'towards the future' on the TV screen, in the Western world. The opposite is to the perceived past... This left side of the screen we see is also the negative or 'sinister' side, Latin for left-handed, even though that's your right side!

When you present it means:

Your right side is the past/negative...

...Your left side is the future/positive.

If you talk about *past/future* or *starting/ending* or *growing or moving forwards* and move or gesture it in the wrong direction...

We will not know why... but it will seem wrong when we watch.

Have a go to check you understand what I mean...

As you are standing during filming, turn yourself slightly towards the side the text will appear and you can gesture to it with your appropriate hand.

Oh yes, and it is vice versa for the Eastern world where they read right to left!

This is top level Confidence on Camera upskilling here, but you're worth it!

Edit tip – you can actually reverse the filmed image in editing – so you could swap from side to side if you really want! Or you can just as easily be dead centre shot if captions will scroll beneath you – simply remember your Visual Impact M^3 + OBE!

Where Visuals Show on Screen
Here's a visual example of what I mean with you, a logo, a pop-up text box and a lower third banner framing:

Western World Pop-up Framing   Eastern World Pop-up Framing

You probably won't have all these pop-ups at once, but you can see what I mean by framing for additional text captions or visuals. You can plan this or you can fit them in during post-production where they look best.

Reality vs Reverse Image on the Studio Monitor

If you are ever watching a live TV monitor *during* filming, what you do in front of the camera is actually a *reverse image* when you see it on screen live. It is not a mirror image!

But when it is on screen it will appear exactly as if someone is looking at you like the pictures here.

Production Planning – Setting the Scene with Confidence A&E

So now, when you have to DIY your own set-up for your production, you can find a number of forms online to help you do so, from a Production Planning Sheet, to a Production Checklist and a Set the Scene Checklist. I've also added a simple Story Board doc there in case you really want to go all pro with your planning!

DO also remember – as more and more videos are viewed on mobiles and tablets, you need to think of close-up framing so they can actually see you on a small screen.

Too many visuals in frame will be too much or not visible.

KISS mobile targeted marketing videos!

Camera Positions in a Pro Studio or when you go on TV

What happens when you have to go into an actual television or professional studio?

Well, the main thing is not to look silly or be cocky and be as polite, smiley, helpful and friendly as you can possibly be! Pay attention and always make sure with the floor manager (FM) – you'll know who they are in the TV Techie Lingo section!

A small pro studio can have one to three cameras, though there may be up to 10 in a TV studio. Each camera will record a different POV (Point of View) or angle, and the finished programme will cut between different cameras to give a variety of shots. This is usually done in editing, but in a TV studio is done live by the director/producer in the studio 'box' – the live editing room next to the studio.

Live TV doesn't always mean LIVE!

As I mentioned, we used to record shows in Hong Kong to make it look like live TV. My director would be in the box choosing which of the three or four cameras to move the camera angle shot to next, for me and my guests. I had to look out for the **tally light** – the red light on top of each camera which shows which camera is recording at any one time; the camera guys would move the cameras into the next position and my floor manager (FM) would get a countdown in their earpiece for which camera was going to record next. It was 1990s English kids' TV in Hong Kong, so far too cheap for me to have an earpiece too! The FM would give me a three-second visual countdown with a big swish-point of the arm and hand to the next camera.

It was very theatrical, but it worked!

These days presenters usually have earpieces direct from the director to indicate which camera to use. As a guest you probably won't.

Many TV studios across the globe don't even have camera people as they are all automated.

If you're on a show in that situation, you look out for the camera with the big red light and you'll know which one to talk to when you want to address the audience, or which one to angle your body and gesture towards while you talk to your host, and with your viewer.

If you DO end up connecting with that camera lens and the viewers outside, remember to look straight into the camera with your Emotional Connection Confidence, move on cue to the next red tally light if they change camera on you, and never hesitate!

Keep holding that camera lens and maintain your connection.

Hold your *"I love you, I love you!"* smile or expression at the end… until you see the tally light go off!

If you are in a studio with a director, FM or camera guys and girls, **never look at them when recording unless you plan to film that way** – i.e. as if you are being interviewed. Reminder codicil here – the interview style video, where you look to the side of the camera as if talking to a person (i.e. the camera person) works well – but not if you do it every time. We want to see the whites of your eyes to trust and fully believe you and if you never talk directly to us, subliminally we are never fully connected to or confident and invested in you…

TV TECHIE LINGO – what does that camera crew mean?

AKA Broadcast TERMINOLOGY AND SIGNALS

There are loads of techie terms in TV to bamboozle the uninitiated! You don't need to know them all, but a little knowledge of terminology for a camera person, director/producer or editor can go a long way. Do look and sound like you know what you're doing, but always be guided and let yourself be directed by the pros so you never come across as cocky on camera!

⅄ Don't know your Voxpops from your Time Span? What a VT/LS/MS/CU is?

⅄ Or where On Set is or where Transitions go or who to give the Credits?

⅄ Or why that FM over there is waving his hands at you in a big circle?

Well then – online you'll find an extensive list of key terms from my ATV World TV days that might prove useful to know when you get to appear on TV or work with a production team in studio.

Seeing as I've got into techie lingo for editing, let's move on now to Post-Production, or as it is usually called, simply 'Post'.

STAGE 6: Post-Production

Post-Production = POST is everything that happens AFTER you film your video shoot.

Most people forget that once the camera stops rolling on you, there is still a HUGE amount of work left to create the final glorious technicolour production that is your online video!

From processing the RAW footage to the final backing up of all your edits and promoting it online.

As discussed, edits can be simple **Top & Tail** – my favourite quick and easy PTC edit, or can be complicated montage edits with lots of different shots you have filmed according to your original storyboard plan. You CAN have whatever shots you want from what you've filmed, just remember complicated = more time = more money!

Once again, you WILL waste huge amounts of time and money if you keep changing your mind. And don't think it won't happen – it has happened to us all, so only you can choose what is good enough for you and when to STOP tinkering!

Go Pro Editing

Hiring a pro video editor costs anything from £/€/$ 200-1,000 per day depending on experience and your project. Often the same person who films you will be editing on a package deal. Always check. Most editors are trained to know what shots, texts and images work when they look at them, so trust them when they tell you so, but you can ask about a specific shot if you really want to use it.

You can also hold out to keep a specific PTC when you feel it is the best presenting you do.

They are trained to look for the best *overall* shot, background, lighting, sound and storyboard, not to look at *how* you are presenting. So trust yourself too.

When working with an editor, you don't have to be there but communicate well, use an **Edit Sheet** *(sample online)* to help, with details of each shot you want to use and any additional visuals and audio you want to use, and stick to your agreed timetable. This should enable you to get your first edit as close as possible to what you want, so that re-edits are a matter of checking timings and adding the 'Extras' overlays like logos, titles, captions, text and In/Out titles or slides. You must advise of all Extras text font, RGB colour codes and style, when and where you want in shot – the editor will re-size text to fit in the frame.

DIY Editing

Do also remember that there are many **Enhancements** you can make in **YouTube** too: Trim the start and end, improve the lighting, colour, contrast, add music, captions, text, annotations, subtitles.

You can even edit your YouTube clips together to form one video in your **Creator Suite** with the **YouTube Video Editor** options.

So if you don't have any editing apps, film three to four 15" PTC shots, upload and edit them together on YouTube. Be aware to check story flow as you do though!

Caption Fonts

It is important to note that not all **caption fonts** work on video so if in doubt:

1. Stick to **non-serif fonts:** Calibri, Verdana, Myriad Pro and Arial.
2. Avoid **serif fonts** – like Times New Roman.
3. Two serif fonts that do work, but may be overused, are Adobe Caslon Pro and Georgia.
4. You can match your marketing material or preferred font.
5. Play to see if you prefer Regular or **Bold.**
6. Too much italic can be hard to read – especially on mobiles.
7. You shouldn't need too much text to pop up – save it for Keywords x three lines only.

Insert Slides

If you have too much text, do an **insert** slide.

Or if you have asked and answered a question, you can type it as an insert.

Transition it in and out – this can cover mistakes too!

This can give enough variety to your visuals.

DIY Editing Tools

Once you have learned what works for you – whether to DIY or Go Pro for editing – you may want to invest in editing software or use the free versions of Windows Movie Maker, iMovie or YouTube/Vimeo/Instagram tools to edit them yourself.

For the most up-to-date Editing Software List + Tips, again go online.

The free ones you'll have on your PC or Mac are:

- **Windows Movie Maker** – installed free on every Windows PC – OK but limited
- **iMovie** – installed free on every Apple Mac computer – amazing options and functions
- Plus the other funsmartphone video apps I've shared already.

I use Adobe Premier Elements on my laptop, bought with Photoshop.

Between those and PowerPoint I can design most visuals I need.

NOTE: Not all visuals online are free – do check copyright status – YouTube may have to remove your video if not.

If you have a Mac or a teenager, you probably have access to loads of editing help and YouTube/Vimeo are making it easier every day to edit and improve the look of your videos once you've posted them online.

BONUS: Keep Attention with an 'Outro' Slide or End Plate

A lot of businesses have extended **Outro** slides – the animations or links images to advertise your contact details, social media links and CTA next steps. They can be known as **End Plates**.

The idea is to keep the viewer on *your* products and services for the '20" mental overlap'. YouTube analytics geniuses designated that's the psychological link time between hearing your offering and the conscious decision to act.

The logic is that Outros help stop viewers from being distracted by other videos, advertised by YouTube, long enough to click through or go on to your links in your VSEO.

The best Outro/End Plates stop on your contact details, of course!

I'm not mad on the 20" superlong Outros myself, but I can see the purpose.

To me they can smack of over-salesy, but check out those you like and emulate them.

Plan the Outro you will use before editing.

The app Intro Designer could also be used to make Outros or Splasheo.com can create fantastic Intro/Outro/Links/Lower Thirds/Banners – all the branded artwork you need as a package. You can always edit it down if you feel it is too long.

The 7 Step 'Simple' Edit Process

I've broken my editing process into seven 'simple' steps for clients – of course what it entails may look far from simple, but one of the most time-consuming things are the camera download, imports into editing software, converting and compressing the raw footage before even starting the edits. Then the save, export and upload of the finished product.

You can leave that happening on your computer overnight.

YouTube also lets you upload multiple videos – but check you have set uploading to be Unlisted or Private in your YouTube Settings Upload Defaults – youtube.com/upload_defaults.

This is why smartphone video tools are so exciting – you can film, upload and enhance online within a matter of minutes, when you're as confident with your DIY tools as you are with your presenting!

My 7 Steps are...

1. **Raw footage Importing and Review.**
2. **The Edit Plan** – after reviewing the footage, to see what footage to use:
   - ⋏ **Top Tip** is to keep notes as you film, so you are very clear with what you want
3. **The First Edit** – the editor pulls together images and sound to fit as one video clip.
4. **Upload for Review** – editors can share the first edit in a number of ways, as you prefer.
5. **Client Feedback** – can be done face-to-face (quickest) or via the phone or email.
6. **The Re-Edit + Sign off** – when your editor fixes up what you want/need.
7. **Upload for Sign off and VSEO:**
   - ⋏ basic 'How to VSEO for YouTube' is in the next section on Video Promotion

This is a step-by-step process mostly for your understanding. It may be done in other ways by others, but it is a process you can fairly easily follow and cross-check for yourself when DIY editing. PTC quick video tips or client testimonials should only really need Top & Tail edits + the extras you can add in YouTube – all instructions are in the YouTube Video Editor.

STAGE 7:   Video Promotion

So the final step once you've got your final video made is to share it out there with the world with confidence with your relevant Video SEO – the part that helps your search engine rankings and is the start of you promoting your video to get more views and create the impact you want.

We know Google own YouTube, so you're crazy not to have a channel linked back to your website and your social media, even if Vimeo is more aesthetically pleasing for your brand.

We started this chapter with YouTube stats, so here are three more marketing focused reasons I love using YouTube …

Basic VSEO for Google + YouTube

1. Together they are used by more people in the world to find what they want and year on year more people are going to YT to help them do just that – another reason having a YT Channel is so important = marketing reach!

2. You can also improve VSEO with other hosts like Vimeo by using the same VSEO tricks.

3. Many of these hosting tools are free and you can use them to store your videos rather than on your own website – simply get your web designer to paste the link on the appropriate page where you have chosen to place the screen.

I've also mentioned the **YouTube Capture App** created in 2013 for smartphones – the free app tool to film, edit, enhance, add music and upload direct to your YT Channel. Plus all the YT enhancement capabilities, editing, copyright-free music, analytics, partnerships, video monetisation, sharing options… really there is so much there, books are already out about it. I'm not going to rant on, just give you a MUST DO VSEO process and ask you…

Why wouldn't you go with the biggest online video site to help promote your business videos and have them make a bigger impact for you?

Do Your YouTube VSEO

If you're worried about getting lost in YT, a sure-fire way to help yourself is to *do what so many others don't bother with* – the **Video SEO**! The specific rules for YT VSEO rankings keep changing and are very much linked to advertising now, so ensure your Google Analytics is connected to your YT channel. You must also ensure you own all copyrights to your video content and music is paid for or copyright-free – your videos can be blocked by YT with any complaint and you will not know until you go there to find it gone.

As video voice recognition technology gets better, YT will also be searching videos to ensure the Description VSEO does match the content – but don't just scribe exactly what you say, that does not help or serve your viewer. Think of the Description as being a mini-blog and include all your social media links and links to anyone else who appears with you for more YT/Google brownie points – they like it when we help and support others, not just ourselves!

Print out the Basic YouTube VSEO Rules for your workbook for easy access.

You **need** to complete all three sections in YT when you upload a video to get the benefit and the linkage back to the Google search. Only make the video Public when this is complete…

> **BASIC YOUTUBE VSEO RULES:**
> 1. **Title** – is the first point of VSEO search – use your, your company name + key video content in title.
> 2. **Description** – what the video is actually about, Minimum 150 words + 5 links. Always start with your URL – your website you want to promote with this video.
> 3. **Keywords** – use the same words you have used for the Title + Description and your website connector key words, but avoid a long list = keyword stuffing!

As I said earlier, video tools and rules change day by day, so if you're reading this in 10 years' time and wondering what I'm talking about here, you've probably got your own best VSEO tool to help you promote and market your videos out to the world!

Once done, you can make the video live – before you opt for Public and click Publish, make sure you have filled in the **Also share on** social media box to tweet and Google+ – you only get this one chance to do this before you publish. If you UnList the video again, this option is not possible again.

Please be Ethically Social Media Minded!

Remember Facebook and Twitter are also clamouring for your videos – choose the platform that will do the most marketing for your business. You can always schedule uploads or use multiple upload tools such as Hootsuite to plan your video posting programme.

Please do always be ethical – only post and share videos you know have copyright ownership by the people who post them, credit contributors who help you, advise where you source your music in your Description. This sentence is always useful at the bottom of each video:

> 'All visuals owned outright or ethically sourced with music copyright/ royalty free from…
>
> No unintentional copyright infringement is intended – please contact us if otherwise advised.'

Bonus Video Marketing News…

Video Marketing is not my field of expertise, though I do keep up to date with what's new and update Viewers, Followers and Members with vlogs and blogs on my social media, with news, **views and reviews here:**

- **YouTube Channel – Lottie Hearn Video Coach**
- **Facebook – @Press Play Presentations @Lottie Hearn Ross**
- **Twitter – Lottie Hearn @PressPlayPres**
- **LinkedIn – Lottie Hearn, The Video Coach**
- **www.ConfidenceOn.Camera – your online club.**

So do come check out the latest tips I find from video marketing experts I've already mentioned, look online for your own and do let me know when you find something fantastic we can share together out there for the Video World!

Remember, the technology will always move on, but the Presenting with Impact and Confidence on Camera will stay very much the same.

Production *and* Promotion Tools
Review A&E Notes

My Playlist for a Confident on Camera Me

As there is so much information and so many technical things to think about in this chapter, have a flick back now over the seven sections to jot down the key items you need to work on…

My Learning Stage Notes:

1. My Video Myths to check…

2. My Confidence in Production Planning – Go Pro or No?…

3. My Pre-Production DIY - Get Set, Get Gear, Get Video Tooled!..

4. My Guide to Looking Good On Screen…

5. My Production Planning…

6. My Post-Production Planning…

7. My Video Promotion…

And remember no matter what - you presenting YOU is your No.1 Production Value!

Remember all the planning, production and promotion worksheets can be found online if you haven't downloaded them already ☺

(sidebar) My Playlist for a Confident on Camera Me! Online

Wrap Up, CTA *and* Close

> *Film is incredibly democratic and accessible,*
> *it's probably the best option if you actually want*
> *to change the world, not just redecorate it.*
>
> **Banksy**

So it's the last scene – we've filmed our acts, we've played our parts and I trust you've played with your camera, and learned loads about your confidence along the way? Make it your tool to make you more accessible to the world – it's not just the best option, it's going to be *the* option for global business communication before too long.

So now's the time to put the book down and if you've read this straight through – *phew, you #SuperGreat superstar!* But please… go get your camera out now and get filming. I'd love to see your videos online so please do get in touch on social media, now you know exactly where I am. I'm a little more demanding of you when you want to work live, but we still do get to play!

We started this journey with Shakespeare and thinking that talking to a machine was not a natural thing to do and I trust now that while it still might not be 100% natural *(yet!)*, it can be one heck of a lot of new business fun!

So I'll leave you with a message from one of my other superfavourite scribes Christopher Robin in *Winnie the Pooh* by AA Milne:

> *If ever there is tomorrow when we're not together... there*
> *is something you must always remember. You are braver*
> *than you believe, stronger than you seem, and smarter*
> *than you think. But the most important thing is, even if*
> *we're apart... I'll always be with you.*

I'm with you, because I'm in your hands right now my
#ConfidentonCamera press playmate!

Director's Note: End scene with confident voice, OBE and glorious gestures to say...

THAT'S A WRAP FOLKS – STAY PLAYFUL!

Possibilities are only out there because you have the guts to dream them.

Lottie's Story

The Story of my Mind Behind the Machine

I first started coaching, designing and developing presenter training courses in the late 1990s at TV Pro Global in Sydney, Australia, with the wonderful Sharon Lynne. She is a powerhouse South African star of stage and screen, who had set up life in Oz as a TV presenter agent and ran the first TV presenter training course in the country. Sharon became my agent on arriving in Oz, equipped with my very British accent; a successful TV presenting, voice-over and creative writing career; an acting CV from drama at university in the UK and work in London, to touring on stage across New Zealand and Sydney; and from Hong Kong, where successful Youth Arts Festivals, pro theatre productions, global voice-overs, radio interviews and corporate gigs were my norm. While amazing auditions came up for me for great TV shows, it was about 10 years too early for an English accent on Aussie TV! So Sharon invited me to help train new TV presenters with her.

While I'd also taught English, done drama coaching and lots of directing/ producer work in HK, I'd never *actually* trained other TV presenters. So just as I started out on TV, I simply had a go! As my confidence grew, I revised ideas and ways of working, and started asking what and how people wanted to learn. It was great fun developing my training confidence, knowledge and skills to help them go on to successful careers themselves on TV.

The pride and joy from helping other people become more Confident on Camera, watching their presenter success, credibility and charisma shine was an inspiration to me. I knew I'd found something else I loved to do, as much as appearing on stage or screen myself. As my soul spirit angel mates would say *(you know who you are!)* I'd found my purpose in life – though it would take a while yet to get to where we are today!

I spent seven years on and off with Sharon, developing and expanding the training, creating new courses and coaching other presenter trainers too. I was making it up as I went along, learning from my students, really discovering details of different presenter styles. I started expanding my own theories of what works on camera and the habits that distract, and found that giving people the freedom to play and be real, just like I had on screen, was the biggest confidence booster that they'd need. And they didn't have to make their mistakes on air, they could hone their presenting skills in a safe, supportive environment.

But I was still missing official qualifications. So to gain 'Government approved qualifications' I went to the largest film and TV casting agency in Oz *(and the folks who cast my fave TV shows Neighbours and Home and Away – watching, always watching!)*, where I met and worked for the casting legend herself, Maura Faye Associates. Their on-the-job trainer training was invaluable to actually understand how adults learn and develop skills. But because all of us Maura Faye trainers were professional actors too, we were all training from the same performance perspective that I loved, using acting techniques to improve live presentations skills. Over the years I've trained a vast variety of corporate business presenters from Star City Casino to Cathay Pacific, from Omega to Diageo, from Coca-Cola, Irish politics and wizards of the financial world to a world champion or two!

Acting exercises and performance theories have huge relevance in the corporate presenting world, and while actors spend days and weeks perfecting a specific skill, accent, voice, body movement, we can simplify the concepts and distil performance down to trainable, practical and easy steps for presenters of all levels in all business fields. I've seen similar techniques used by some of the world's best professional speakers from National Speaking Associations and as President of the Professional Speaking Association in Dublin, Ireland today.

Developing my skills and qualifications as a corporate trainer and pro speaker reinforced my belief that there is nothing quite like doing it. Practising, performing, improving; constructing feedback methods to boost confidence, in a truly positive way. Always encouraging other people *to have another go* to develop their M³, 3 Cs, 3 Vs and loads of *'real mes'* at work, at home and across the world, both live and online!

Even when I eventually got my Train The Trainer qualifications and an Online Marketing Diploma in Ireland much more recently, I found those lessons learned and the skills developed starting *last century* are still so utterly relevant. With the gargantuan growth of video and virtual meetings online, the on-camera coaching simply seemed the logical thing to do now. Performance techniques don't really change *(I've gone to enough acting classes to know!)* but the mediums to share the performance are changing day by day.

That's why I'm now **Lottie Hearn, The Video Coach** empowering your Confidence on Camera.

My passion is now to serve you – to help you project your power online and make the connections you need on screen. To share Play tools developed and learned through my varied global networks and with best buddies both on and off stage! Thank you all very much for allowing me to be part of your journey.

Stay Playful!

Lottie
xx

AWESOME REVIEWS

"When you commit to following this book, you commit to building your confidence on camera."

Shelley Taylor-Smith, 7-time World Champion Marathon Swimmer, Author, Swim and Business Coach & Global Motivational Speaker

"This work has a lot of information packed into it. It comes across as a wonderful resource guide and reference, something we who create videos will want to refer to on a regular basis. Thank you."

Terry Brock, USA Hall of Fame Speaker, Digital Marketing Expert & Author

"Lottie writes with vibrancy and positivity along with a helpful easy how-to feel for the reader."

Carole Smith, Synneo.ie, Online Marketing Solutions for SMEs

"Lottie has been coaching our team for conferences, training and webinars both live and on camera for a number of years. With her book Confidence on Camera, we now have a step-by-step guide to share with staff across the world that will enable us to maintain our competitive edge when connecting with our customers."

Joe Hannon, CEO Scale-Up Systems Ltd @DynoChem, software provider to over 40 countries

"Working with Lottie not only increased my confidence on camera, but gave me more confidence in all areas of my life."

Ciara Conlon, Productivity Consultant, Speaker and Author www.ciaraconlon.com @ciaraconlon

"Uncover the Secrets to Speaking on Camera Without Fear!

There's a world of a difference between speaking to an audience that's right there in front of you – where you can see whether you're connecting with them straight away – and trying to share something interesting to the same audience via an inanimate and cold video camera lens. If you don't know the tricks of the trade, it can feel clumsy, unnatural, and downright overwhelming. But fear not. Lottie Hearn has written a first rate, step-by-step guide that will help you to create videos like a pro. And, she makes it wonderfully easy.

From what it takes to create winning scripts to making the right equipment choices, from how to add energy to your voice to insights on connecting through the lens, from the importance of your attitude to secrets from the world of TV presenting...

This is a must have guide if you need to create confident and interesting videos! I can't recommend it highly enough.

I was lucky enough to be given a review copy of this book and I'm so glad I did; It's awesome."

Eamonn O'Brien, Founder of The Reluctant Speakers Club, President of PSA Ireland, and author of How to Make Powerful Speeches

"Having known Lottie and been trained by her many years ago, I know how invaluable her advice working on camera is when you just have to go for it! Lottie gave me the confidence and skills to perform on screen. Over eight years as part of a market leading IT team for a Top 10 international financial institution, weekly meetings and interacting are on a more personal level with our global virtual teams in the UK, Singapore, Chennai and Hong Kong now all on video conferencing. 'Confidence on Camera' enables me to plan and present better for all our on screen communications. Recently it has also empowered me to add Vlog posts to my personal rock-climbing blog summitupdownunder.wordpress.com"

Craig Hitchcock, software lead tester with Australian multinational bank across Asia, USA & UK and international travel/climbing blogger

"Lottie creates the best 'real you' on camera. I have been complimented so many times by my clients and new clients have been attracted by the honest and warm video created by Lottie"

Valerie Pierce, ClearThinkinginAction.com Creator of worldwide 'Clear & Critical Thinking' training and coaching modules

Lightning Source UK Ltd.
Milton Keynes UK
UKOW06f0619230915

259121UK00002B/208/P